# The Scheme Programming Language

## Third Edition

## DATE DUE

R. KENT DYBVIG

# The Scheme Programming Language
## Third Edition

Illustrations by Jean-Pierre Hébert

The MIT Press
Cambridge, Massachusetts
London, England

Library of Congress Cataloging-in-Publication Data

Dybvig, R. Kent.
    The Scheme programming language / R. Kent Dybvig; illustrations
    by Jean-Pierre Hébert—3rd ed.
        p.   cm
    Includes bibliographical references and index.
    ISBN 0-262-54148-3 (pbk. : alk. paper)
    1. Scheme (Computer Programming Language)   I. Title

QA76.73.S34D93 2003
005.13′3—dc21                                                    2003046449

# Contents

Preface                                                                          ix

1. Introduction                                                                   1
    1.1. Scheme Syntax . . . . . . . . . . . . . . . . . . . . . . .               6
    1.2. Scheme Naming Conventions . . . . . . . . . . . . . .                     7
    1.3. Typographical and Notational Conventions . . . . . . . . . . . . . . .    8

2. Getting Started                                                               11
    2.1. Interacting with Scheme . . . . . . . . . . . . . . . . . .              13
    2.2. Simple Expressions . . . . . . . . . . . . . . . . . . . .               15
    2.3. Evaluating Scheme Expressions . . . . . . . . . . . . . .                21
    2.4. Variables and Let Expressions . . . . . . . . . . . . . .                22
    2.5. Lambda Expressions . . . . . . . . . . . . . . . . . . .                 25
    2.6. Top-Level Definitions . . . . . . . . . . . . . . . . . . .              29
    2.7. Conditional Expressions . . . . . . . . . . . . . . . . .                33
    2.8. Simple Recursion . . . . . . . . . . . . . . . . . . . . .               39
    2.9. Assignment . . . . . . . . . . . . . . . . . . . . . . . .               45

3. Going Further                                                                 55
    3.1. Syntactic Extension . . . . . . . . . . . . . . . . . . . .              57
    3.2. More Recursion . . . . . . . . . . . . . . . . . . . . . .               62
    3.3. Continuations . . . . . . . . . . . . . . . . . . . . . . .              70
    3.4. Continuation Passing Style . . . . . . . . . . . . . . . .               75
    3.5. Internal Definitions . . . . . . . . . . . . . . . . . . . .             77

**4. Procedures and Variable Bindings**                                    **83**

   4.1. Variable References . . . . . . . . . . . . . . . . . . . . . . . . 85

   4.2. Lambda . . . . . . . . . . . . . . . . . . . . . . . . . . . . . . 86

   4.3. Local Binding . . . . . . . . . . . . . . . . . . . . . . . . . . 87

   4.4. Variable Definitions . . . . . . . . . . . . . . . . . . . . . . . 89

   4.5. Assignment . . . . . . . . . . . . . . . . . . . . . . . . . . . 91

**5. Control Operations**                                                  **93**

   5.1. Procedure Application . . . . . . . . . . . . . . . . . . . . . 95

   5.2. Sequencing . . . . . . . . . . . . . . . . . . . . . . . . . . . 96

   5.3. Conditionals . . . . . . . . . . . . . . . . . . . . . . . . . . 97

   5.4. Recursion, Iteration, and Mapping . . . . . . . . . . . . . . 100

   5.5. Continuations . . . . . . . . . . . . . . . . . . . . . . . . . 104

   5.6. Delayed Evaluation . . . . . . . . . . . . . . . . . . . . . . 108

   5.7. Multiple Values . . . . . . . . . . . . . . . . . . . . . . . . 110

   5.8. Eval . . . . . . . . . . . . . . . . . . . . . . . . . . . . . . . 116

**6. Operations on Objects**                                               **119**

   6.1. Constants and Quotation . . . . . . . . . . . . . . . . . . . 121

   6.2. Generic Equivalence and Type Predicates . . . . . . . . . . . 122

   6.3. Lists and Pairs . . . . . . . . . . . . . . . . . . . . . . . . . 132

   6.4. Numbers . . . . . . . . . . . . . . . . . . . . . . . . . . . . 139

   6.5. Characters . . . . . . . . . . . . . . . . . . . . . . . . . . . 153

   6.6. Strings . . . . . . . . . . . . . . . . . . . . . . . . . . . . . 158

   6.7. Vectors . . . . . . . . . . . . . . . . . . . . . . . . . . . . . 164

   6.8. Symbols . . . . . . . . . . . . . . . . . . . . . . . . . . . . . 166

**7. Input and Output**                                                    **169**

   7.1. Input Operations . . . . . . . . . . . . . . . . . . . . . . . 171

   7.2. Output Operations . . . . . . . . . . . . . . . . . . . . . . . 175

   7.3. Loading Programs . . . . . . . . . . . . . . . . . . . . . . . 179

   7.4. Transcript Files . . . . . . . . . . . . . . . . . . . . . . . . . 179

**8. Syntactic Extension**      **181**

     8.1. Keyword Bindings . . . . . . . . . . . . . . . . . . . . . 184

     8.2. Syntax-Rules Transformers . . . . . . . . . . . . . . . . 187

     8.3. Syntax-Case Transformers . . . . . . . . . . . . . . . . 190

     8.4. Examples . . . . . . . . . . . . . . . . . . . . . . . . . . 200

**9. Extended Examples**      **211**

     9.1. Matrix and Vector Multiplication . . . . . . . . . . . . . 213

     9.2. Sorting . . . . . . . . . . . . . . . . . . . . . . . . . . . 218

     9.3. A Set Constructor . . . . . . . . . . . . . . . . . . . . . 220

     9.4. Word Frequency Counting . . . . . . . . . . . . . . . . 224

     9.5. Scheme Printer . . . . . . . . . . . . . . . . . . . . . . . 228

     9.6. Formatted Output . . . . . . . . . . . . . . . . . . . . . 231

     9.7. A Meta-Circular Interpreter for Scheme . . . . . . . . . 234

     9.8. Defining Abstract Objects . . . . . . . . . . . . . . . . 238

     9.9. Fast Fourier Transform . . . . . . . . . . . . . . . . . . 242

     9.10. A Unification Algorithm . . . . . . . . . . . . . . . . . 247

     9.11. Multitasking with Engines . . . . . . . . . . . . . . . . 250

**Bibliography**      **259**

**Answers to Selected Exercises**      **261**

**Formal Syntax of Scheme**      **277**

**Summary of Forms**      **281**

**Index**      **289**

# Preface

Scheme was introduced in 1975 by Gerald J. Sussman and Guy L. Steele Jr. [20, 21], and was the first dialect of Lisp to fully support lexical scoping, first-class procedures, and continuations. In its earliest form it was a very small language intended primarily for research and teaching, supporting only a handful of predefined syntactic forms and procedures. Scheme is now a complete general-purpose programming language, though it still derives its power from a small set of key concepts. Early implementations of the language were interpreter-based and slow, but some current Scheme implementations boast sophisticated compilers that generate code on par with code generated by the best optimizing compilers for lower-level languages such as C and Fortran.

This book is intended to provide an introduction to the Scheme programming language but not an introduction to programming in general. The reader is expected to have had some experience programming and to be familiar with terms commonly associated with computers and programming languages. The author recommends that readers unfamiliar with Scheme or Lisp also read *The Little Schemer* [8] to become familiar with the concepts of list processing and recursion. Readers new to programming should begin with an introductory text on programming.

Scheme has been standardized both formally and informally. The "IEEE Standard for the Scheme Programming Language" [13], describes the formal ANSI/IEEE Standard for Scheme. A related series of reports, the "Revised Reports on the Algorithmic Language Scheme," document an evolving informal standard that most implementations support. The current report in this series is the "Revised⁵ Report on the Algorithmic Language Scheme" [14].

This book covers everything in both standards. Features included in the Revised⁵ Report but not in the ANSI/IEEE standard are identified as such when they are described. This book also documents the portable "syntax-case" syntactic abstraction system that has been adopted by many Scheme implementations. Features specific to particular implementations are not included. In particular, features specific to the author's *Chez Scheme* and *Petite Chez Scheme* are described separately in the *Chez Scheme User's Guide* [5].

A large number of small- to medium-sized examples are spread throughout the text, and one entire chapter is dedicated to the presentation of a set of longer examples. Many of the examples show how a standard Scheme syntactic form or procedure might be implemented; others implement useful extensions. Nearly all Scheme systems are interactive, and all of the examples can be entered directly from the keyboard into an interactive Scheme session.

This book is organized into nine chapters, plus appendices. Chapter 1 describes the properties and features of Scheme that make it a useful and enjoyable language to use. Chapter 1 also describes Scheme's notational conventions and the typographical conventions employed in this book.

Chapter 2 is an introduction to Scheme programming for the novice Scheme programmer that leads the reader through a series of examples, beginning with simple Scheme expressions and working toward progressively more difficult ones. Each section of Chapter 2 introduces a small set of related features, and the end of each section contains a set of exercises for further practice. The reader will learn the most from Chapter 2 by sitting at the keyboard and typing in the examples and trying the exercises.

Chapter 3 continues the introduction but covers more advanced features and concepts. Even readers with prior Scheme experience may wish to work through the examples and exercises found there.

Chapters 4 through 8 make up the reference portion of the text. They present each of Scheme's primitive procedures and syntactic forms in turn, grouping them into short sections of related procedures and forms. Chapter 4 describes operations for creating procedures and variable bindings; Chapter 5, program control operations; Chapter 6, operations on the various object types (including lists, numbers, and strings); Chapter 7, input and output operations; and Chapter 8, syntactic extension.

Chapter 9 contains a collection of complete example programs or packages, each with a short overview, some examples of its use, the implementation with brief explanation, and a set of exercises for further work. Each of these programs demonstrates a particular set of features, and together they illustrate an appropriate style for programming in Scheme.

Following Chapter 9 are a bibliography, answers to selected exercises, a detailed description of the formal syntax of Scheme programs and data, a concise summary of Scheme syntactic forms and procedures, and the index. The summary of forms and procedures is a useful first stop for programmers unsure of the structure of a syntactic form or the arguments expected by a primitive procedure. The page numbers appearing in the summary of forms and procedures and the italicized page numbers appearing in the index indicate the locations in the text where forms and procedures are defined.

Because the reference portion describes a number of aspects of the language not covered by the introductory chapters along with a number of interesting short examples, most readers will find it profitable to read through most of the material to become familiar with each feature and how it relates to other features. Chapter 6 is lengthy, however, and may be skimmed and later referenced as needed.

An online version of this book is available at *http://www.scheme.com/tspl/*. The summary of forms and index in the online edition include page numbers for the printed version and are thus useful as searchable indices.

*About the illustrations:* The cover illustration and the illustrations at the front of each chapter are monohedral tilings created by artist Jean-Pierre Hébert. In a monohedral tiling, all tiles are congruent: they have the same size and shape but may be flipped. The base tile is called the prototile of the tiling. Many familiar and trivial monohedral tilings are known, but no known algorithm exists to decide whether a tile is the prototile of a monohedral tiling.

Some of the most interesting tilings are spiral shaped, and the spirals may have from one to many arms. They come from a number of known prototiles, the first one having been discovered by Voderberg in 1936. Illustrations of the curious Voderberg tile (on the cover and at the front of Chapter 3) show how two tiles can surround one or even two similar ones and how they can be assembled to generate straight lines, arcs or circles, random paths, or regular paths.

For each of the illustrations, a Scheme program was used to define tiles and placement rules for these tiles, resulting in diverse monohedral spiral and non-spiral tilings of the plane. Monohedral tilings were output directly as plane geometries in Postscript to produce the illustrations appearing at the front of Chapters 1, 4, and 7. For the remaining illustrations, the tilings were warped in various ways and augmented with the help of Geomview (Geometry Center, Minneapolis), which allows for spatial manipulations, insertions, and adjustments in color, perspective, light, and material.

*Acknowledgements:* Many individuals contributed in one way or another to the preparation of one or more editions of this book, including Bruce Smith, Eugene Kohlbecker, Matthias Felleisen, Dan Friedman, Bruce Duba, Phil Dybvig, Guy Steele, Bob Hieb, Chris Haynes, Dave Plaisted, Joan Curry, Frank Silbermann, Pavel Curtis, John Wait, Carl Bruggeman, Sam Daniel, Oscar Waddell, Mike Ashley, John LaLonde, John Zuckerman, and John Simmons. Many others have offered minor corrections and suggestions. Oscar Waddell helped create the typesetting system used to format the printed and online versions of this book. Fred is no longer with us, but his faithful companionship is not forgotten. Finally and most importantly, my wife, Susan Dybvig, suggested that I write this book in the first place and lent her expertise and assistance to the production and publication of all three editions.

R. Kent Dybvig
Bloomington, Indiana

# CHAPTER 1

# *Introduction*

*Concentric rings from a crescent shaped prototile.*

Scheme is a general-purpose computer programming language. It is a high-level language, supporting operations on structured data such as strings, lists, and vectors, as well as operations on more traditional data such as numbers and characters. While Scheme is often identified with symbolic applications, its rich set of data types and flexible control structures make it a truly versatile language. Scheme has been employed to write text editors, optimizing compilers, operating systems, graphics packages, expert systems, numerical applications, financial analysis packages, virtual reality systems, and practically every other type of application imaginable. Scheme is a fairly simple language to learn, since it is based on a handful of syntactic forms and semantic concepts and since the interactive nature of most implementations encourages experimentation. Scheme is a challenging language to understand fully, however; developing the ability to use its full potential requires careful study and practice.

Scheme programs are highly portable across implementations of the same Scheme system on different machines, because machine dependencies are almost completely hidden from the programmer. Also, because of two related Scheme standardization efforts, it is possible to write programs that are portable across different Scheme implementations. A formal ANSI/IEEE standard is described in the "IEEE Standard for the Scheme Programming Language" [13]. The ANSI/IEEE standard grew out of an ongoing effort by a group of Scheme designers, who have published a series of less formal reports, the "Revised Reports" on Scheme. The most recent, the "Revised[5] Report" [14], extends the ANSI/IEEE standard in several useful ways.

Although some early Scheme systems were inefficient and slow, many newer compiler-based implementations are fast, with programs running on par with equivalent programs written in lower-level languages. The relative inefficiency that sometimes remains results from run-time checks that support generic arithmetic and help programmers detect and correct various common programming errors. These checks may be disabled in most implementations.

Scheme supports many types of data values, or *objects*, including characters, strings, symbols, lists or vectors of objects, and a full set of numeric data types, including complex, real, and arbitrary-precision rational numbers.

The storage required to hold the contents of an object is dynamically allocated as necessary and retained until no longer needed, then automatically deallocated, typically by a *garbage collector* that periodically recovers the storage used by inaccessible objects. Simple atomic values, such as small integers, characters, booleans, and the empty list, are typically represented as immediate values and thus incur no allocation or deallocation overhead.

Regardless of representation, all objects are *first-class* data values; because they are retained indefinitely, they may be passed freely as arguments to procedures, returned as values from procedures, and combined to form new objects. This is in contrast with many other languages where composite data values such as arrays are either statically allocated and never deallocated, allocated on entry to a block of code and unconditionally deallocated on exit from the block, or explicitly allocated *and* deallocated by the programmer.

Scheme is a call-by-value language, but for mutable objects (objects that can be modified) at least, the values are pointers to the actual storage. These pointers remain behind the scenes, however, and programmers need not be conscious of them except to understand that the storage for an object is not copied when an object is passed to or returned from a procedure.

At the heart of the Scheme language is a small core of syntactic forms from which all other forms are built. These core forms, a set of extended syntactic forms derived from them, and a library of primitive procedures make up the full Scheme language. An interpreter or compiler for Scheme can be quite small and potentially fast and highly reliable. The extended syntactic forms and many primitive procedures can be defined in Scheme itself, simplifying the implementation and increasing reliability.

Scheme programs share a common printed representation with Scheme data structures. As a result, any Scheme program has a natural and obvious internal representation as a Scheme object. For example, variables and syntactic keywords correspond to symbols, while structured syntactic forms correspond to lists. This representation is the basis for the syntactic extension facilities provided by Scheme for the definition of new syntactic forms in terms of existing syntactic forms and procedures. It also facilitates the implementation of interpreters, compilers, and other program transformation tools for Scheme directly in Scheme, as well as program transformation tools for other languages in Scheme.

Scheme variables and keywords are *lexically scoped*, and Scheme programs are *block-structured*. Identifiers may be bound at top level (as are the names of primitive Scheme procedures and syntactic forms) or locally, within a given block of code. A local binding is visible only lexically, i.e., within the program text that makes up the particular block of code. An occurrence of an identifier of the same name outside this block refers to a different binding; if no binding for the identifier exists outside the block, then the reference is invalid. Blocks may be nested, and a binding in one block may *shadow* a binding for an identifier of the same name in a surrounding block. The *scope* of a binding is the block in which the bound identifier is visible minus any portions of the block in which the identifier is shadowed. Block structure and lexical scoping help create programs that are modular, easy to read, easy to maintain, and reliable. Efficient code for lexical scoping is possible because a compiler can determine before program evaluation the scope of all bindings and the binding to which each identifier reference resolves. This does not mean, of course, that a compiler can determine the values of all variables, since the actual values are not computed in most cases until the program executes.

In most languages, a procedure definition is simply the association of a name with a block of code. Certain variables local to the block are the parameters of the procedure. In some languages, a procedure definition may appear within another block or procedure so long as the procedure is invoked only during execution of the enclosing block. In others, procedures can be defined only at top level. In Scheme, a procedure definition may appear within another block or procedure, and the procedure may be invoked at any time thereafter, even if the enclosing block has completed its execution. To support lexical scoping, a procedure carries the lexical context (environment) along with its code.

Furthermore, Scheme procedures are not always named. Instead, procedures are first-class data objects like strings or numbers, and variables are bound to procedures in the same way they are bound to other objects.

As with procedures in most other languages, Scheme procedures may be recursive. That is, any procedure may invoke itself directly or indirectly. Many algorithms are most elegantly or efficiently specified recursively. A special case of recursion, called tail recursion, is used to express iteration, or looping. A *tail call* occurs when one procedure directly returns the result of invoking another procedure; *tail recursion* occurs when a procedure recursively tail calls itself, directly or indirectly. Scheme implementations are required to implement tail calls as jumps (gotos), so the storage overhead normally associated with recursion is avoided. As a result, Scheme programmers need master only simple procedure calls and recursion and need not be burdened with the usual assortment of looping constructs.

Scheme supports the definition of arbitrary control structures with *continuations*. A continuation is a procedure that embodies the remainder of a program at a given point in the program. A continuation may be obtained at any time during the execution of a program. As with other procedures, a continuation is a first-class object and may be invoked at any time after its creation. Whenever it is invoked, the program immediately continues from the point where the continuation was obtained. Continuations allow the implementation of complex control mechanisms including explicit backtracking, multithreading, and coroutines.

Scheme also allows programmers to define new syntactic forms in terms of existing syntactic forms using a convenient high-level pattern language. Syntactic extensions are useful for defining new language constructs, for emulating language constructs found in other languages, for achieving the effects of in-line code expansion, and even for emulating entire languages in Scheme. Most large Scheme programs are built from a mix of syntactic extensions and procedure definitions.

Scheme evolved from the Lisp language and is considered to be a dialect of Lisp. Scheme inherited from Lisp the treatment of values as first-class objects, several important data types, including symbols and lists, and the representation of programs as objects, among other things. Lexical scoping and block structure are features taken from Algol 60 [16]. Scheme was the first Lisp dialect to adopt lexical scoping and block structure, the notion of first-class procedures, treatment of tail calls as jumps, and continuations.

Common Lisp [19] and Scheme are both contemporary Lisp languages, and the development of each has been influenced by the other. Like Scheme but unlike earlier Lisp languages, Common Lisp adopted lexical scoping and first-class procedures, although the Common Lisp's syntactic extension facility does not respect lexical scoping. Common Lisp's evaluation rules for procedures are different from the evaluation rules for other objects, however, and it maintains a separate namespace for procedure variables, thereby inhibiting the use of procedures as first-class objects. Also, Common Lisp does not support continuations or require proper treatment of tail calls, but it does support several less general control structures not found in Scheme. While the two languages are similar, Common Lisp includes more specialized operators, while Scheme includes more general-purpose building blocks out of which such operators (and others) may be built.

The remainder of this chapter describes Scheme's syntax and naming conventions and the typographical conventions used throughout this book.

## 1.1. Scheme Syntax

Scheme programs are made up of keywords, variables, structured forms, constant data (numbers, characters, strings, quoted vectors, quoted lists, quoted symbols, etc.), whitespace, and comments.

Keywords, variables, and symbols are collectively called identifiers. Identifiers may be formed from the following set of characters:

- the lower-case letters `a` through `z`,
- the upper-case letters `A` through `Z`,
- the digits `0` through `9`, and
- the characters `? ! . + - * / < = > : $ % ^ & _ ~ @`.

Identifiers normally cannot start with any character that may start a number, i.e., a digit, plus sign ( `+` ), minus sign ( `-` ), or decimal point ( `.` ). Exceptions are `+`, `-`, and `...`, which are valid identifiers. For example, `hi`, `Hello`, `n`, `x`, `x3`, and `?$&*!!!` are all identifiers. Identifiers must be delimited by whitespace, parentheses, a string (double) quote ( `"` ), or the comment character ( `;` ). All implementations must recognize as identifiers any sequences of characters that adhere to these rules. Other sequences of characters, such as `-1234a`, that do not represent numbers or other syntactic entities may be recognized as identifiers in some implementations, although it is best to avoid such identifiers in code that may need to run in more than one Scheme system.

There is no inherent limit on the length of a Scheme identifier; programmers may use as many characters as necessary. Long identifiers are no substitute for comments, however, and frequent use of long identifiers can make a program difficult to format and consequently difficult to read.

Identifiers may be written in any mix of upper-case and lower-case letters. The case is not important, in that two identifiers differing only in case are identical. For example, `abcde`, `Abcde`, `AbCdE`, and `ABCDE` all refer to the same identifier. Scheme systems typically print an identifier in either all upper-case or all lower-case letters regardless of the way it is entered.

Structured forms and list constants are enclosed within parentheses, e.g., `(a b c)` or `(* (- x 2) y)`. The empty list is written `()`. Some implementations permit the use of brackets ( `[ ]` ) in place of parentheses, and brackets are sometimes used to set off particular subexpressions for readability.

The boolean values representing *true* and *false* are written as `#t` and `#f`. Scheme conditional expressions actually treat `#f` as false and all other objects as true, so `3`, `()`, `"false"`, and `nil` all count as true.

Vectors are written similarly to lists, except that they are preceded by `#(` and terminated by `)`, e.g., `#(this is a vector of symbols)`. Strings are enclosed in double quotation marks, e.g., `"I am a string"`. Characters are preceded by `#\`, e.g., `#\a`. Case is important within character and string constants, unlike within identifiers. Numbers may be written as integers, e.g., -123, as ratios, e.g., 1/2, in floating-point or scientific notation, e.g., 1.3 or 1e23, or as complex numbers in rectangular or polar notation, e.g., 1.3-2.7i or -1.2@73. Details of the syntax for each type of constant data are given in the individual sections of Chapter 6 and in the formal syntax of Scheme given in the back of the book.

Scheme expressions may span several lines, and no explicit terminator is required. Since the number of whitespace characters (spaces and newlines) between expressions is not significant, Scheme programs are normally indented to show the structure of the code in a way that is pleasing to the author of the program. Comments may appear on any line of a Scheme program, between a semicolon ( `;` ) and the end of the line. Comments explaining a particular Scheme expression are normally placed at the same indentation level as the expression, on the line before the expression. Comments explaining a procedure or group of procedures are normally placed before the procedures, without indentation. Multiple comment characters are often used to set off the latter kind of comment, e.g., `;;; The following procedures ....`

## 1.2. Scheme Naming Conventions

Scheme's naming conventions are designed to provide a high degree of regularity. The following is a list of these naming conventions:

- Predicate names end in a question mark ( ? ). Predicates are procedures that return a true or false answer, such as `eq?`, `zero?`, and `string=?`. The common numeric comparators `=`, `<`, `>`, `<=`, and `>=` are exceptions to this naming convention.

- Type predicates, such as `pair?`, are created from the name of the type, in this case `pair`, and the question mark.

- The names of most character, string, and vector procedures start with the prefix `char-`, `string-`, and `vector-`, e.g., `string-append`. (The names of some list procedures start with `list-`, but most do not.)

- The names of procedures that convert an object of one type into an object of another type are written as $type_1$->$type_2$, e.g., `vector->list`.

- The names of procedures and syntactic forms that cause side effects end with an exclamation point ( ! ). These include `set!` and `vector-set!`. Procedures that perform input or output technically cause side effects, but their names are exceptions to this rule.

Programmers should employ these same conventions in their own code whenever possible.

## 1.3. Typographical and Notational Conventions

Often, the value of a procedure or syntactic form is said to be *unspecified*. This means that an implementation is free to return any Scheme object as the value of the procedure or syntactic form. Do not count on this value being the same across implementations, the same across versions of the same implementation, or even the same across two uses of the procedure or syntactic form. Some Scheme systems routinely use a special object to represent unspecified values. Printing of this object is often suppressed by interactive Scheme systems, so that the values of expressions returning unspecified values are not printed.

Scheme expressions usually evaluate to a single value, although the multiple values mechanism described in Section 5.7 allows an expression to evaluate to zero or more than one value. To simplify the presentation, this book usually refers to the result of an expression as a single value even if the expression may in fact evaluate to zero or more than one value.

This book sometimes says "it is an error" or "an error will be signaled" when describing a circumstance in violation of the rules of Scheme. Something that is an error is not valid in Scheme, and the behavior of a Scheme implementation in such a case is not specified. A signaled error results in the invocation of an implementation-dependent error handler, which typically results in an error message being printed and a reset of the interactive programming system or entry into a debugging subsystem.

The typographic conventions used in this book are straightforward. All Scheme objects are printed in a `typewriter` typeface, just as they are to be typed at the keyboard. This includes syntactic keywords, variables, constant objects, Scheme expressions, and example programs. An *italic* typeface is used to set off syntax variables in the descriptions of syntactic forms and arguments in the descriptions of procedures. Italics are also used to set off technical terms the first time they appear. In general, names of syntactic forms and procedures are never capitalized, even at the beginning of a sentence. The same is true for syntax variables written in italics.

In the description of a syntactic form or procedure, a pattern shows the syntactic form or the application of the procedure. The syntax keyword or procedure name is given in typewriter font, as are parentheses. The remaining pieces of the syntax or arguments are shown in italics, using a name that implies the type of expression or argument expected by the syntactic form or procedure. Ellipses are used to specify zero or more occurrences of a subexpression or argument. For example, (`or` *exp* ...) describes the `or` syntactic form, which has zero or more subexpressions, and (`member` *obj list*) describes the `member` procedure, which expects two arguments, an object and a list.

# CHAPTER 2

# *Getting Started*

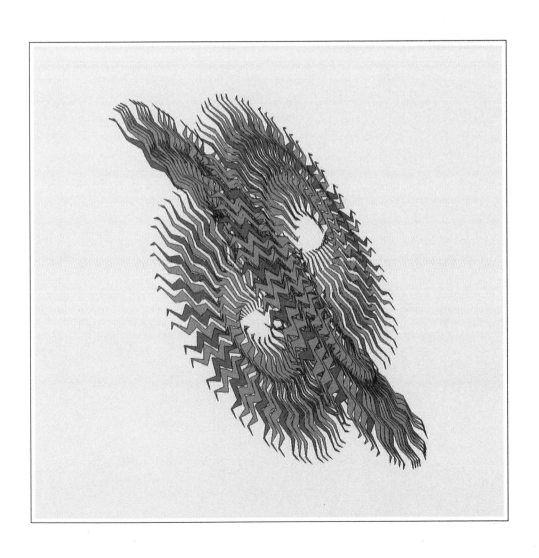

*Two warped, two-armed spirals.*

This chapter is an introduction to Scheme for programmers who are new to the language. You will get more from this chapter if you are sitting in front of an interactive Scheme system, trying out the examples as you go.

After reading this chapter and working the exercises, you should be able to start using Scheme. You will have learned the syntax of Scheme programs and how they are executed, along with how to use simple data structures and control mechanisms.

## 2.1. Interacting with Scheme

Most Scheme systems provide an interactive programming environment that simplifies program development and experimentation. The simplest interaction with Scheme follows a "read-evaluate-print" cycle. A program (often called a *read-evaluate-print loop*, or REPL) reads each expression you type at the keyboard, evaluates it, and prints its value.

With an interactive Scheme system, you can type an expression at the keyboard and see its value immediately. You can define a procedure and apply it to arguments to see how it works. You can even type in an entire program consisting of a set of procedure definitions and test it without leaving the system. When your program starts getting longer, it will be more convenient to type it into a file (using a text editor), load the file (using `load`), and test it interactively. Preparing your program in a file has several advantages: you have a chance to compose your program more carefully, you can correct errors without retyping the program, and you can retain a copy for later use. Scheme treats expressions loaded from a file the same as expressions typed from the keyboard.

While Scheme provides various input and output procedures, the REPL takes care of reading expressions and printing their values. Furthermore, if you need to save the results for later use, you can make a transcript (using `transcript-on` and `transcript-off`; see Section 7.4) of an interactive session. This frees you to concentrate on writing your program without worrying about how its results will be displayed or saved.

The examples in this chapter and in the rest of the book follow a regular format. An expression you might type from your keyboard is given first, possibly spanning several lines. The value of the expression is given after the ⇒, to be read as "evaluates to." The ⇒ is omitted when the value of the expression is unspecified, e.g., for variable definitions.

The example programs are formatted in a style that "looks nice" and conveys the structure of the program. The code is easy to read because the relationship between each expression and its subexpressions is clearly shown. Scheme ignores indentation and line breaks, however, so there is no need to follow a particular style. The important thing is to establish one style and keep to it. Scheme sees each program as if it were on a single line, with its subexpressions ordered from left to right.

If you have access to an interactive Scheme system, it might be a good idea to start it up now and type in the examples as you read. One of the simplest Scheme expressions is a string constant. Try typing "Hi Mom!" (including the double quotes) in response to the prompt. The system should respond with "Hi Mom!"; the value of any constant is the constant itself.

```
"Hi Mom!"  ⇒  "Hi Mom!"
```

Here is a set of expressions, each with Scheme's response. They are explained in later sections of this chapter, but for now use them to practice interacting with Scheme.

```
"hello"  ⇒  "hello"
42  ⇒  42
22/7  ⇒  22/7
3.141592653  ⇒  3.141592653
+  ⇒  #<procedure>
(+ 76 31)  ⇒  107
'(a b c d)  ⇒  (a b c d)
```

Be careful not to miss any single quotes ( ' ), double quotes, or parentheses. If you left off a single quote in the last expression, you probably received an error message. Just try again. If you left off a closing parenthesis or double quote, the system may still be waiting for it.

Here are a few more expressions to try. You can try to figure out on your own what they mean or wait to find out later in the chapter.

```
(car '(a b c))  ⇒  a
(cdr '(a b c))  ⇒  (b c)
(cons 'a '(b c))  ⇒  (a b c)
(cons (car '(a b c))
      (cdr '(d e f)))  ⇒  (a e f)
```

As you can see, Scheme expressions may span more than one line. The Scheme system knows when it has an entire expression by matching double quotes and parentheses.

Next, let's try defining a procedure.

```
(define square
  (lambda (n)
    (* n n)))
```

The procedure **square** computes the square $n^2$ of any number $n$. We say more about the expressions that make up this definition later in this chapter. For now it suffices to say that **define** establishes variable bindings, **lambda** creates procedures,

and * names the multiplication procedure. Note the form of these expressions. All
structured forms are enclosed in parentheses and written in *prefix notation*, i.e.,
the operator precedes the arguments. As you can see, this is true even for simple
arithmetic operations such as *.

Try using `square`.

```
(square 5)  ⇒  25
(square -200)  ⇒  40000
(square 0.5)  ⇒  0.25
(square -1/2)  ⇒  1/4
```

Scheme systems that do not support exact ratios internally may print `0.25` for
`(square -1/2)`.

Even though the next definition is short, you might enter it into a file. Let's
assume you call the file "reciprocal.ss."

```
(define reciprocal
  (lambda (n)
    (if (= n 0)
        "oops!"
        (/ 1 n))))
```

This procedure, `reciprocal`, computes the quantity $1/n$ for any number $n \neq 0$. For
$n = 0$, `reciprocal` returns the string `"oops!"`. Return to Scheme and try loading
your file with the procedure `load`.

```
(load "reciprocal.ss")
```

Finally, try using the procedure we have just defined.

```
(reciprocal 10)  ⇒  1/10
(reciprocal 1/10)  ⇒  10
(reciprocal 0)  ⇒  "oops!"
(reciprocal (reciprocal 1/10))  ⇒  1/10
```

In the next section we will discuss Scheme expressions in more detail. Throughout this chapter, keep in mind that your Scheme system is one of the most useful
tools for learning Scheme. Whenever you try one of the examples in the text, follow
it up with your own examples. In an interactive Scheme system, the cost of trying
something out is relatively small—usually just the time to type it in.

## 2.2. Simple Expressions

The simplest Scheme expressions are constant data objects, such as strings, numbers, symbols, and lists. Scheme supports other object types, but these four are
enough for many programs. We saw some examples of strings and numbers in the
preceding section.

Let's discuss numbers in a little more detail. Numbers are constants. If you enter a number, Scheme echoes it back to you. The following examples show that Scheme supports several types of numbers.

```
123456789987654321  ⇒  123456789987654321
3/4  ⇒  3/4
2.718281828  ⇒  2.718281828
2.2+1.1i  ⇒  2.2+1.1i
```

Scheme numbers include exact and inexact integer, rational, real, and complex numbers. Exact integers and rational numbers have arbitrary precision, i.e., they can be of arbitrary size. Inexact numbers are usually represented internally using IEEE standard floating-point representations. Scheme implementations, however, need not support all types of numbers and have great freedom where internal representations are concerned. Experiment to determine what kind of numbers the Scheme system you are using supports.

Scheme provides the names +, -, *, and / for the corresponding arithmetic procedures. Each procedure accepts two numeric arguments. The expressions below are called *procedure applications*, because they specify the application of a procedure to a set of arguments.

```
(+ 1/2 1/2)  ⇒  1
(- 1.5 1/2)  ⇒  1.0

(* 3 1/2)  ⇒  3/2
(/ 1.5 3/4)  ⇒  2.0
```

Scheme employs prefix notation even for common arithmetic operations. Any procedure application, whether the procedure takes zero, one, two, or more arguments, is written as (*procedure arg* ...). This regularity simplifies the syntax of expressions; one notation is employed regardless of the operation, and there are no complicated rules regarding the precedence or associativity of operators.

Procedure applications may be nested, in which case the innermost values are computed first. We can thus nest applications of the arithmetic procedures given above to evaluate more complicated formulas.

```
(+ (+ 2 2) (+ 2 2))  ⇒  8
(- 2 (* 4 1/3))  ⇒  2/3
(* 2 (* 2 (* 2 (* 2 2))))  ⇒  32
(/ (* 6/7 7/2) (- 4.5 1.5))  ⇒  1.0
```

These examples demonstrate everything you need to use Scheme as a four-function desk calculator. While we will not discuss them in this chapter, Scheme supports many other arithmetic procedures. Now might be a good time to turn to Section 6.4 and experiment with some of them.

Simple numeric objects are sufficient for many tasks, but sometimes aggregate data structures containing two or more values are needed. In many languages, the basic aggregate data structure is the array. In Scheme, it is the *list*. Lists are written as sequences of objects surrounded by parentheses. For instance, (1 2 3 4 5) is a list of numbers, and ("this" "is" "a" "list") is a list of strings. Lists need not contain only one type of object, so (4.2 "hi") is a valid list containing a number and a string. Lists may be nested (may contain other lists), so ((1 2) (3 4)) is a valid list with two elements, each of which is a list of two elements.

You may notice that lists look just like procedure applications and wonder how Scheme tells them apart. That is, how does Scheme distinguish between a list of objects, (*obj₁ obj₂* ...), and a procedure application, (*procedure arg* ...)?

In some cases, the distinction may seem obvious. The list of numbers (1 2 3 4 5) could hardly be confused with a procedure application, since 1 is a number, not a procedure. So, the answer might be that Scheme looks at the first element of the list or procedure application and makes its decision based on whether that first element is a procedure or not. This answer is not good enough, since we may even want to treat a valid procedure application such as (+ 3 4) as a list. The answer is that we must tell Scheme explicitly to treat a list as data rather than as a procedure application. We do this with **quote**.

```
(quote (1 2 3 4 5))  ⇒  (1 2 3 4 5)
(quote ("this" "is" "a" "list"))  ⇒  ("this" "is" "a" "list")
(quote (+ 3 4))  ⇒  (+ 3 4)
```

The **quote** forces the list to be treated as data. Try entering the above expressions without the quote; you will likely receive an error message for the first two and an incorrect answer (7) for the third.

Because **quote** is required fairly frequently in Scheme code, Scheme recognizes a single quotation mark ( ' ) preceding an expression as an abbreviation for **quote**.

```
'(1 2 3 4)  ⇒  (1 2 3 4)
'((1 2) (3 4))  ⇒  ((1 2) (3 4))
'(/ (* 2 -1) 3)  ⇒  (/ (* 2 -1) 3)
```

Both forms are referred to as **quote** expressions. We often say an object is *quoted* when it is enclosed in a **quote** expression.

A **quote** expression is *not* a procedure application, since it inhibits the evaluation of its subexpression. It is an entirely different syntactic form. Scheme supports several other syntactic forms in addition to procedure applications and **quote** expressions. Each syntactic form is evaluated differently. Fortunately, the number of different syntactic forms is small. We will see more of them later in this chapter.

Not all **quote** expressions involve lists. Try the following expression with and without the **quote**.

```
(quote hello)  ⇒  hello
```

The symbol `hello` must be quoted in order to prevent Scheme from treating `hello` as a *variable*. Symbols and variables in Scheme are similar to symbols and variables in mathematical expressions and equations. When we evaluate the mathematical expression $1 - x$ for some value of $x$, we think of $x$ as a variable. On the other hand, when we consider the algebraic equation $x^2 - 1 = (x - 1)(x + 1)$, we think of $x$ as a symbol (in fact, we think of the whole equation symbolically). Just as quoting a list tells Scheme to treat a parenthesized form as a list rather than as a procedure application, quoting an identifier tells Scheme to treat the identifier as a symbol rather than as a variable. While symbols are commonly used to represent variables in symbolic representations of equations or programs, symbols may also be used, for example, as words in the representation of natural language sentences.

You might wonder why applications and variables share notations with lists and symbols. The shared notation allows Scheme programs to be represented as Scheme data, simplifying the writing of interpreters, compilers, editors, and other tools in Scheme. This is demonstrated by the Scheme interpreter given in Section 9.7, which is itself written in Scheme. Many people believe this to be one of the most important features of Scheme.

Numbers and strings may be quoted, too.

```
'2  ⇒  2
'2/3  ⇒  2/3
(quote "Hi Mom!")  ⇒  "Hi Mom!"
```

Numbers and strings are treated as constants in any case, however, so quoting them is unnecessary.

Now let's discuss some Scheme procedures for manipulating lists. There are two basic procedures for taking lists apart: `car` and `cdr` (pronounced *could-er*). `car` returns the first element of a list, and `cdr` returns the remainder of the list. (The names "car" and "cdr" are derived from operations supported by the first computer on which a Lisp language was implemented, the IBM 704.) Each requires a nonempty list as its argument.

```
(car '(a b c))  ⇒  a
(cdr '(a b c))  ⇒  (b c)
(cdr '(a))  ⇒  ()

(car (cdr '(a b c)))  ⇒  b
(cdr (cdr '(a b c)))  ⇒  (c)

(car '((a b) (c d)))  ⇒  (a b)
(cdr '((a b) (c d)))  ⇒  ((c d))
```

The first element of a list is often called the "car" of the list, and the rest of the list is often called the "cdr" of the list. The cdr of a list with one element is (), the *empty list*.

The procedure **cons** constructs lists. It takes two arguments. The second argument is usually a list, and in that case **cons** returns a list.

```
(cons 'a '())  ⇒  (a)
(cons 'a '(b c))  ⇒  (a b c)
(cons 'a (cons 'b (cons 'c '()))))  ⇒  (a b c)
(cons '(a b) '(c d))  ⇒  ((a b) c d)

(car (cons 'a '(b c)))  ⇒  a
(cdr (cons 'a '(b c)))  ⇒  (b c)
(cons (car '(a b c))
      (cdr '(d e f)))  ⇒  (a e f)
(cons (car '(a b c))
      (cdr '(a b c)))  ⇒  (a b c)
```

Just as "car" and "cdr" are often used as nouns, "cons" is often used as a verb. Creating a new list by adding an element to the beginning of a list is referred to as *consing* the element onto the list.

Notice the word "usually" in the description of **cons**'s second argument. The procedure **cons** actually builds *pairs*, and there is no reason that the cdr of a pair must be a list. A list is a sequence of pairs; each pair's cdr is the next pair in the sequence.

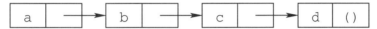

The cdr of the last pair in a *proper list* is the empty list. Otherwise, the sequence of pairs forms an *improper list*. More formally, the empty list is a proper list, and any pair whose cdr is a proper list is a proper list.

An improper list is printed in *dotted-pair notation*, with a period, or *dot*, preceding the final element of the list.

```
(cons 'a 'b)  ⇒  (a . b)
(cdr '(a . b))  ⇒  b
(cons 'a '(b . c))  ⇒  (a b . c)
```

Because of its printed notation, a pair whose cdr is not a list is often called a *dotted pair*. Even pairs whose cdrs are lists can be written in dotted-pair notation, however, although the printer always chooses to write proper lists without dots.

```
'(a . (b . (c . ()))))  ⇒  (a b c)
```

The procedure **list** is similar to **cons**, except that it takes an arbitrary number of arguments and always builds a proper list.

```
(list 'a 'b 'c)  ⇒  (a b c)
(list 'a)  ⇒  (a)
(list)  ⇒  ()
```

   Section 6.3 provides more information on lists and the Scheme procedures for manipulating them. This might be a good time to turn to that section and familiarize yourself with the other procedures given there.

**Exercise 2.2.1.** Convert the following arithmetic expressions into Scheme expressions and evaluate them.

   a. $1.2 \times (2 - 1/3) + -8.7$
   b. $(2/3 + 4/9) \div (5/11 - 4/3)$
   c. $1 + 1 \div (2 + 1 \div (1 + 1/2))$
   d. $1 \times -2 \times 3 \times -4 \times 5 \times -6 \times 7$

**Exercise 2.2.2.** Experiment with the procedures +, -, *, and / to determine Scheme's rules for the type of value returned by each when given different types of numeric arguments.

**Exercise 2.2.3.** Determine the values of the following expressions. Use your Scheme system to verify your answers.

   a. `(cons 'car 'cdr)`
   b. `(list 'this '(is silly))`
   c. `(cons 'is '(this silly?))`
   d. `(quote (+ 2 3))`
   e. `(cons '+ '(2 3))`
   f. `(car '(+ 2 3))`
   g. `(cdr '(+ 2 3))`
   h. `cons`
   i. `(quote cons)`
   j. `(quote (quote cons))`
   k. `(car (quote (quote cons)))`
   l. `(+ 2 3)`
   m. `(+ '2 '3)`
   n. `(+ (car '(2 3)) (car (cdr '(2 3))))`
   o. `((car (list + - * /)) 2 3)`

**Exercise 2.2.4.** `(car (car '((a b) (c d))))` yields a. Determine which compositions of `car` and `cdr` applied to `((a b) (c d))` yield b, c, and d.

**Exercise 2.2.5.** Write a Scheme expression that evaluates to the following internal list structure.

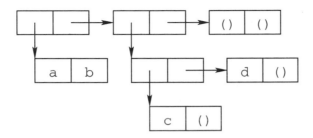

**Exercise 2.2.6.** Draw the internal list structure produced by the expression below.

`(cons 1 (cons '(2 . ((3) . ())) (cons '(()) (cons 4 5))))`

**Exercise 2.2.7.** The behavior of `(car (car (car '((a b) (c d)))))` is undefined because `(car '((a b) (c d)))` is `(a b)`, `(car '(a b))` is `a`, and `(car 'a)` is undefined. Determine all legal compositions of `car` and `cdr` applied to `((a b) (c d))`.

**Exercise 2.2.8.** Try to explain how Scheme expressions are evaluated. Does your explanation cover the last example in Exercise 2.2.3?

## 2.3. Evaluating Scheme Expressions

Let's turn to a discussion of how Scheme evaluates the expressions you type. We have already established the rules for constant objects such as strings and numbers; the object itself is the value. You have probably also worked out in your mind a rule for evaluating procedure applications of the form (*procedure* $arg_1$ ... $arg_n$). Here, *procedure* is an expression representing a Scheme procedure, and $arg_1$ ... $arg_n$ are expressions representing its arguments. One possibility is the following.

- Find the value of *procedure*.
- Find the value of $arg_1$.

  ⋮

- Find the value of $arg_n$.
- Apply the value of *procedure* to the values of $arg_1$ ... $arg_n$.

For example, consider the simple procedure application (+ 3 4). The value of + is the addition procedure, the value of 3 is the number 3, and the value of 4 is the number 4. Applying the addition procedure to 3 and 4 yields 7, so our value is the object 7.

By applying this process at each level, we can find the value of the nested expression (* (+ 3 4) 2). The value of * is the multiplication procedure, the value of (+ 3 4) we can determine to be the number 7, and the value of 2 is the number 2. Multiplying 7 by 2 we get 14, so our answer is 14.

This rule works for procedure applications but not for quote expressions because the subexpressions of a procedure application are evaluated, whereas the subexpression of a quote expression is not. The evaluation of a quote expression is more similar to the evaluation of constant objects. The value of a quote expression of the form (quote *object*) is simply *object*.

Constant objects, procedure applications, and quote expressions are only three of the many syntactic forms provided by Scheme. Fortunately, only a few of the other syntactic forms need to be understood directly by a Scheme programmer; these are referred to as *core* syntactic forms. The remaining syntactic forms are *syntactic extensions* defined, ultimately, in terms of the core syntactic forms. We will discuss the remaining core syntactic forms and a few syntactic extensions in the remaining sections of this chapter. Section 3.1 summarizes the core syntactic forms and introduces the syntactic extension mechanism.

Before we go on to more syntactic forms and procedures, two points related to the evaluation of procedure applications are worthy of note. First, the process given above is overspecified, in that it requires the subexpressions to be evaluated from left to right. That is, *procedure* is evaluated before $arg_1$, $arg_1$ is evaluated before $arg_2$, and so on. This need not be the case. A Scheme evaluator is free to evaluate the expressions in any order—left to right, right to left, or any other sequential order. In fact, the subexpressions may be evaluated in different orders for different applications even in the same implementation.

The second point is that *procedure* is evaluated in the same manner as $arg_1$ ... $arg_n$. While *procedure* is often a variable that names a particular procedure, this need not be the case. Exercise 2.2.3 had you determine the value of ((car (list + - * /)) 2 3). Here, *procedure* is (car (list + - * /)). The value of (car (list + - * /)) is the addition procedure, just as if *procedure* were simply the variable +.

**Exercise 2.3.1.** Write down the steps necessary to evaluate the expression below.

((car (cdr (list + - * /))) 17 5)

# 2.4. Variables and Let Expressions

Suppose *expr* is a Scheme expression that contains a variable *var*. Suppose, additionally, that we would like *var* to have the value *val* when we evaluate *expr*. For example, we might like x to have the value 2 when we evaluate (+ x 3). Or,

we might want y to have the value 3 when we evaluate (+ 2 y). The following
examples demonstrate how to do this using Scheme's let syntactic form.

```
(let ((x 2))
  (+ x 3))  ⇒  5
(let ((y 3))
  (+ 2 y))  ⇒  5
(let ((x 2) (y 3))
  (+ x y))  ⇒  5
```

The let syntactic form includes a list of variable-expression pairs, along with a
sequence of expressions referred to as the *body* of the let. The general form of a
let expression is

```
(let ((var val) ...) exp₁ exp₂ ...)
```

We say the variables are *bound* to the values by the let. We refer to variables
bound by let as let-*bound* variables.

A let expression is often used to simplify an expression that would contain
two identical subexpressions. Doing so also ensures that the value of the common
subexpression is computed only once.

```
(+ (* 4 4) (* 4 4))  ⇒  32
(let ((a (* 4 4)))
  (+ a a))  ⇒  32
(let ((list1 '(a b c)) (list2 '(d e f)))
  (cons (cons (car list1)
              (car list2))
        (cons (car (cdr list1))
              (car (cdr list2)))))  ⇒  ((a . d) b . e)
```

Since expressions in the first position of a procedure application are evaluated no
differently from other expressions, a let-bound variable may be used there as well.

```
(let ((f +))
  (f 2 3))  ⇒  5
(let ((f +) (x 2))
  (f x 3))  ⇒  5
(let ((f +) (x 2) (y 3))
  (f x y))  ⇒  5
```

The variables bound by let are visible only within the body of the let.

```
(let ((+ *))
  (+ 2 3))  ⇒  6
(+ 2 3)  ⇒  5
```

This is fortunate, because we would not want the value of + to be the multiplication procedure everywhere.

It is possible to nest `let` expressions.

```
(let ((a 4) (b -3))
  (let ((a-squared (* a a))
        (b-squared (* b b)))
    (+ a-squared b-squared)))  ⇒  25
```

When nested `let` expressions bind the same variable, only the binding created by the inner `let` is visible within its body.

```
(let ((x 1))
  (let ((x (+ x 1)))
    (+ x x)))  ⇒  4
```

The outer `let` expression binds x to 1 within its body, which is the second `let` expression. The inner `let` expression binds x to (+ x 1) within its body, which is the expression (+ x x). What is the value of (+ x 1)? Since (+ x 1) appears within the body of the outer `let` but not within the body of the inner `let`, the value of x must be 1 and hence the value of (+ x 1) is 2. What about (+ x x)? It appears within the body of both `let` expressions. Only the inner binding for x is visible, so x is 2 and (+ x x) is 4.

The inner binding for x is said to *shadow* the outer binding. A `let`-bound variable is visible everywhere within the body of its `let` expression except where it is shadowed. The region where a variable binding is visible is called its *scope*. The scope of the first x in the example above is the body of the outer `let` expression minus the body of the inner `let` expression, where it is shadowed by the second x. This form of scoping is referred to as *lexical scoping*, since the scope of each binding can be determined by a straightforward textual analysis of the program.

Shadowing may be avoided by choosing different names for variables. The expression above could be rewritten so that the variable bound by the inner `let` is `new-x`.

```
(let ((x 1))
  (let ((new-x (+ x 1)))
    (+ new-x new-x)))  ⇒  4
```

Although choosing different names can sometimes prevent confusion, shadowing can help prevent the accidental use of an "old" value. For example, with the original version of the preceding example, it would be impossible for us to mistakenly refer to the outer x within the body of the inner `let`.

**Exercise 2.4.1.** Rewrite the following expressions, using `let` to remove common subexpressions and to improve the structure of the code. Do not perform any algebraic simplifications.

   *a.* `(+ (- (* 3 a) b) (+ (* 3 a) b))`
   *b.* `(cons (car (list a b c)) (cdr (list a b c)))`

**Exercise 2.4.2.** Determine the value of the following expression. Explain how you derived this value.

```
(let ((x 9))
  (* x
     (let ((x (/ x 3)))
       (+ x x))))
```

**Exercise 2.4.3.** Rewrite the following expressions to give unique names to each different `let`-bound variable so that none of the variables is shadowed. Verify that the value of your expression is the same as that of the original expression.

   *a.*
```
(let ((x 'a) (y 'b))
  (list (let ((x 'c)) (cons x y))
        (let ((y 'd)) (cons x y))))
```
   *b.*
```
(let ((x '((a b) c)))
  (cons (let ((x (cdr x)))
          (car x))
        (let ((x (car x)))
          (cons (let ((x (cdr x)))
                  (car x))
                (cons (let ((x (car x)))
                        x)
                      (cdr x))))))
```

## 2.5. Lambda Expressions

In the expression `(let ((x (* 3 4))) (+ x x))`, the variable `x` is bound to the value of `(* 3 4)`. What if we would like the value of `(+ x x)` where `x` is bound to the value of `(/ 99 11)`? Where `x` is bound to the value of `(- 2 7)`? In each case we need a different `let` expression. When the body of the `let` is complicated, however, having to repeat it can be inconvenient.

    Instead, we can use the syntactic form `lambda` to create a new procedure that has `x` as a parameter and has the same body as the `let` expression.

`(lambda (x) (+ x x))` ⇒ `#<procedure>`

The general form of a `lambda` expression is

`(lambda (`*var* `...)` *exp*$_1$ *exp*$_2$ `...)`

The variables *var* ... are the *formal parameters* of the procedure, and the sequence of expressions *exp*$_1$ *exp*$_2$ ... is its body. (Actually, the true general form is somewhat more general than this, as you will see later.)

A procedure is just as much an object as a number, string, symbol, or pair. It does not have any meaningful printed representation as far as Scheme is concerned, however, so this book uses the notation #<procedure> to show that the value of an expression is a procedure.

The most common operation to perform on a procedure is to apply it to one or more values.

```
((lambda (x) (+ x x)) (* 3 4))  ⇒  24
```

This is no different from any other procedure application. The procedure is the value of (lambda (x) (+ x x)), and the only argument is the value of (* 3 4), or 12. The argument values, or *actual parameters*, are bound to the formal parameters within the body of the lambda expression in the same way as let-bound variables are bound to their values. In this case, x is bound to 12, and the value of (+ x x) is 24. Thus, the result of applying the procedure to the value 12 is 24.

Because procedures are objects, we can establish a procedure as the value of a variable and use the procedure more than once.

```
(let ((double (lambda (x) (+ x x))))
  (list (double (* 3 4))
        (double (/ 99 11))
        (double (- 2 7))))  ⇒  (24 18 -10)
```

Here, we establish a binding for double to a procedure, then use this procedure to double three different values.

The procedure expects its actual parameter to be a number, since it passes the actual parameter on to +. In general, the actual parameter may be any sort of object. Consider, for example, a similar procedure that uses cons instead of +.

```
(let ((double-cons (lambda (x) (cons x x))))
  (double-cons 'a))  ⇒  (a . a)
```

Noting the similarity between double and double-cons, you should not be surprised to learn that they may be collapsed into a single procedure by adding an additional argument.

```
(let ((double-any (lambda (f x) (f x x))))
  (list (double-any + 13)
        (double-any cons 'a)))  ⇒  (26 (a . a))
```

This demonstrates that procedures may accept more than one argument and that arguments passed to a procedure may themselves be procedures.

As with let expressions, lambda expressions become somewhat more interesting when they are nested within other lambda or let expressions.

```
(let ((x 'a))
  (let ((f (lambda (y) (list x y))))
    (f 'b)))  ⇒  (a b)
```

The occurrence of x within the lambda expression refers to the x outside the lambda that is bound by the outer let expression. The variable x is said to *occur free* in the lambda expression or to be a *free variable* of the lambda expression. The variable y does not occur free in the lambda expression since it is bound by the lambda expression. A variable that occurs free in a lambda expression should be bound by an enclosing lambda or let expression, unless the variable is (like the names of primitive procedures) bound at top level, as we discuss in the following section.

What happens when the procedure is applied somewhere outside the scope of the bindings for variables that occur free within the procedure, as in the following expression?

```
(let ((f (let ((x 'sam))
           (lambda (y z) (list x y z)))))
  (f 'i 'am))  ⇒  (sam i am)
```

The answer is that the same bindings that were in effect when the procedure was created are in effect again when the procedure is applied. This is true even if another binding for x is visible where the procedure is applied.

```
(let ((f (let ((x 'sam))
           (lambda (y z) (list x y z)))))
  (let ((x 'not-sam))
    (f 'i 'am)))  ⇒  (sam i am)
```

In both cases, the value of x within the procedure named f is sam.

Incidentally, a let expression is nothing more than the direct application of a lambda expression to a set of argument expressions. For example, the two expressions below are equivalent.

```
(let ((x 'a)) (cons x x)) ≡ ((lambda (x) (cons x x)) 'a)
```

In fact, a let expression is a syntactic extension defined in terms of lambda and procedure application, which are both core syntactic forms. In general, any expression of the form

```
(let ((var val) ...) exp₁ exp₂ ...)
```

is equivalent to the following.

```
((lambda (var ...) exp₁ exp₂ ...)
  val ...)
```

See Section 3.1 for more about core forms and syntactic extensions.

As mentioned above, the general form for `lambda` is a bit more complicated than the form we saw earlier, in that the formal parameter specification, (*var* ...), need not be a proper list, or indeed even a list at all. The formal parameter specification can be in any of the following three forms.

- a proper list of variables, ($var_1$ ... $var_n$), such as we have already seen,

- a single variable, $var_r$, or

- an improper list of variables, ($var_1$ ... $var_n$ . $var_r$).

In the first case, exactly $n$ actual parameters must be supplied, and each variable is bound to the corresponding actual parameter. In the second, any number of actual parameters is valid; all of the actual parameters are put into a single list and the single variable is bound to this list. The third case is a hybrid of the first two cases. At least $n$ actual parameters must be supplied. The variables $var_1$ ... $var_n$ are bound to the corresponding actual parameters, and the variable $var_r$ is bound to a list containing the remaining actual parameters. In the second and third cases, $var_r$ is sometimes referred to as a "rest" parameter because it holds the rest of the actual parameters beyond those that are individually named.

Let's consider a few examples to help clarify the more general syntax of `lambda` expressions.

```
(let ((f (lambda x x)))
  (f 1 2 3 4))  ⇒  (1 2 3 4)
(let ((f (lambda x x)))
  (f))  ⇒  ()
(let ((g (lambda (x . y) (list x y))))
  (g 1 2 3 4))  ⇒  (1 (2 3 4))
(let ((h (lambda (x y . z) (list x y z))))
  (h 'a 'b 'c 'd))  ⇒  (a b (c d))
```

In the first two examples, the procedure named `f` accepts any number of arguments. These arguments are automatically formed into a list to which the variable `x` is bound; the value of `f` is this list. In the first example, the arguments are 1, 2, 3, and 4, so the answer is (1 2 3 4). In the second, there are no arguments, so the answer is the empty list (). The value of the procedure named `g` in the third example is a list whose first element is the first argument and whose second element is a list containing the remaining arguments. The procedure named `h` is similar but separates out the second argument. While `f` accepts any number of arguments, `g` must receive at least one and `h` must receive at least two.

**Exercise 2.5.1.** Determine the values of the expressions below.

*a.* ```
(let ((f (lambda (x) x)))
  (f 'a))
```
*b.* ```
(let ((f (lambda x x)))
  (f 'a))
```
*c.* ```
(let ((f (lambda (x . y) x)))
  (f 'a))
```
*d.* ```
(let ((f (lambda (x . y) y)))
  (f 'a))
```

**Exercise 2.5.2.** How might the primitive procedure `list` be defined?

**Exercise 2.5.3.** List the variables that occur free in each of the `lambda` expressions below. Do not omit variables that name primitive procedures such as + or cons.

*a.* ```
(lambda (f x) (f x))
```
*b.* ```
(lambda (x) (+ x x))
```
*c.* ```
(lambda (x y) (f x y))
```
*d.* ```
(lambda (x)
  (cons x (f x y)))
```
*e.* ```
(lambda (x)
  (let ((z (cons x y)))
    (x y z)))
```
*f.* ```
(lambda (x)
  (let ((y (cons x y)))
    (x y z)))
```

# 2.6. Top-Level Definitions

The variables bound by `let` and `lambda` expressions are not visible outside the bodies of these expressions. Suppose you have created an object, perhaps a procedure, that must be accessible anywhere, like + or `cons`. What you need is a *top-level definition*, which may be established with `define`. Top-level definitions are visible in every expression you enter, except where shadowed by another binding.

Let's establish a top-level definition of the **double-any** procedure of the last section.

```
(define double-any
  (lambda (f x)
    (f x x)))
```

The variable **double-any** now has the same status as **cons** or the name of any other primitive procedure. We can use **double-any** as if it were a primitive procedure.

```
(double-any + 10)  ⇒  20
(double-any cons 'a)  ⇒  (a . a)
```

A top-level definition may be established for any object, not just for procedures.

```
(define sandwich "peanut-butter-and-jelly")
```

```
sandwich  ⇒  "peanut-butter-and-jelly"
```

Most often, though, top-level definitions are used for procedures.

As suggested above, top-level definitions may be shadowed by `let` or `lambda` bindings.

```
(define xyz '(x y z))
(let ((xyz '(z y x)))
  xyz)  ⇒  (z y x)
```

Variables with top-level definitions act almost as if they were bound by a `let` expression enclosing all of the expressions you type.

Given only the simple tools you have read about up to this point, it is already possible to define some of the primitive procedures provided by Scheme and described later in this book. If you completed the exercises from the last section, you should already know how to define `list`.

```
(define list (lambda x x))
```

Also, Scheme provides the abbreviations `cadr` and `cddr` for the compositions of `car` with `cdr` and `cdr` with `cdr`. That is, (`cadr` *list*) is equivalent to (`car` (`cdr` *list*)), and, similarly, (`cddr` *list*) is equivalent to (`cdr` (`cdr` *list*)). They are easily defined as follows.

```
(define cadr
  (lambda (x)
    (car (cdr x))))
(define cddr
  (lambda (x)
    (cdr (cdr x))))
```

```
(cadr '(a b c))  ⇒  b
(cddr '(a b c))  ⇒  (c)
```

Any definition (`define` *var* *exp*) where *exp* is a `lambda` expression can be written in a shorter form that suppresses the `lambda`. The exact syntax depends upon the format of the `lambda` expression's formal parameter specifier, i.e., whether it is a proper list of variables, a single variable, or an improper list of variables. A definition of the form

```
(define var₀
  (lambda (var₁ ... varₙ)
    e₁ e₂ ...))
```

may be abbreviated

```
(define (var_0 var_1 ... var_n)
  e_1 e_2 ...)
```

while

```
(define var_0
  (lambda var_r
    e_1 e_2 ...))
```

may be abbreviated

```
(define (var_0 . var_r)
  e_1 e_2 ...)
```

and

```
(define var_0
  (lambda (var_1 ... var_n . var_r)
    e_1 e_2 ...))
```

may be abbreviated

```
(define (var_0 var_1 ... var_n . var_r)
  e_1 e_2 ...)
```

For example, the definitions of cadr and list may be written as follows.

```
(define (cadr x)
  (car (cdr x)))
```

```
(define (list . x) x)
```

This book does not often employ this alternative syntax. Although it is shorter, it tends to mask the reality that procedures are not intimately tied to variables, or names, as they are in many other languages. This syntax is often referred to, somewhat pejoratively, as the "defun" syntax for define, after the defun form provided by Lisp languages in which procedures are more closely tied to their names.

Top-level definitions make it easier for us to experiment with a procedure interactively because we need not retype the procedure each time it is used. Let's try defining a somewhat more complicated variation of double-any, one that turns an "ordinary" two-argument procedure into a "doubling" one-argument procedure.

```
(define doubler
  (lambda (f)
    (lambda (x) (f x x))))
```

doubler accepts one argument, f, which must be a procedure that accepts two arguments. The procedure returned by doubler accepts one argument, which it uses for both arguments in an application of f. We can define, with doubler, the simple double and double-cons procedures of the last section.

```
(define double (doubler +))
(double 13/2)   ⇒   13

(define double-cons (doubler cons))
(double-cons 'a)   ⇒   (a . a)
```

We can also define **double-any** with **doubler**.

```
(define double-any
  (lambda (f x)
    ((doubler f) x)))
```

Within **double** and **double-cons**, **f** has the appropriate value, i.e., **+** or **cons**, even though the procedures are clearly applied outside the scope of **f**.

What happens if you attempt to use a variable that is not bound by a **let** or **lambda** expression and that does not have a top-level definition? Try using the variable **i-am-not-defined** to see what happens.

```
(i-am-not-defined 3)
```

Most Scheme systems print an error message to inform you that the variable is unbound or undefined.

The system will not complain about the appearance of an undefined variable within a **lambda** expression, until and unless the resulting procedure is applied. The following should *not* cause an error, even though we have not yet established a top-level definition of **proc2**.

```
(define proc1
  (lambda (x y)
    (proc2 y x)))
```

If you try to apply **proc1** before defining **proc2**, you should get an error message. Let's give **proc2** a top-level definition and try **proc1**.

```
(define proc2 cons)
(proc1 'a 'b)   ⇒   (b . a)
```

When you define **proc1**, the system accepts your promise to define **proc2**, and does not complain unless you use **proc1** before defining **proc2**. This allows you to define procedures in any order you please. This is especially useful when you are trying to organize a file full of procedure definitions in a way that makes your program more readable. It is necessary when two procedures defined at top level depend upon each other; we will see some examples of this later.

**Exercise 2.6.1.** What would happen if you were to type

```
(double-any double-any double-any)
```

given the definition of **double-any** from the beginning of this section?

**Exercise 2.6.2.** A more elegant (though possibly less efficient) way to define `cadr` and `cddr` than given in this section is to define a procedure that composes two procedures to create a third. Write the procedure `compose`, such that (`compose` $p_1$ $p_2$) is the composition of $p_1$ and $p_2$ (assuming both take one argument). That is, (`compose` $p_1$ $p_2$) should return a new procedure of one argument that applies $p_1$ to the result of applying $p_2$ to the argument. Use `compose` to define `cadr` and `cddr`.

**Exercise 2.6.3.** Scheme also provides `caar`, `cdar`, `caaar`, `caadr`, and so on, with any combination of up to four a's (representing `car`) and d's (representing `cdr`) between the `c` and the `r` (see Section 6.3). Define each of these with the `compose` procedure of the preceding exercise.

## 2.7. Conditional Expressions

So far we have considered expressions that perform a given task unconditionally. Suppose that we wish to write the procedure `abs`. If its argument $x$ is negative, `abs` returns $-x$; otherwise, it returns $x$. The most straightforward way to write `abs` is to determine whether the argument is negative and if so negate it, using the `if` syntactic form.

```
(define abs
  (lambda (n)
    (if (< n 0)
        (- 0 n)
        n)))
```

```
(abs 77)   ⇒   77
(abs -77)  ⇒   77
```

An `if` expression has the form (`if` *test consequent alternative*), where *consequent* is the expression to evaluate if *test* is true and *alternative* is the expression to evaluate if *test* is false. In the expression above, *test* is (`< n 0`), *consequent* is (`- 0 n`), and *alternative* is `n`.

The procedure `abs` could be written in a variety of other ways. Any of the following are valid definitions of `abs`.

```
(define abs
  (lambda (n)
    (if (>= n 0)
        n
        (- 0 n)))))
```

```
(define abs
  (lambda (n)
    (if (not (< n 0))
        n
        (- 0 n)))))
(define abs
  (lambda (n)
    (if (or (> n 0) (= n 0))
        n
        (- 0 n)))))
(define abs
  (lambda (n)
    (if (= n 0)
        0
        (if (< n 0)
            (- 0 n)
            n)))))
(define abs
  (lambda (n)
    ((if (>= n 0) + -)
     0
     n)))
```

The first of these definitions asks if **n** is greater than or equal to zero, inverting the test. The second asks if **n** is not less than zero, using the procedure **not** with <. The third asks if **n** is greater than zero or **n** is equal to zero, using the syntactic form **or**. The fourth treats zero separately, though there is no benefit in doing so. The fifth is somewhat tricky; **n** is either added to or subtracted from zero, depending upon whether **n** is greater than or equal to zero.

Why is **if** a syntactic form and not a procedure? In order to answer this, let's revisit the definition of **reciprocal** from the first section of this chapter.

```
(define reciprocal
  (lambda (n)
    (if (= n 0)
        "oops!"
        (/ 1 n)))))
```

When the second argument to the division procedure is zero, the behavior is unspecified, and many implementations signal an error. Our definition of **reciprocal** avoids this problem by testing for zero before dividing. Were **if** a procedure, its arguments (including (/ 1 n)) would be evaluated before it had a chance to choose between the consequent and alternative. Like **quote**, which does not evaluate its only subexpression, if does not evaluate all of its subexpressions and so cannot be a procedure.

The syntactic form or operates in a manner similar to if. The general form of an or expression is (or *exp* ...). If there are no subexpressions, i.e., the expression is simply (or), the value is false. Otherwise, each *exp* is evaluated in turn until either (a) one of the expressions evaluates to true or (b) no more expressions are left. In case (a), the value is true; in case (b), the value is false.

To be more precise, in case (a), the value of the or expression is the value of the last subexpression evaluated. This clarification is necessary because there are many possible true values. Usually, the value of a test expression is one of the two objects #t, for true, or #f, for false.

```
(< -1 0)  ⇒  #t
(> -1 0)  ⇒  #f
```

Every Scheme object, however, is considered to be either true or false by conditional expressions and by the procedure not. Only #f is considered false; all other objects are considered true.

```
(if #t 'true 'false)  ⇒  true
(if #f 'true 'false)  ⇒  false
(if '() 'true 'false)  ⇒  true
(if 1 'true 'false)  ⇒  true
(if '(a b c) 'true 'false)  →  true

(not #t)  ⇒  #f
(not "false")  ⇒  #f
(not #f)  ⇒  #t

(or)  ⇒  #f
(or #f)  ⇒  #f
(or #f #t)  ⇒  #t
(or #f 'a #f)  ⇒  a
```

The and syntactic form is similar in form to or, but an and expression is true if all its subexpressions are true, and false otherwise. In the case where there are no subexpressions, i.e., the expression is simply (and), the value is true. Otherwise, the subexpressions are evaluated in turn until either no more subexpressions are left or the value of a subexpression is false. The value of the and expression is the value of the last subexpression evaluated.

Using and, we can define a slightly different version of reciprocal.

```
(define reciprocal
  (lambda (n)
    (and (not (= n 0))
         (/ 1 n))))
```

```
(reciprocal 3)  ⇒  1/3
(reciprocal 0.5)  ⇒  2.0
(reciprocal 0)  ⇒  #f
```

In this version, the value is #f if n is zero and 1/n otherwise.

The procedures =, <, >, <=, and >= are called *predicates*. A predicate is a procedure that answers a specific question about its arguments and returns one of the two values #t or #f. The names of most predicates end with a question mark ( ? ); the common numeric procedures listed above are exceptions to this rule. Not all predicates require numeric arguments, of course. The predicate null? returns true if its argument is the empty list () and false otherwise.

```
(null? '())  ⇒  #t
(null? 'abc)  ⇒  #f
(null? '(x y z))  ⇒  #f
(null? (cdddr '(x y z)))  ⇒  #t
```

It is an error to pass the procedure cdr anything other than a pair, and most implementations signal an error when this happens. Common Lisp, however, defines (cdr '()) to be (). The following procedure, lisp-cdr, is defined using null? to return () if its argument is ().

```
(define lisp-cdr
  (lambda (x)
    (if (null? x)
        '()
        (cdr x))))
(lisp-cdr '(a b c))  ⇒  (b c)
(lisp-cdr '(c))  ⇒  ()
(lisp-cdr '())  ⇒  ()
```

Another useful predicate is eqv?, which requires two arguments. If the two arguments are equivalent, eqv? returns true. Otherwise, eqv? returns false.

```
(eqv? 'a 'a)  ⇒  #t
(eqv? 'a 'b)  ⇒  #f
(eqv? #f #f)  ⇒  #t
(eqv? #t #t)  ⇒  #t
(eqv? #f #t)  ⇒  #f
(eqv? 3 3)  ⇒  #t
(eqv? 3 2)  ⇒  #f
(let ((x "Hi Mom!"))
  (eqv? x x))  ⇒  #t
(let ((x (cons 'a 'b)))
  (eqv? x x))  ⇒  #t
(eqv? (cons 'a 'b) (cons 'a 'b))  ⇒  #f
```

As you can see, eqv? returns true if the arguments are the same symbol, boolean, number, pair, or string. Two pairs are not the same by eqv? if they are created by different calls to cons, even if they have the same contents. Detailed equivalence rules for eqv? are given in Section 6.2.

Scheme also provides a set of *type predicates* that return true or false depending on the type of the object, e.g., pair?, symbol?, number?, and string?. The predicate pair?, for example, returns true only if its argument is a pair.

```
(pair? '(a . c))  ⇒  #t
(pair? '(a b c))  ⇒  #t
(pair? '())  ⇒  #f
(pair? 'abc)  ⇒  #f
(pair? "Hi Mom!")  ⇒  #f
(pair? 1234567890)  ⇒  #f
```

Type predicates are useful for deciding if the argument passed to a procedure is of the appropriate type. For example, the following version of reciprocal checks first to see that its argument is a number before testing against zero or performing the division.

```
(define reciprocal
  (lambda (n)
    (if (and (number? n) (not (= n 0)))
        (/ 1 n)
        "oops!")))
(reciprocal 2/3)  ⇒  3/2
(reciprocal 'a)  ⇒  "oops!"
```

By the way, the code that uses reciprocal must check to see that the returned value is a number and not a string. It is usually better to report the error, using whatever error-reporting facilities your Scheme implementation provides. For example, *Chez Scheme* provides the procedure error for reporting errors; we might use error in the definition of reciprocal as follows.

```
(define reciprocal
  (lambda (n)
    (if (and (number? n) (not (= n 0)))
        (/ 1 n)
        (error 'reciprocal "improper argument ~s" n))))
(reciprocal .25)  ⇒  4.0
(reciprocal 0)  ⇒  Error in reciprocal: improper argument 0.
(reciprocal 'a)  ⇒  Error in reciprocal: improper argument a.
```

The first argument to error is a symbol identifying where the message originates, the second is a string describing the error, and the third and subsequent arguments are objects to be inserted into the error message. The message string must contain one ~s for each object; the position of each ~s within the string determines the placement of the corresponding object in the resulting error message.

Let's consider one more conditional expression, cond, that is often useful in place of if. cond is similar to if except that it allows multiple test and alternative expressions. A cond expression usually takes the following form.

(cond (*test exp*) ... (else *exp*))

Consider the following definition of sign, which returns -1 for negative inputs, +1 for positive inputs, and 0 for zero.

```
(define sign
  (lambda (n)
    (if (< n 0)
        -1
        (if (> n 0)
            +1
            0))))
```

```
(sign -88.3)  ⇒  -1
(sign 0)  ⇒  0
(sign 333333333333)  ⇒  1
(* (sign -88.3) (abs -88.3))  ⇒  -88.3
```

The two if expressions may be replaced by a single cond expression as follows.

```
(define sign
  (lambda (n)
    (cond
      ((< n 0) -1)
      ((> n 0) +1)
      (else 0))))
```

Sometimes it is clearer to leave out the else clause. This should be done only when there is no possibility that all the tests will fail, as in the new version of sign below.

```
(define sign
  (lambda (n)
    (cond
      ((< n 0) -1)
      ((> n 0) +1)
      ((= n 0) 0))))
```

These definitions of sign do not depend on the order in which the tests are performed, since only one of the tests can be true for any value of n. The following procedure computes the tax on a given amount of income in a progressive tax system with breakpoints at 10,000, 20,000, and 30,000 dollars.

```
(define income-tax
  (lambda (income)
    (cond
      ((<= income 10000) (* income .05))
      ((<= income 20000) (+ (* (- income 10000) .08) 500.00))
      ((<= income 30000) (+ (* (- income 20000) .13) 1300.00))
      (else (+ (* (- income 30000) .21) 2600.00)))))
```

```
(income-tax 5000)   ⇒   250.0
(income-tax 15000)  ⇒   900.0
(income-tax 25000)  ⇒   1950.0
(income-tax 50000)  ⇒   8600.0
```

In this example, the order in which the tests are performed, left to right (top to bottom), is significant.

**Exercise 2.7.1.** Define the predicate atom?, which returns true if its argument is not a pair and false if it is.

**Exercise 2.7.2.** The procedure length returns the length of its argument, which must be a list. For example, (length '(a b c)) is 3. Using length, define the procedure shorter, which returns the shorter of two list arguments. Have it return the first list if they have the same length.

```
(shorter '(a b) '(c d e))  ⇒  (a b)
(shorter '(a b) '(c d))    ⇒  (a b)
(shorter '(a b) '(c))      ⇒  (c)
```

## 2.8. Simple Recursion

We have seen how we can control whether or not expressions are evaluated with if, and, or, and cond. We can also perform an expression more than once by creating a procedure containing the expression and invoking the procedure more than once. What if we need to perform some expression repeatedly, say for all the elements of a list or all the numbers from one to ten? We can do so via recursion. Recursion is a simple concept: the application of a procedure from within that procedure. It can be tricky to master recursion at first, but once mastered it provides expressive power far beyond ordinary looping constructs.

A *recursive procedure* is a procedure that applies itself. Perhaps the simplest recursive procedure is the following, which we will call **goodbye**.

```
(define goodbye
  (lambda ()
    (goodbye)))
```

```
(goodbye)  ⇒
```

This procedure takes no arguments and simply applies itself immediately. There is no value after the ⇒ because **goodbye** never returns.

Obviously, to make practical use out of a recursive procedure, we must have some way to terminate the recursion. Most recursive procedures should have at least two basic elements, a *base case* and a *recursion step*. The base case terminates the recursion, giving the value of the procedure for some base argument. The recursion step gives the value in terms of the value of the procedure applied to a different argument. In order for the recursion to terminate, the different argument must be closer to the base argument in some way.

Let's consider the problem of finding the length of a list recursively. We need a base case and a recursion step. The logical base argument for recursion on lists is nearly always the empty list. The length of the empty list is zero, so the base case should give the value zero for the empty list. In order to become closer to the empty list, the natural recursion step involves the cdr of the argument. A nonempty list is one element longer than its cdr, so the recursion step gives the value as one more than the length of the cdr of the list.

```
(define length
  (lambda (ls)
    (if (null? ls)
        0
        (+ (length (cdr ls)) 1))))
```

```
(length '())    ⇒  0
(length '(a))   ⇒  1
(length '(a b)) ⇒  2
```

The **if** expression asks if the list is empty. If so, the value is zero. This is the base case. If not, the value is one more than the length of the cdr of the list. This is the recursion step.

Most Scheme implementations allow you to trace the execution of a procedure to see how it operates. In *Chez Scheme*, for example, one way to trace a procedure is to type (**trace** *name*), where *name* is the name of a procedure you have defined at top level. If you trace **length** as defined above and pass it the argument '(a b c d), you should see something like this:

```
|(length (a b c d))
|  (length (b c d))
|  |(length (c d))
|  |  (length (d))
|  |  |(length ())
|  |  |0
|  |  1
|  |2
|  3
|4
```

The indentation shows the nesting level of the recursion; the vertical lines associate applications visually with their values. Notice that on each application of length the list gets smaller until it finally reaches (). The value at () is 0, and each outer level adds 1 to arrive at the final value.

Let's write a procedure, list-copy, that returns a copy of its argument, which must be a list. That is, list-copy returns a new list consisting of the elements (but not the pairs) of the old list. Making a copy may be useful if either the original list or the copy may be altered via set-car! or set-cdr!, which we discuss later.

```
(list-copy '())  ⇒  ()
(list-copy '(a b c))  ⇒  (a b c)
```

See if you can define list-copy before studying the definition below.

```
(define list-copy
  (lambda (ls)
    (if (null? ls)
        '()
        (cons (car ls)
              (list-copy (cdr ls))))))
```

The definition of list-copy is similar to the definition of length. The test in the base case is the same, (null? ls). The value in the base case is (), however, not 0, because we are building up a list, not a number. The recursive call is the same, but instead of adding one, list-copy conses the car of the list onto the value of the recursive call.

There is no reason why there cannot be more than one base case. The procedure memv takes two arguments, an object and a list. It returns the first sublist, or *tail*, of the list whose car is equal to the object, or #f if the object is not found in the list. The value of memv may be used as a list or as a truth value in a conditional expression.

```
(define memv
  (lambda (x ls)
    (cond
      ((null? ls) #f)
      ((eqv? (car ls) x) ls)
      (else (memv x (cdr ls))))))
```

```
(memv 'a '(a b b d))  ⇒  (a b b d)
(memv 'b '(a b b d))  ⇒  (b b d)
(memv 'c '(a b b d))  ⇒  #f
(memv 'd '(a b b d))  ⇒  (d)
(if (memv 'b '(a b b d))
    "yes"
    "no")  ⇒  "yes"
```

Here there are two conditions to check, hence the use of cond. The first cond clause
checks for the base value of (); no object is a member of (), so the answer is #f.
The second clause asks if the car of the list is the object, in which case the list is
returned, being the first tail whose car contains the object. The recursion step just
continues down the list.

There may also be more than one recursion case. Like memv, the procedure remv
defined below takes two arguments, an object and a list. It returns a new list with
all occurrences of the object removed from the list.

```
(define remv
  (lambda (x ls)
    (cond
      ((null? ls) '())
      ((eqv? (car ls) x) (remv x (cdr ls)))
      (else (cons (car ls) (remv x (cdr ls)))))))
```

```
(remv 'a '(a b b d))  ⇒  (b b d)
(remv 'b '(a b b d))  ⇒  (a d)
(remv 'c '(a b b d))  ⇒  (a b b d)
(remv 'd '(a b b d))  ⇒  (a b b)
```

This definition is similar to the definition of memv above, except remv does not quit
once it finds the element in the car of the list. Rather, it continues, simply ignoring
the element. If the element is not found in the car of the list, remv does the same
thing as list-copy above: it conses the car of the list onto the recursive value.

Up to now, the recursion has been only on the cdr of a list. It is sometimes
useful, however, for a procedure to recur on the car as well as the cdr of the list.
The procedure tree-copy defined below treats the structure of pairs as a tree rather
than as a list, with the left subtree being the car of the pair and the right subtree
being the cdr of the pair. It performs a similar operation to list-copy, building
new pairs while leaving the elements (leaves) alone.

```
(define tree-copy
  (lambda (tr)
    (if (not (pair? tr))
        tr
        (cons (tree-copy (car tr))
              (tree-copy (cdr tr)))))))
```

(tree-copy '((a . b) . c))   ⇒   ((a . b) . c)

The natural base argument for a tree structure is anything that is not a pair, since the recursion traverses pairs rather than lists. The recursive step in this case is *doubly recursive*, finding the value recursively for the car as well as the cdr of the argument.

At this point, readers who are familiar with other languages that provide special iteration constructs, e.g., *while* or *for* loops, may wonder whether similar constructs are required in Scheme. Such constructs are unnecessary; iteration in Scheme is expressed more clearly and succinctly via recursion. Recursion is more general and eliminates the need for the variable assignments required by many other languages' iteration constructs, resulting in code that is more reliable and easier to follow. Some recursion is essentially iteration and executes as such; Section 3.2 has more to say about this. Often, there is no need to make a distinction, however. Concentrate instead on writing clear, concise, and correct programs.

Before we leave the topic of recursion, let's consider a special form of repetition called *mapping*. Consider the following procedure, abs-all, that takes a list of numbers as input and returns a list of their absolute values.

```
(define abs-all
  (lambda (ls)
    (if (null? ls)
        '()
        (cons (abs (car ls))
              (abs-all (cdr ls)))))))
```

(abs-all '(1 -2 3 -4 5 -6))   ⇒   (1 2 3 4 5 6)

This procedure forms a new list from the input list by applying the procedure abs to each element. We say that abs-all *maps* abs over the input list to produce the output list. Mapping a procedure over a list is a fairly common thing to do, so Scheme provides the procedure map, which maps its first argument, a procedure, over its second, a list. We can use map to define abs-all.

```
(define abs-all
  (lambda (ls)
    (map abs ls)))
```

We really do not need `abs-all`, however, since the corresponding direct application of `map` is just as short and perhaps clearer.

```
(map abs '(1 -2 3 -4 5 -6))  ⇒  (1 2 3 4 5 6)
```

Of course, we can use `lambda` to create the procedure argument to `map`, e.g., to square the elements of a list of numbers.

```
(map (lambda (x) (* x x))
     '(1 -3 -5 7))  ⇒  (1 9 25 49)
```

We can map a multiple-argument procedure over multiple lists, as in the following example.

```
(map cons '(a b c) '(1 2 3))  ⇒  ((a . 1) (b . 2) (c . 3))
```

The lists must be of the same length, and the procedure must accept as many arguments as there are lists. Each element of the output list is the result of applying the procedure to corresponding members of the input list.

Looking at the first definition of `abs-all` above, you should be able to derive, before studying it, the following definition of `map1`, a restricted version of `map` that maps a one-argument procedure over a single list.

```
(define map1
  (lambda (p ls)
    (if (null? ls)
        '()
        (cons (p (car ls))
              (map1 p (cdr ls)))))))

(map1 abs '(1 -2 3 -4 5 -6))  ⇒  (1 2 3 4 5 6)
```

All we have done is to replace the call to `abs` in `abs-all` with a call to the new parameter `p`. A definition of the more general `map` is given in Section 5.4.

**Exercise 2.8.1.** Describe what would happen if you switched the order of the arguments to `cons` in the definition of `tree-copy`.

**Exercise 2.8.2.** Consult Section 6.3 for the description of `append` and define a two-argument version of it. What would happen if you switched the order of the arguments in the call to `append` within your definition of `append`?

**Exercise 2.8.3.** Define the procedure `make-list`, which takes a nonnegative integer $n$ and an object and returns a new list, $n$ long, each element of which is the object.

```
(make-list 7 '())  ⇒  (() () () () () () ())
```

[*Hint*: The base test should be (= *n* 0), and the recursion step should involve (- *n* 1). Whereas () is the natural base case for recursion on lists, 0 is the natural base case for recursion on nonnegative integers. Similarly, subtracting 1 is the natural way to bring a nonnegative integer closer to 0.]

**Exercise 2.8.4.** The procedures `list-ref` and `list-tail` return the *nth* element and *nth* tail of a list *ls*.

```
(list-ref '(1 2 3 4) 0)  ⇒  1
(list-tail '(1 2 3 4) 0)  ⇒  (1 2 3 4)
(list-ref '(a short (nested) list) 2)  ⇒  (nested)
(list-tail '(a short (nested) list) 2)  ⇒  ((nested) list)
```

Define both procedures.

**Exercise 2.8.5.** Exercise 2.7.2 had you use `length` in the definition of `shorter`, which returns the shorter of its two list arguments, or the first if the two have the same length. Write `shorter` without using `length`. [*Hint*: Define a recursive helper, `shorter?`, and use it in place of the length comparison.]

**Exercise 2.8.6.** All of the recursive procedures shown so far have been directly recursive. That is, each procedure directly applies itself to a new argument. It is also possible to write two procedures that use each other, resulting in indirect recursion. Define the procedures `odd?` and `even?`, each in terms of the other. [*Hint*: What should each return when its argument is 0?]

```
(even? 17)  ⇒  #f
(odd? 17)  ⇒  #t
```

**Exercise 2.8.7.** Use `map` to define a procedure, `transpose`, that takes a list of pairs and returns a pair of lists as follows.

```
(transpose '((a . 1) (b . 2) (c . 3)))  ⇒  ((a b c) 1 2 3)
```

[*Hint*: ((a b c) 1 2 3) is the same as ((a b c) . (1 2 3)).]

## 2.9. Assignment

Although many programs can be written without them, assignments to top-level variables or `let`-bound and `lambda`-bound variables are sometimes useful. Assignments do not create new bindings, as with `let` or `lambda`, but rather change the values of existing bindings. Assignments are performed with `set!`.

```
(define abcde '(a b c d e))
abcde  ⇒  (a b c d e)
(set! abcde (cdr abcde))
abcde  ⇒  (b c d e)
(let ((abcde '(a b c d e)))
  (set! abcde (reverse abcde))
  abcde)  ⇒  (e d c b a)
```

Many languages require the use of assignments to initialize local variables, separate from the declaration or binding of the variables. In Scheme, all local variables are given a value immediately upon binding. Besides making the separate assignment to initialize local variables unnecessary, it ensures that the programmer cannot forget to initialize them, a common source of errors in most languages.

In fact, most of the assignments that are either necessary or convenient in other languages are both unnecessary and inconvenient in Scheme, since there is typically a clearer way to express the same algorithm without assignments. One common practice in some languages is to sequence expression evaluation with a series of assignments, as in the following procedure that finds the roots of a quadratic equation.

```
(define quadratic-formula
  (lambda (a b c)
    (let ((root1 0) (root2 0) (minusb 0) (radical 0) (divisor 0))
      (set! minusb (- 0 b))
      (set! radical (sqrt (- (* b b) (* 4 (* a c)))))
      (set! divisor (* 2 a))
      (set! root1 (/ (+ minusb radical) divisor))
      (set! root2 (/ (- minusb radical) divisor))
      (cons root1 root2))))
```

The roots are computed according to the well-known quadratic formula,

$$\frac{-b \pm \sqrt{b^2 - 4ac}}{2a}$$

which yields the solutions to the equation $0 = ax^2 + bx + c$. The let expression in this definition is employed solely to establish the variable bindings, corresponding to the declarations required in other languages. The first three assignment expressions compute subpieces of the formula, namely $-b$, $\sqrt{b^2 - 4ac}$, and $2a$. The last two assignment expressions compute the two roots in terms of the subpieces. A pair of the two roots is the value of quadratic-formula. For example, the two roots of $2x^2 - 4x - 6$ are $x = 3$ and $x = -1$.

```
(quadratic-formula 2 -4 -6)  ⇒  (3 . -1)
```

The definition above works, but it can be written more clearly without the assignments, as shown below.

```
(define quadratic-formula
  (lambda (a b c)
    (let ((minusb (- 0 b))
          (radical (sqrt (- (* b b) (* 4 (* a c)))))
          (divisor (* 2 a)))
      (let ((root1 (/ (+ minusb radical) divisor))
            (root2 (/ (- minusb radical) divisor)))
        (cons root1 root2)))))
```

In this version, the set! expressions are gone, and we are left with essentially the same algorithm. By employing two let expressions, however, the definition makes clear the dependency of root1 and root2 on the values of minusb, radical, and divisor. Equally important, the let expressions make clear the *lack* of dependencies among minusb, radical, and divisor and between root1 and root2.

Assignments do have some uses in Scheme, otherwise the language would not support them. Consider the following version of cons that counts the number of times it is called, storing the count in a variable named cons-count. It uses set! to increment the count; there is no way to achieve the same behavior without assignments.

```
(define cons-count 0)

(define cons
  (let ((old-cons cons))
    (lambda (x y)
      (set! cons-count (+ cons-count 1))
      (old-cons x y))))
```

```
(cons 'a '(b c))  ⇒  (a b c)
cons-count  ⇒  1
(cons 'a (cons 'b (cons 'c '())))  ⇒  (a b c)
cons-count  ⇒  4
```

set! is used both to establish the new top-level value for cons and to update the variable cons-count each time cons is invoked.

Assignments are commonly used to implement procedures that must maintain some internal state. For example, suppose we would like to define a procedure that returns 0 the first time it is called, 1 the second time, 2 the third time, and so on indefinitely. We could write something similar to the definition of cons-count above:

```
(define next 0)

(define count
  (lambda ()
    (let ((v next))
      (set! next (+ next 1))
      v)))
```

```
(count)  ⇒  0
(count)  ⇒  1
```

This solution is somewhat undesirable in that the variable **next** is visible at top level even though it need not be. Since it is visible at top level, any code in the system can change its value, perhaps inadvertently affecting the behavior of **count** in a subtle way. We can solve this problem by **let**-binding **next** outside of the **lambda** expression:

```
(define count
  (let ((next 0))
    (lambda ()
      (let ((v next))
        (set! next (+ next 1))
        v))))
```

The latter solution also generalizes easily to provide multiple counters, each with its own local counter. The procedure **make-counter**, defined below, returns a new counting procedure each time it is called.

```
(define make-counter
  (lambda ()
    (let ((next 0))
      (lambda ()
        (let ((v next))
          (set! next (+ next 1))
          v)))))
```

Since **next** is bound inside of **make-counter** but outside of the procedure returned by **make-counter**, each procedure it returns maintains its own unique counter.

```
(define count1 (make-counter))
(define count2 (make-counter))
```

```
(count1)  ⇒  0
(count2)  ⇒  0
(count1)  ⇒  1
(count1)  ⇒  2
(count2)  ⇒  1
```

If a state variable must be shared by more than one procedures defined at top-level, but we do not want the state variable to be visible at top-level, we can use **let** to bind the variable and **set!** to make the procedures visible at top level.

```
(define shhh #f)
(define tell #f)
(let ((secret 0))
  (set! shhh
    (lambda (message)
      (set! secret message)))
  (set! tell
    (lambda ()
      message)))
```

```
(shhh "sally likes harry")
(tell)   ⇒  "sally likes harry"
secret   ⇒  Error: variable secret is not bound
```

Variables must be defined before they can be assigned, so we define shhh and tell to be #f initially. (Any initial value would do.) We'll see this structure again in Chapter 3.

Local state is sometimes useful for caching computed values or allowing a computation to be evaluated *lazily*, i.e., only once and only on demand. The procedure lazy below accepts a *thunk*, or zero-argument procedure, as an argument. Thunks are often used to "freeze" computations that must be delayed for some reason, which is exactly what we need to do in this situation. When passed a thunk $t$, lazy returns a new thunk that, when invoked, returns the value of invoking $t$. Once computed, the value is saved in a local variable so that the computation need not be performed again. A boolean flag is used to record whether $t$ has been invoked and its value saved.

```
(define lazy
  (lambda (t)
    (let ((val #f) (flag #f))
      (lambda ()
        (if (not flag)
            (begin (set! val (t))
                   (set! flag #t)))
        val))))
```

The syntactic form begin, used here for the first time, evaluates its subexpressions in sequence from left to right and returns the value of the last subexpression, like the body of a let or lambda expression. We also see that the *alternative* subexpression of an if expression can be omitted. This should be done only when the value of the if is discarded, as it is in this case.

Lazy evaluation is especially useful for values that require considerable time to compute. By delaying the evaluation, we may avoid computing the value altogether, and by saving the value, we avoid computing it more than once.

The operation of lazy can best be illustrated by printing a message from within a thunk passed to lazy.

```
(define p
  (lazy (lambda ()
          (display "Ouch!")
          (newline)
          "got me")))
```

The first time p is invoked, the message Ouch! is printed and the string "got me" is returned. Thereafter, "got me" is returned but the message is not printed. The procedures display and newline are the first examples of explicit input/output we have seen; display prints the string without quotation marks, and newline prints a newline character.

To further illustrate the use of set!, let's consider the implementation of stack objects whose internal workings are not visible on the outside. A stack object accepts one of four *messages*: empty?, which returns #t if the stack is empty; push!, which adds an object to the top of the stack; top, which returns the object on the top of the stack; and pop!, which removes the object on top of the stack. The procedure make-stack given below creates a new stack each time it is called in a manner similar to make-counter.

```
(define make-stack
  (lambda ()
    (let ((ls '()))
      (lambda (msg . args)
        (cond
          ((eqv? msg 'empty?) (null? ls))
          ((eqv? msg 'push!)
           (set! ls (cons (car args) ls)))
          ((eqv? msg 'top) (car ls))
          ((eqv? msg 'pop!)
           (set! ls (cdr ls)))
          (else "oops"))))))
```

Each stack is stored as a list bound to the variable ls; set! is used to change this binding for push! and pop!. Notice that the argument list of the inner lambda expression uses the improper list syntax to bind args to a list of all arguments but the first. This is useful here because in the case of empty?, top, and pop! there is only one argument (the message), but in the case of push! there are two (the message and the object to push onto the stack).

```
(define stack1 (make-stack))
(define stack2 (make-stack))

(stack1 'empty?)  ⇥  #t
(stack2 'empty?)  ⇒  #t
```

```
(stack1 'push! 'a)
(stack1 'empty?)   ⇒   #f
(stack2 'empty?)   ⇒   #t

(stack1 'push! 'b)
(stack2 'push! 'c)
(stack1 'top)   ⇒   b
(stack2 'top)   ⇒   c

(stack1 'pop!)
(stack2 'empty?)   ⇒   #f
(stack1 'top)   ⇒   a

(stack2 'pop!)
(stack2 'empty?)   ⇒   #t
```

As with the counters created by make-counter, the state maintained by each stack object is directly accessible only within the object. Each reference or change to this state is made explicitly by the object itself. One important benefit is that we can change the internal structure of the stack, perhaps to use a vector (see Section 6.7) instead of a list to hold the elements, without changing its external behavior. Because the behavior of the object is known abstractly (not operationally), it is known as an *abstract object*. See Section 9.8 for more about creating abstract objects.

In addition to changing the values of variables, we can also change the values of the car and cdr fields of a pair, using the procedures set-car! and set-cdr!.

```
(define p (list 1 2 3))
(set-car! (cdr p) 'two)
p   ⇒   (1 two 3)
(set-cdr! p '())
p   ⇒   (1)
```

We can use these operators to define a queue datatype, which is like a stack except that new elements are added at one end and extracted from the other. The following implementation of a queue uses a *tconc* structure, borrowed from old Lisp systems. A tconc consists of a nonempty list and a header. The header is a pair whose car points to the first pair (head) of the list and whose cdr points to the last pair (end) of the list.

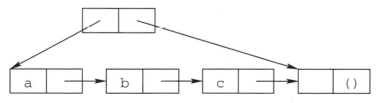

The last element of the list is a placeholder and not considered part of the queue.

Four operations on queues are defined below: `make-queue`, which constructs a queue, `putq!`, which adds an element to the end of a queue, `getq`, which retrieves the element at the front of a queue, and `delq!`, which removes the element at the front of a queue.

```
(define make-queue
  (lambda ()
    (let ((end (cons 'ignored '())))
      (cons end end))))
(define putq!
  (lambda (q v)
    (let ((end (cons 'ignored '())))
      (set-car! (cdr q) v)
      (set-cdr! (cdr q) end)
      (set-cdr! q end))))
(define getq
  (lambda (q)
    (car (car q))))
(define delq!
  (lambda (q)
    (set-car! q (cdr (car q)))))
```

All are simple operations except for `putq!`, which modifies the end pair to contain the new value and adds a new end pair.

```
(define myq (make-queue))
(putq! myq 'a)
(putq! myq 'b)
(getq myq)  ⇒  a
(delq! myq)
(getq myq)  ⇒  b
(delq! myq)
(putq! myq 'c)
(putq! myq 'd)
(getq myq)  ⇒  c
(delq! myq)
(getq myq)  ⇒  d
```

**Exercise 2.9.1.** Modify `make-counter` to take two arguments: an initial value for the counter to use in place of 0 and an amount to increment the counter by each time.

**Exercise 2.9.2.** Look up the description of `case` in Section 5.3. Replace the `cond` expression in `make stack` with an equivalent case expression. Add `mt?` as a second name for the `empty?` message.

**Exercise 2.9.3.** Modify the `stack` object to allow the two messages `ref` and `set!`. (*stack* `'ref` *i*) should return the *i*th element from the top of the stack; (*stack* `'ref` 0) should be equivalent to (*stack* `'top`). (*stack* `'set!` *i* *v*) should change the *i*th element from the top of the stack to *v*.

```
(define stack (make-stack))

(stack 'push! 'a)
(stack 'push! 'b)
(stack 'push! 'c)

(stack 'ref 0)   ⇒   c
(stack 'ref 2)   ⇒   a
(stack 'set! 1 'd)
(stack 'ref 1)   ⇒   d
(stack 'top)     ⇒   c
(stack 'pop!)
(stack 'top)     ⇒   d
```

[*Hint*: Use `list-ref` to implement `ref` and `list-tail` with `set-car!` to implement `set!`.]

**Exercise 2.9.4.** Scheme supports *vectors* as well as lists. Like lists, vectors are aggregate objects that contain other objects. Unlike lists, vectors have a fixed size and are laid out in one flat block of memory, typically with a header containing the length of the vector, as in the ten-element vector below.

| 10 | a | b | c | d | e | f | g | h | i | j |
|----|---|---|---|---|---|---|---|---|---|---|

This makes vectors more suitable for applications needing fast access to any element of the aggregate but less suitable for applications needing data structures that grow and shrink as needed.

Look up the basic vector operations in Section 6.7 and reimplement the `stack` object to use a vector instead of a list to hold the stack contents. Include the `ref` and `set!` messages of Exercise 2.9.3. Have the new `make-stack` accept a size argument *n* and make the vector length *n*, but do not otherwise change the external (abstract) interface.

**Exercise 2.9.5.** Define a predicate, `emptyq?`, for determining if a queue is empty. Modify `getq` and `delq!` to signal an error when an empty queue is found, using the error signaling facility provided by your implementation of Scheme.

**Exercise 2.9.6.** In the queue implementation, the last pair in the encapsulated list is a placeholder, i.e., it never holds anything useful. Recode the queue operators to avoid this wasted pair. Make sure that the series of queue operations given earlier works with the new implementation. Which implementation do you prefer?

**Exercise 2.9.7.** Using `set-cdr!`, it is possible to create *cyclic lists*. For example, the following expression evaluates to a list whose car is the symbol **a** and whose cdr is the list itself.

```
(let ((ls (cons 'a '())))
  (set-cdr! ls ls)
  ls)
```

What happens when you enter the above expression during an interactive Scheme session? What will the implementation of `length` on page 40 do when given a cyclic list? What does the built-in `length` primitive do?

**Exercise 2.9.8.** Define the predicate `list?`, which returns `#t` if its argument is a proper list and `#f` otherwise (see Section 6.3). It should return `#f` for cyclic lists as well as for lists terminated by objects other than ().

```
(list? '())      ⇒  #t
(list? '(1 2 3)) ⇒  #t
(list? '(a . b)) ⇒  #f
(list? (let ((ls (cons 'a '())))
         (set-cdr! ls ls)
         ls))    ⇒  #f
```

First write a simplified version of `list?` that does not handle cyclic lists, then extend this to handle cyclic lists correctly. Revise your definition until you are satisfied that it is as clear and concise as possible. [*Hint*: Use the following "hare and tortoise" algorithm to detect cycles. Define a recursive help procedure of two arguments, the hare and the tortoise. Start both the hare and the tortoise at the beginning of the list. Have the hare advance by two cdrs each time the tortoise advances by one cdr. If the hare catches the tortoise, there must be a cycle.]

# CHAPTER 3

# *Going Further*

*Assemblies of spirals from the Voderberg prototile.*

The preceding chapter prepared you to write Scheme programs using a small set of the most useful primitive syntactic forms and procedures. This chapter introduces a number of additional features and programming techniques that will allow you to write more sophisticated and efficient programs.

## 3.1. Syntactic Extension

As we saw in Section 2.5, the `let` syntactic form is merely a *syntactic extension* defined in terms of a `lambda` expression and a procedure application, both core syntactic forms. At this point, you might be wondering which syntactic forms are core forms and which are syntactic extensions, and how new syntactic extensions may be defined. This section provides some answers to these questions.

In truth, it is not necessary for us to draw a distinction between core forms and syntactic extensions, since once defined, a syntactic extension has exactly the same status as a core form. Drawing a distinction, however, makes understanding the language easier, since it allows us to focus attention on the core forms and to understand all others in terms of them.

It *is* necessary for a Scheme implementation to distinguish between core forms and syntactic extensions. A Scheme implementation expands syntactic extensions into core forms as the first step of compilation or interpretation, allowing the rest of the compiler or interpreter to focus only on the core forms. The set of core forms remaining after expansion to be handled directly by the compiler or interpreter is implementation-dependent, however, and may be different from the set of forms described as core here.

The exact set of syntactic forms making up the core of the language is thus subject to debate, although it must be possible to derive all other forms from any set of forms declared to be core forms. The set described here is among the simplest for which this constraint is satisfied. It also closely matches the set described as "primitive" in the ANSI/IEEE Scheme standard and Revised Reports.

The core syntactic forms include top-level `define` forms, constants, variables, procedure applications, `quote` expressions, `lambda` expressions, `if` expressions, and `set!` expressions. The grammar below describes the core syntax of Scheme in terms of these definitions and expressions. In the grammar, vertical bars ( | ) separate alternatives, and a form followed by an asterisk ( * ) represents zero or more occurrences of the form. ⟨variable⟩ is any Scheme identifier. ⟨datum⟩ is any Scheme object, such as a number, list, symbol, or vector. ⟨boolean⟩ is either #t or #f, ⟨number⟩ is any number, ⟨character⟩ is any character, and ⟨string⟩ is any string. We have already seen examples of numbers, strings, lists, symbols, and booleans. See Chapter 6 or the more detailed grammar at the back of this book for more on the object-level syntax of these and other objects.

⟨program⟩ ⟶ ⟨form⟩*
⟨form⟩ ⟶ ⟨definition⟩ | ⟨expression⟩
⟨definition⟩ ⟶ ⟨variable definition⟩ | (**begin** ⟨definition⟩*)
⟨variable definition⟩ ⟶ (**define** ⟨variable⟩ ⟨expression⟩)
⟨expression⟩ ⟶ ⟨constant⟩
     | ⟨variable⟩
     | (**quote** ⟨datum⟩)
     | (**lambda** ⟨formals⟩ ⟨expression⟩ ⟨expression⟩*)
     | (**if** ⟨expression⟩ ⟨expression⟩ ⟨expression⟩)
     | (**set!** ⟨variable⟩ ⟨expression⟩)
     | ⟨application⟩
⟨constant⟩ ⟶ ⟨boolean⟩ | ⟨number⟩ | ⟨character⟩ | ⟨string⟩
⟨formals⟩ ⟶ ⟨variable⟩
     | (⟨variable⟩*)
     | (⟨variable⟩ ⟨variable⟩* . ⟨variable⟩)
⟨application⟩ ⟶ (⟨expression⟩ ⟨expression⟩*)

The grammar is ambiguous in that the syntax for procedure applications conflicts with the syntaxes for **quote**, **lambda**, **if**, and **set!** expressions. In order to qualify as a procedure application, the first ⟨expression⟩ must not be one of these keywords, unless the keyword has been redefined or locally bound.

The "defun" syntax for **define** given in Section 2.6 is not included in the core, since definitions in that form are straightforwardly translated into the simpler **define** syntax. Similarly, the core syntax for **if** does not permit the *alternative* to be omitted, as did one example in Section 2.9. An **if** expression lacking an *alternative* can be translated into the core syntax for **if** merely by replacing the missing subexpression with an arbitrary constant, such as **#f**.

A **begin** that contains only definitions is considered to be a definition in the grammar; this is permitted in order to allow syntactic extensions to expand into more than one definition. **begin** expressions, i.e., **begin** forms containing expressions, are not considered core forms. A **begin** expression of the form

(**begin** $e_1$ $e_2$ ...)

is equivalent to the **lambda** application

((**lambda** () $e_1$ $e_2$ ...))

and hence need not be considered core.

Now that we have established a set of core syntactic forms, let's turn to a discussion of syntactic extensions. Syntactic extensions are so called because they extend the syntax of Scheme beyond the core syntax. All syntactic extensions in a Scheme program must ultimately be derived from the core forms. One syntactic extension, however, may be defined in terms of another syntactic extension, as long as the latter is in some sense "closer" to the core syntax. Syntactic forms may

appear anywhere an expression or definition is expected, as long as the extended
form expands into a definition or expression as appropriate.

Syntactic extensions are defined with `define-syntax`. `define-syntax` is similar
to `define`, except that `define-syntax` associates a syntactic transformation procedure, or *transformer*, with a keyword (such as `let`), rather than associating a value
with a variable. Here is how we might define `let` with `define-syntax`.

```
(define-syntax let
  (syntax-rules ()
    ((_ ((x v) ...) e1 e2 ...)
     ((lambda (x ...) e1 e2 ...) v ...))))
```

The identifier appearing after `define-syntax` is the name, or keyword, of the syntactic extension being defined, in this case `let`. The `syntax-rules` form is an
expression that evaluates to a transformer. The item following `syntax-rules` is
a list of *auxiliary keywords* and is nearly always (). An example of an auxiliary
keyword is the `else` of `cond`. (Examples requiring the use of auxiliary keywords are
given in Chapter 8.) Following the list of auxiliary keywords is a sequence of one
or more *rules*, or *pattern/template* pairs. Only one rule appears in our definition
of `let`. The pattern part of a rule specifies the form that the input must take, and
the template specifies to what the input should be transformed.

The pattern should always be a structured expression whose first element is an
underscore ( _ ). (As we shall see in Chapter 8, the use of _ is only a convention,
but it is a good one to follow.) If more than one rule is present, the appropriate one
is chosen by matching the patterns, in order, against the input during expansion.
An error is signaled if none of the patterns match the input.

Identifiers appearing within a pattern are *pattern variables*, unless they are listed
as auxiliary keywords. Pattern variables match any substructure and are bound to
that substructure within the corresponding template. The notation *pat* ... in the
pattern allows for zero or more expressions matching the ellipsis prototype *pat* in
the input. Similarly, the notation *exp* ... in the template produces zero or more
expressions from the ellipsis prototype *exp* in the output. The number of *pats* in
the input determines the number of *exps* in the output; in order for this to work,
any ellipsis prototype in the template must contain at least one pattern variable
from an ellipsis prototype in the pattern.

The single rule in our definition of `let` should be fairly self-explanatory, but a few
points are worth mentioning. First, the syntax of `let` requires that the body contain
at least one expression; hence, we have specified `e1 e2 ...` instead of `e ...`, which
might seem more natural. On the other hand, `let` does not require that there be
at least one variable/value pair, so we were able to use, simply, `(x v) ....` Second,
the pattern variables `x` and `v`, though together within the same prototype in the
pattern, are separated in the template; any sort of rearrangement or recombination
is possible. Finally, the three pattern variables `x`, `v`, and `e2` that appear in ellipsis

prototypes in the pattern also appear in ellipsis prototypes in the template. This is not a coincidence; it is a requirement. In general, if a pattern variable appears within an ellipsis prototype in the pattern, it cannot appear outside an ellipsis prototype in the template.

The definition of **and** below is somewhat more complex than the one for **let**.

```
(define-syntax and
  (syntax-rules ()
    ((_) #t)
    ((_ e) e)
    ((_ e1 e2 e3 ...)
     (if e1 (and e2 e3 ...) #f))))
```

This definition is recursive and involves more than one rule. Recall that (and) evaluates to #t; the first rule takes care of this case. The second and third rules specify the base case and recursion steps of the recursion and together translate **and** expressions with two or more subexpressions into nested **if** expressions. For example, (and a b c) expands first into

```
(if a (and b c) #f)
```

then

```
(if a (if b (and c) #f) #f)
```

and finally

```
(if a (if b c #f) #f)
```

With this expansion, if a and b evaluate to a true value, then the value is the value of c, otherwise #f, as desired.

The version of **and** below is simpler but, unfortunately, incorrect.

```
(define-syntax and ; incorrect!
  (syntax-rules ()
    ((_) #t)
    ((_ e1 e2 e3 ...)
     (if e1 (and e2 e3 ...) #f))))
```

The expression

```
(and (not (= x 0)) (/ 1 x))
```

which should return the value of (/ 1 x) when x is not zero. With the incorrect version of **and**, the expression expands as follows.

```
(if (not (= x 0)) (and (/ 1 x)) #f)   →
  (if (not (= x 0)) (if (/ 1 x) (and) #f) #f)   →
  (if (not (= x 0)) (if (/ 1 x) #t #f) #f)
```

The final answer if x is not zero is #t, not the value of (/ 1 x).

The definition of or below is similar to the one for and except that a temporary variable must be introduced for each intermediate value so that we can both test the value and return it if it is a true value. (A similar temporary is not needed for and since there is only one false value, #f.)

```
(define-syntax or
  (syntax-rules ()
    ((_) #f)
    ((_ e) e)
    ((_ e1 e2 e3 ...)
     (let ((t e1))
       (if t t (or e2 e3 ...))))))
```

Like variables bound by lambda or let, identifiers introduced by a template are lexically scoped, i.e., visible only within expressions introduced by the template. Thus, even if one of the expressions e2 e3 ... contains a reference to t, the introduced binding for t does not "capture" those references. This is typically accomplished via automatic renaming of introduced identifiers.

As with the simpler version of and given above, the simpler version of or below is incorrect.

```
(define-syntax or
  (syntax-rules ()
    ((_) #f)
    ((_ e1 e2 e3 ...)
     (let ((t e1))
       (if t t (or e2 e3 ...))))))
```

The reason is more subtle, however, and is the subject of Exercise 3.2.6.

**Exercise 3.1.1.** Write out the expansion steps necessary to expand

```
(let ((x (memv 'a ls)))
  (and x (memv 'b x)))
```

into core forms.

**Exercise 3.1.2.** Write out the expansion steps necessary to expand

```
(or (memv x '(a b c)) (list x))
```

into core forms.

**Exercise 3.1.3.** let* is similar to let but evaluates its bindings in sequence. Each of the right-hand-side expressions is within the scope of the earlier bindings.

```
(let* ((a 5) (b (+ a a)) (c (+ a b)))
  (list a b c))   ⇒   (5 10 15)
```

let* can be implemented as nested let expressions. For example, the let* expression above is equivalent to the nested let expressions below.

```
(let ((a 5))
  (let ((b (+ a a)))
    (let ((c (+ a b)))
      (list a b c))))  ⇒  (5 10 15)
```

Define let* with define-syntax.

**Exercise 3.1.4.** As we saw in Section 2.9, it is legal to omit the third, or *alternative*, subexpression of an if expression. Doing so, however, often leads to confusion. Some Scheme systems provide two syntactic forms, when and unless, that may be used in place of such "one-armed" if expressions.

```
(when test exp₁ exp₂ ...)
(unless test exp₁ exp₂ ...)
```

With both forms, test is evaluated first. For when, if test evaluates to true, the remaining forms are evaluated in sequence as if enclosed in an implicit begin expression. If test evaluates to false, the remaining forms are not evaluated, and the result is unspecified. unless is similar except that the remaining forms are evaluated only if test evaluates to false.

```
(let ((x 3))
  (unless (= x 0) (set! x (+ x 1)))
  (when (= x 4) (set! x (* x 2)))
  x)  ⇒  8
```

Define when as a syntactic extension in terms of if and begin, and define unless in terms of when.

## 3.2. More Recursion

In Section 2.8, we saw how to define recursive procedures using top-level definitions. Before that, we saw how to create local bindings for procedures using let. It is natural to wonder whether a let-bound procedure can be recursive. The answer is no, at least not in a straightforward way. If you try to evaluate the expression

```
(let ((sum (lambda (ls)
             (if (null? ls)
                 0
                 (+ (car ls) (sum (cdr ls)))))))
  (sum '(1 2 3 4 5)))
```

you will probably receive an error message to the effect that sum is undefined. This is because the variable sum is visible only within the body of the let expression and not within the lambda expression whose value is bound to sum. We can get around this problem by passing the procedure sum to itself as follows.

```
(let ((sum (lambda (sum ls)
             (if (null? ls)
                 0
                 (+ (car ls) (sum sum (cdr ls))))))))
  (sum sum '(1 2 3 4 5)))  ⇒  15
```

This works and is a clever solution, but there is an easier way, using letrec. Like let, the letrec syntactic form includes a set of variable-value pairs, along with a sequence of expressions referred to as the *body* of the letrec.

```
(letrec ((var val) ...) exp₁ exp₂ ...)
```

Unlike let, the variables *var* ... are visible not only within the body of the letrec but also within *val* .... Thus, we can rewrite the expression above as follows.

```
(letrec ((sum (lambda (ls)
               (if (null? ls)
                   0
                   (+ (car ls) (sum (cdr ls)))))))
  (sum '(1 2 3 4 5)))  ⇒  15
```

Using letrec, we can also define mutually recursive procedures, such as the procedures even? and odd? that were the subject of Exercise 2.8.6.

```
(letrec ((even?
           (lambda (x)
             (or (= x 0)
                 (odd? (- x 1)))))
         (odd?
           (lambda (x)
             (and (not (= x 0))
                  (even? (- x 1))))))
  (list (even? 20) (odd? 20)))  ⇒  (#t #f)
```

In a letrec expression, *val* ... are most commonly lambda expressions, though this need not be the case. One restriction on the expressions must be obeyed, however. It must be possible to evaluate each *val* without evaluating any of the variables *var* .... This restriction is always satisfied if the expressions are all lambda expressions, since even though the variables may appear within the lambda expressions, they cannot be evaluated until the resulting procedures are invoked in the body of the letrec. The following letrec expression obeys this restriction.

```
(letrec ((f (lambda () (+ x 2)))
         (x 1))
   (f))  ⇒  3
```

while the following does not.

```
(letrec ((y (+ x 2))
         (x 1))
   y)
```

The behavior in this case depends upon the implementation. The expression may return 3, it may return any other value, or it may result in an error being signaled.

We can use letrec to hide the definitions of "help" procedures so that they do not clutter the top-level name space. This is demonstrated by the definition of list? below, which follows the "hare and tortoise" algorithm outlined in Exercise 2.9.8.

```
(define list?
  (lambda (x)
    (letrec ((race
               (lambda (h t)
                 (if (pair? h)
                     (let ((h (cdr h)))
                       (if (pair? h)
                           (and (not (eq? h t))
                                (race (cdr h) (cdr t)))
                           (null? h)))
                     (null? h)))))
      (race x x))))
```

When a recursive procedure is called in only one place outside the procedure, as in the example above, it is often clearer to use a *named* let expression. Named let expressions take the following form.

```
(let name ((var val) ...)
  exp₁ exp₂ ...)
```

Named let is similar to unnamed let in that it binds the variables *var* ... to the values of *val* ... within the body *exp₁ exp₂* .... As with unnamed let, the variables are visible only within the body and not within *val* .... In addition, the variable *name* is bound within the body to a procedure that may be called to recur; the arguments to the procedure become the new values for the variables *var* ....

The definition of `list?` has been rewritten below to use named `let`.

```
(define list?
  (lambda (x)
    (let race ((h x) (t x))
      (if (pair? h)
          (let ((h (cdr h)))
            (if (pair? h)
                (and (not (eq? h t))
                     (race (cdr h) (cdr t)))
                (null? h)))
          (null? h)))))
```

Just as `let` can be expressed as a simple direct application of a `lambda` expression to arguments, named `let` can be expressed as the application of a recursive procedure to arguments. A named `let` of the form

```
(let name ((var val) ...)
  exp₁ exp₂ ...)
```

can be rewritten in terms of `letrec` as follows.

```
((letrec ((name (lambda (var ...) exp₁ exp₂ ...)))
   name)
 val ...)
```

Alternatively, it can be rewritten as

```
(letrec ((name (lambda (var ...) exp₁ exp₂ ...)))
  (name val ...))
```

provided that the variable *name* does not appear free within *val* ....

As we discussed in Section 2.8, some recursion is essentially iteration and executes as such. When a procedure call is in tail position (see below) with respect to a `lambda` expression, it is considered to be a *tail call*, and Scheme systems must treat it *properly*, as a "goto" or jump. When a procedure tail calls itself or calls itself indirectly through a series of tail calls, the result is *tail recursion*. Because tail calls are treated as jumps, tail recursion can be used for indefinite iteration in place of the more restrictive iteration constructs provided by other programming languages, without fear of overflowing any sort of recursion stack.

A call is in tail position with respect to a `lambda` expression if its value is returned directly from the `lambda` expression, i.e., if nothing is left to do after the call but to return from the `lambda` expression. For example, a call is in tail position if it is the last expression in the body of a `lambda` expression, the *consequent* or *alternative* part of an `if` expression in tail position, the last subexpression of an `and` or `or` expression in tail position, the last expression in the body of a `let` or `letrec` in tail position, etc. Each of the calls to `f` in the expressions below are tail calls, but the calls to `g` are not.

```
(lambda () (f (g)))
(lambda () (if (g) (f) (f)))
(lambda () (let ((x 4)) (f)))
(lambda () (or (g) (f)))
```

In each case, the values of the calls to f are returned directly, whereas the calls to g are not.

Recursion in general and named let in particular provide a natural way to implement many algorithms, whether iterative, recursive, or partly iterative and partly recursive; the programmer is not burdened with two distinct mechanisms.

The following two definitions of **factorial** use named let expressions to compute the factorial, $n!$, of a nonnegative integer $n$. The first employs the recursive definition $n! = n \times (n-1)!$, where 0! is defined to be 1.

```
(define factorial
  (lambda (n)
    (let fact ((i n))
      (if (= i 0)
          1
          (* i (fact (- i 1)))))))
```

```
(factorial 0)   ⇒   1
(factorial 1)   ⇒   1
(factorial 2)   ⇒   2
(factorial 3)   ⇒   6
(factorial 10)  ⇒   3628800
```

The second is an iterative version that employs the iterative definition $n! = n \times (n-1) \times (n-2) \times \ldots \times 1$, using an accumulator, a, to hold the intermediate products.

```
(define factorial
  (lambda (n)
    (let fact ((i n) (a 1))
      (if (= i 0)
          a
          (fact (- i 1) (* a i))))))
```

A similar problem is to compute the $n$th Fibonacci number for a given $n$. The *Fibonacci numbers* are an infinite sequence of integers, 0, 1, 1, 2, 3, 5, 8, etc., in which each number is the sum of the two preceding numbers in the sequence. A procedure to compute the $n$th Fibonacci number is most naturally defined recursively as follows.

```
(define fibonacci
  (lambda (n)
    (let fib ((i n))
      (cond
        ((= i 0) 0)
        ((= i 1) 1)
        (else (+ (fib (- i 1)) (fib (- i 2)))))))))
```

```
(fibonacci 0)    ⇒    0
(fibonacci 1)    ⇒    1
(fibonacci 2)    ⇒    1
(fibonacci 3)    ⇒    2
(fibonacci 4)    ⇒    3
(fibonacci 5)    ⇒    5
(fibonacci 6)    ⇒    8
(fibonacci 20)   ⇒    6765
(fibonacci 30)   ⇒    832040
```

This solution requires the computation of the two preceding Fibonacci numbers at each step and hence is *doubly recursive*. For example, to compute (`fibonacci 4`) requires the computation of both (`fib 3`) and (`fib 2`), to compute (`fib 3`) requires computing both (`fib 2`) and (`fib 1`), and to compute (`fib 2`) requires computing both (`fib 1`) and (`fib 0`). This is very inefficient, and it becomes more inefficient as n grows. A more efficient solution is to adapt the accumulator solution of the `factorial` example above to use two accumulators, `a1` for the current Fibonacci number and `a2` for the preceding one.

```
(define fibonacci
  (lambda (n)
    (if (= n 0)
        0
        (let fib ((i n) (a1 1) (a2 0))
          (if (= i 1)
              a1
              (fib (- i 1) (+ a1 a2) a1)))))))
```

Here, zero is treated as a special case, since there is no preceding value. This allows us to use the single base case (`= i 1`). The time it takes to compute the $n$th Fibonacci number using this iterative solution grows linearly with $n$, which makes a significant difference when compared to the doubly recursive version. To get a feel for the difference, try computing (`fibonacci 30`) and (`fibonacci 35`) using both definitions to see how long each takes.

We can also get a feel for the difference by looking at a trace for each on small inputs. The first trace below shows the calls to `fib` in the non-tail-recursive version of `fibonacci`, with input 5.

```
|(fib 5)
| (fib 4)
| |(fib 3)
| | (fib 2)
| | |(fib 1)
| | |1
| | |(fib 0)
| | |0
| | 1
| | (fib 1)
| | 1
| |2
| |(fib 2)
| | (fib 1)
| | 1
| | (fib 0)
| | 0
| |1
| 3
| (fib 3)
| |(fib 2)
| | (fib 1)
| | 1
| | (fib 0)
| | 0
| |1
| |(fib 1)
| |1
| 2
|5
```

Notice how there are several calls to `fib` with arguments 2, 1, and 0. The second trace shows the calls to `fib` in the tail-recursive version, again with input 5.

```
|(fib 5 1 0)
|(fib 4 1 1)
|(fib 3 2 1)
|(fib 2 3 2)
|(fib 1 5 3)
|5
```

Clearly, there is quite a difference.

The named `let` examples shown so far are either tail-recursive or not tail-recursive. It often happens that one recursive call within the same expression is tail-recursive while another is not. The definition of **factor** below computes the prime factors of its nonnegative integer argument. The first call to f is not tail-recursive, but the second one is.

```
(define factor
  (lambda (n)
    (trace-let f ((n n) (i 2))
      (cond
        ((>= i n) (list n))
        ((integer? (/ n i))
         (cons i (f (/ n i) i)))
        (else (f n (+ i 1)))))))
```

```
(factor 0)  ⇒  (0)
(factor 1)  ⇒  (1)
(factor 12)  ⇒  (2 2 3)
(factor 3628800)  ⇒  (2 2 2 2 2 2 2 3 3 3 3 5 5 7)
(factor 9239)  ⇒  (9239)
```

The trace of the calls to f in the evaluation of (factor 120) below highlights the difference between the nontail calls and the tail calls.

```
|(f 120 2)
| (f 60 2)
| |(f 30 2)
| | (f 15 2)
| | (f 15 3)
| | |(f 5 3)
| | |(f 5 4)
| | |(f 5 5)
| | |(5)
| | (3 5)
| |(2 3 5)
| (2 2 3 5)
|(2 2 2 3 5)
```

A nontail call to f is shown indented relative to its caller, since the caller is still active, whereas tail calls appear at the same level of indentation.

**Exercise 3.2.1.** Which of the recursive procedures defined in Section 3.2 are tail-recursive, and which are not?

**Exercise 3.2.2.** Rewrite factor using letrec to bind f in place of named let. Which version do you prefer?

**Exercise 3.2.3.** Can the letrec expression below be rewritten using named let? If not, why not? If so, do it.

```
(letrec ((even?
            (lambda (x)
               (or (= x 0)
                    (odd? (- x 1)))))
           (odd?
            (lambda (x)
               (and (not (= x 0))
                    (even? (- x 1)))))))
  (even? 20))
```

**Exercise 3.2.4.** Rewrite both definitions of `fibonacci` given in this section to count the number of recursive calls to `fib`, using a counter similar to the one used in the `cons-count` example of Section 2.9. Count the number of recursive calls made in each case for several input values. What do you notice?

**Exercise 3.2.5.** Augment the definition of `let` given in Section 3.1 to handle named `let` as well as unnamed `let`, using two rules.

**Exercise 3.2.6.** The following definition of `or` is simpler than the one given in Section 3.1.

```
(define-syntax or ; incorrect!
  (syntax-rules ()
    ((_) #f)
    ((_ e1 e2 ...)
     (let ((t e1))
       (if t t (or e2 ...))))))
```

Say why it is not correct. [*Hint*: Think about what would happen if this version of `or` were used in the `even?` and `odd?` example given on page 63 for very large inputs.]

**Exercise 3.2.7.** The definition of `factor` is not the most efficient possible. First, no factors of $n$ besides $n$ itself can possibly be found beyond $\sqrt{n}$. Second, the division (`/ n i`) is performed twice when a factor is found. Third, after 2, no even factors can possibly be found. Recode `factor` to correct all three problems. Which is the most important problem to solve? Are there any additional improvements you can make?

## 3.3. Continuations

During the evaluation of a Scheme expression, the implementation must keep track of two things: (1) what to evaluate and (2) what to do with the value. Consider the evaluation of (`null? x`) within the expression below.

```
(if (null? x) (quote ()) (cdr x))
```

The implementation must first evaluate (null? x) and, based on its value, evaluate either (quote ()) or (cdr x). "What to evaluate" is (null? x), and "what to do with the value" is to make the decision which of (quote ()) and (cdr x) to evaluate and to do so. We call "what to do with the value" the *continuation* of a computation.

Thus, at any point during the evaluation of any expression, there is a continuation ready to complete, or at least *continue*, the computation from that point. Let's assume that x has the value (a b c). Then we can isolate six continuations during the evaluation of (if (null? x) (quote ()) (cdr x)), the continuations waiting for:

1. the value of (if (null? x) (quote ()) (cdr x)),
2. the value of (null? x),
3. the value of null?,
4. the value of x,
5. the value of cdr, and
6. the value of x (again).

The continuation of (cdr x) is not listed because it is the same as the one waiting for (if (null? x) (quote ()) (cdr x)).

Scheme allows the continuation of any expression to be obtained with the procedure call-with-current-continuation, which may be abbreviated call/cc in most implementations.

We use the shorter name here. If the implementation you are using does not recognize call/cc, simply define it as follows

```
(define call/cc call-with-current-continuation)
```

or use the longer name in your code.

call/cc must be passed a procedure $p$ of one argument. call/cc constructs a concrete representation of the the current continuation and passes it to $p$. The continuation itself is represented by a procedure $k$. Each time $k$ is applied to a value, it returns the value to the continuation of the call/cc application. This value becomes, in essence, the value of the application of call/cc.

If $p$ returns without invoking $k$, the value returned by the procedure becomes the value of the application of call/cc.

Consider the simple examples below.

```
(call/cc
  (lambda (k)
    (* 5 4)))  ⇒  20
(call/cc
  (lambda (k)
    (* 5 (k 4))))  ⇒  4
```

```
(+ 2
   (call/cc
     (lambda (k)
       (* 5 (k 4))))) ⇒ 6
```

In the first example, the continuation is obtained and bound to k, but k is never used, so the value is simply the product of 5 and 4. In the second, the continuation is invoked before the multiplication, so the value is the value passed to the continuation, 4. In the third, the continuation includes the addition by 2; thus, the value is the value passed to the continuation, 4, plus 2.

Here is a less trivial example, showing the use of call/cc to provide a nonlocal exit from a recursion.

```
(define product
  (lambda (ls)
    (call/cc
      (lambda (break)
        (let f ((ls ls))
          (cond
            ((null? ls) 1)
            ((= (car ls) 0) (break 0))
            (else (* (car ls) (f (cdr ls))))))))))
```

```
(product '(1 2 3 4 5)) ⇒ 120
(product '(7 3 8 0 1 9 5)) ⇒ 0
```

The nonlocal exit allows product to return immediately, without performing the pending multiplications, when a zero value is detected.

Each of the continuation invocations above returns to the continuation while control remains within the procedure passed to call/cc. The following example uses the continuation after this procedure has already returned.

```
(let ((x (call/cc (lambda (k) k))))
  (x (lambda (ignore) "hi"))) ⇒ "hi"
```

The continuation obtained by this invocation of call/cc may be described as "Take the value, bind it to x, and apply the value of x to the value of (lambda (ignore) "hi")." Since (lambda (k) k) returns its argument, x is bound to the continuation itself; this continuation is applied to the procedure resulting from the evaluation of (lambda (ignore) "hi"). This has the effect of binding x (again!) to this procedure and applying the procedure to itself. The procedure ignores its argument and returns "hi".

The following variation of the example above is probably the most confusing Scheme program of its size; it may be easy to guess what it returns, but it takes some work to verify that guess.

```
(((call/cc (lambda (k) k)) (lambda (x) x)) "HEY!") ⇒ "HEY!"
```

The value of the `call/cc` is its own continuation, as in the preceding example. This is applied to the identity procedure (`lambda (x) x`), so the `call/cc` returns a second time with this value. Then, the identity procedure is applied to itself, yielding the identity procedure. This is finally applied to `"HEY!"`, yielding `"HEY!"`.

Continuations used in this manner are not always so puzzling. Consider the following definition of `factorial` that saves the continuation at the base of the recursion before returning 1, by assigning the top-level variable `retry`.

```
(define retry #f)

(define factorial
  (lambda (x)
    (if (= x 0)
        (call/cc (lambda (k) (set! retry k) 1))
        (* x (factorial (- x 1))))))
```

With this definition, `factorial` works as we expect `factorial` to work, except it has the side effect of assigning `retry`.

```
(factorial 4)  ⇒  24
(retry 1)  ⇒  24
(retry 2)  ⇒  48
```

The continuation bound to `retry` might be described as "Multiply the value by 1, then multiply this result by 2, then multiply this result by 3, then multiply this result by 4." If we pass the continuation a different value, i.e., not 1, we will cause the base value to be something other than 1 and hence change the end result.

```
(retry 2)  ⇒  48
(retry 5)  ⇒  120
```

This mechanism could be the basis for a breakpoint package implemented with `call/cc`; each time a breakpoint is encountered, the continuation of the breakpoint is saved so that the computation may be restarted from the breakpoint (more than once, if desired).

Continuations may be used to implement various forms of multitasking. The simple "light-weight process" mechanism defined below allows multiple computations to be interleaved. Since it is *nonpreemptive*, it requires that each process voluntarily "pause" from time to time in order to allow the others to run.

```
(define lwp-list '())
(define lwp
  (lambda (thunk)
    (set! lwp-list (append lwp-list (list thunk)))))
```

```
(define start
  (lambda ()
    (let ((p (car lwp-list)))
      (set! lwp-list (cdr lwp-list))
      (p))))
(define pause
  (lambda ()
    (call/cc
      (lambda (k)
        (lwp (lambda () (k #f)))
        (start)))))
```

The following light-weight processes cooperate to print an infinite sequence of lines containing "hey!".

```
(lwp (lambda () (let f () (pause) (display "h") (f))))
(lwp (lambda () (let f () (pause) (display "e") (f))))
(lwp (lambda () (let f () (pause) (display "y") (f))))
(lwp (lambda () (let f () (pause) (display "!") (f))))
(lwp (lambda () (let f () (pause) (newline) (f))))
(start)
hey!
hey!
hey!
hey!
⋮
```

See Section 9.11 for an implementation of *engines*, which support preemptive multitasking, with call/cc.

**Exercise 3.3.1.** Use call/cc to write a program that loops indefinitely, printing a sequence of numbers beginning at zero. Do not use any recursive procedures, and do not use any assignments.

**Exercise 3.3.2.** Rewrite product without call/cc, retaining the feature that no multiplications are performed if any of the list elements are zero.

**Exercise 3.3.3.** What would happen if a process created by lwp as defined above were to terminate, i.e., simply return without calling pause? Define a quit procedure that allows a process to terminate without otherwise affecting the lwp system. Be sure to handle the case in which the only remaining process terminates.

**Exercise 3.3.4.** Each time lwp is called, the list of processes is copied because lwp uses append to add its argument to the end of the process list. Modify the original lwp code to use the queue datatype developed in Section 2.9 to avoid this problem.

**Exercise 3.3.5.** The light-weight process mechanism allows new processes to be created dynamically, although the example given in this section does not do so. Design an application that requires new processes to be created dynamically and implement it using the light-weight process mechanism.

## 3.4. Continuation Passing Style

As we discussed in the preceding section, a continuation waits for the value of each expression. In particular, a continuation is associated with each procedure call. When one procedure invokes another via a nontail call, the called procedure receives an implicit continuation that is responsible for completing what is left of the calling procedure's body plus returning to the calling procedure's continuation. If the call is a tail call, the called procedure simply receives the continuation of the calling procedure.

We can make the continuations explicit by encapsulating "what to do" in an explicit procedural argument passed along on each call. For example, the continuation of the call to f in

```
(letrec ((f (lambda (x) (cons 'a x)))
         (g (lambda (x) (cons 'b (f x))))
         (h (lambda (x) (g (cons 'c x)))))
  (cons 'd (h '())))  ⇒  (d b a c)
```

conses the symbol b onto the value returned to it, then returns the result of this cons to the continuation of the call to g. This continuation is the same as the continuation of the call to h, which conses the symbol d onto the value returned to it. We can rewrite this in *continuation-passing style*, or CPS, by replacing these implicit continuations with explicit procedures.

```
(letrec ((f (lambda (x k) (k (cons 'a x))))
         (g (lambda (x k)
              (f x (lambda (v) (k (cons 'b v))))))
         (h (lambda (x k) (g (cons 'c x) k))))
  (h '() (lambda (v) (cons 'd v))))
```

Like the implicit continuation of h and g in the preceding example, the explicit continuation passed to h and on to g,

```
(lambda (v) (cons 'd v))
```

conses the symbol d onto the value passed to it. Similarly, the continuation passed to f,

```
(lambda (v) (k (cons 'b v)))
```

conses b onto the value passed to it, then passes this on to the continuation of g.

Expressions written in CPS are more complicated, of course, but this style of programming has some useful applications. CPS allows a procedure to pass more than one result to its continuation, because the procedure that implements the continuation can take any number of arguments.

```
(define car&cdr
  (lambda (p k)
    (k (car p) (cdr p))))

(car&cdr '(a b c)
  (lambda (x y)
    (list y x)))  ⇒  ((b c) a)
(car&cdr '(a b c) cons)  ⇒  (a b c)
(car&cdr '(a b c a d) memv)  ⇒  (a d)
```

(This can be done with multiple values as well; see Section 5.7.) CPS also allows a procedure to take separate "success" and "failure" continuations, which may accept different numbers of arguments. An example is `integer-divide` below, which passes the quotient and remainder of its first two arguments to its third, unless the second argument (the divisor) is zero, in which case it passes an error message to its fourth argument.

```
(define integer-divide
  (lambda (x y success failure)
    (if (= y 0)
        (failure "divide by zero")
        (let ((q (quotient x y)))
          (success q (- x (* q y)))))))

(integer-divide 10 3 list (lambda (x) x))  ⇒  (3 1)
(integer-divide 10 0 list (lambda (x) x))  ⇒  "divide by zero"
```

The procedure `quotient`, employed by `integer-divide`, returns the quotient of its two arguments, truncated toward zero.

Explicit success and failure continuations can sometimes help to avoid the extra communication necessary to separate successful execution of a procedure from unsuccessful execution. Furthermore, it is possible to have multiple success or failure continuations for different flavors of success or failure, each possibly taking different numbers and types of arguments. See Sections 9.10 and 9.11 for extended examples that employ continuation-passing style.

At this point you may be wondering about the relationship between CPS and the continuations obtained via `call/cc`. It turns out that any program that uses `call/cc` can be rewritten in CPS without `call/cc`, but a total rewrite of the program (sometimes including even system-defined primitives) may be necessary. Try to convert the product example on page 72 into CPS before looking at the version below.

```
(define product
  (lambda (ls k)
    (let ((break k))
      (let f ((ls ls) (k k))
        (cond
          ((null? ls) (k 1))
          ((= (car ls) 0) (break 0))
          (else (f (cdr ls)
                  (lambda (x)
                    (k (* (car ls) x)))))))))))

(product '(1 2 3 4 5) (lambda (x) x))  ⇒  120
(product '(7 3 8 0 1 9 5) (lambda (x) x))  ⇒  0
```

**Exercise 3.4.1.** Rewrite the `reciprocal` example first given in Section 2.1 to accept both success and failure continuations, like `integer-divide` above.

**Exercise 3.4.2.** Rewrite the `retry` example from page 73 to use CPS.

**Exercise 3.4.3.** Rewrite the following expression in CPS to avoid using `call/cc`.

```
(define reciprocals
  (lambda (ls)
    (call/cc
      (lambda (k)
        (map (lambda (x)
               (if (= x 0)
                   (k "zero found")
                   (/ 1 x)))
             ls)))))

(reciprocals '(2 1/3 5 1/4))  ⇒  (1/2 3 1/5 4)
(reciprocals '(2 1/3 0 5 1/4))  ⇒  "zero found"
```

[*Hint*: A single-list version of `map` is defined on page 44.]

## 3.5. Internal Definitions

In Section 2.6, we discussed top-level definitions. Definitions may also appear at the front of a `lambda`, `let`, or `letrec` body, in which case the bindings they create are local to the body.

```
(define f (lambda (x) (* x x)))
(let ((x 3))
  (define f (lambda (y) (+ y x)))
  (f 4))  ⇒  7
(f 4)  ⇒  16
```

Procedures bound by internal definitions can be mutually recursive, as with `letrec`. For example, we can rewrite the **even?** and **odd?** example from Section 3.2 using internal definitions as follows.

```
(let ()
  (define even?
    (lambda (x)
      (or (= x 0)
          (odd? (- x 1)))))
  (define odd?
    (lambda (x)
      (and (not (= x 0))
           (even? (- x 1)))))
  (even? 20))  ⇒  #t
```

Similarly, we can replace the use of `letrec` to bind **race** with an internal definition of **race** in our first definition of `list?`.

```
(define list?
  (lambda (x)
    (define race
      (lambda (h t)
        (if (pair? h)
            (let ((h (cdr h)))
              (if (pair? h)
                  (and (not (eq? h t))
                       (race (cdr h) (cdr t)))
                  (null? h)))
            (null? h))))
    (race x x)))
```

In fact, internal definitions and `letrec` are practically interchangeable. It should not be surprising, therefore, that a `lambda`, `let`, or `letrec` body containing internal definitions can be replaced with an equivalent `letrec` expression. A body of the form

```
(define var  val)
```

$\vdots$

$exp_1$

$exp_2$

$\vdots$

is equivalent to a `letrec` expression binding the defined variables to the associated values in a body comprising the expressions.

(letrec (($var$ $val$) ...) $exp_1$ $exp_2$ ...)

Conversely, a `letrec` of the form

(letrec (($var$ $val$) ...) $exp_1$ $exp_2$ ...)

can be replaced with a `let` expression containing internal definitions and the expressions from the body as follows.

```
(let ()
  (define var val)
     ⋮
  exp₁
  exp₂
     ⋮
)
```

The seeming lack of symmetry between these transformations is due to the fact that `letrec` expressions can appear anywhere an expression is valid, whereas internal definitions can appear only at the front of a body. Thus, in replacing a `letrec` with internal definitions, we must generally introduce a `let` expression to hold the definitions.

Syntax definitions may also appear at the front of a `lambda`, `let`, or `letrec` body.

```
(let ((x 3))
  (define-syntax set-x!
    (syntax-rules ()
      ((_ e) (set! x e))))
  (set-x! (+ x x))
  x)  ⇒  6
```

The scope of a syntactic extension established by an internal syntax definition, as with an internal variable definition, is limited to the body in which the syntax definition appears.

Internal definitions may be used in conjunction with top-level definitions and assignments to help modularize programs. Each module of a program should make visible only those bindings that are needed by other modules, while hiding other bindings that would otherwise clutter the top-level namespace and possibly result in unintended use or redefinition of those bindings. A common way of structuring a module is shown below.

```
(define export-var #f)
  .
  .
  .
(let ()
  (define var val)
    .
    .
    .
  init-exp
    .
    .
    .
  (set! export-var export-val)
    .
    .
    .
)
```

The first set of definitions establish top-level bindings for the variables we desire to export (make visible globally). The second set of definitions establish local bindings visible only within the module. The expressions *init-exp* ... perform any initialization that must occur after the local bindings have been established. Finally, the **set!** expressions assign the exported variables to the appropriate values. Some of the extended examples in Chapter 9 use this modularization technique.

One advantage of this form of modularization is that the bracketing **let** expression may be removed or "commented out" during program development, making the internal definitions top-level to facilitate interactive testing.

The following module exports a single variable, **calc**, which is bound to a procedure that implements a simple four-function calculator.

```
(define calc #f)
(let ()
  (define do-calc
    (lambda (ek exp)
      (cond
        ((number? exp) exp)
        ((and (list? exp) (= (length exp) 3))
         (let ((op (car exp)) (args (cdr exp)))
           (case op
             ((add) (apply-op ek + args))
             ((sub) (apply-op ek - args))
             ((mul) (apply-op ek * args))
             ((div) (apply-op ek / args))
             (else (complain ek "invalid operator" op)))))
        (else (complain ek "invalid expression" exp)))))
  (define apply-op
    (lambda (ek op args)
      (op (do-calc ek (car args)) (do-calc ek (cadr args)))))
```

```
(define complain
  (lambda (ek msg exp)
    (ek (list msg exp))))
(set! calc
  (lambda (exp)
    ; grab an error continuation ek
    (call/cc
      (lambda (ek)
        (do-calc ek exp)))))))
(calc '(add (mul 3 2) -4))  ⇒  2
(calc '(div 1/2 1/6))  ⇒  3
(calc '(add (mul 3 2) (div 4)))  ⇒  ("invalid expression" (div 4))
(calc '(mul (add 1 -2) (pow 2 7)))  ⇒  ("invalid operator" pow)
```

This example uses a **case** expression to determine which operator to apply. **case** is similar to **cond** except that the test is always the same: (**memv** *val* (*key* ...)), where *val* is the value of the first **case** subform and (*key* ...) is the list of items at the front of each **case** clause. The **case** expression in the example above could be rewritten using **cond** as follows.

```
(let ((temp op))
  (cond
    ((memv temp '(add)) (apply-op ek + args))
    ((memv temp '(sub)) (apply-op ek - args))
    ((memv temp '(mul)) (apply-op ek * args))
    ((memv temp '(div)) (apply-op ek / args))
    (else (complain ek "invalid operator" op))))
```

**Exercise 3.5.1.** Redefine `complain` in the calc example as an equivalent syntactic extension.

**Exercise 3.5.2.** In the `calc` example, the error continuation `ek` is passed along on each call to `apply-op`, `complain`, and `do-calc`. Move the definitions of `apply-op`, `complain`, and `do-calc` inward as far inward as necessary to eliminate the `ek` argument from the definitions and applications of these procedures.

**Exercise 3.5.3.** Eliminate the `call/cc` from `calc` and rewrite `complain` to signal an error, using the error-reporting facilities provided by your Scheme implementation.

**Exercise 3.5.4.** Extend `calc` to handle unary minus expressions, e.g.,

```
(calc '(minus (add 2 3)))  ⇒  -5
```

and other operators of your choice.

# CHAPTER 4

# Procedures and Variable Bindings

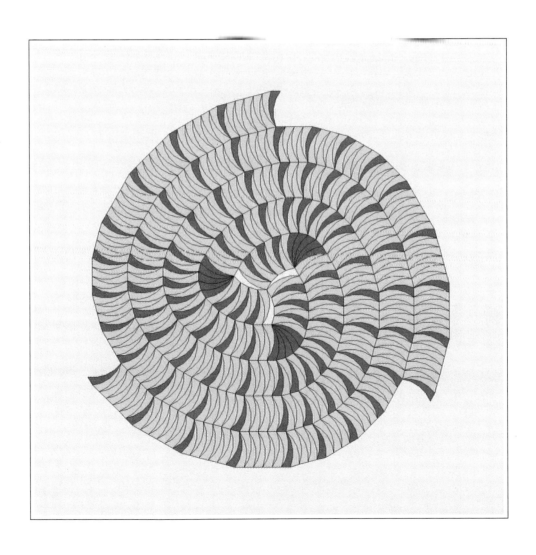

*A three-armed spiral.*

Procedures and variable bindings are the fundamental building blocks of Scheme programs. This chapter describes the small set of syntactic form whose primary purpose is to create procedures and manipulate variable bindings. It begins with two most fundamental building blocks of Scheme programs: variable references and **lambda** expressions, and continues with descriptions of the basic local variable binding forms **let** and **letrec**, top-level and internal **define**, and **set!**.

Various other forms that bind or assign variables for which the binding or assignment is not the primary purpose (such as named **let**) are found in Chapter 5.

## 4.1. Variable References

*variable*                                                            **syntax**
**returns:** the value of *variable*

Any identifier appearing as an expression in a program is a keyword or variable reference. It is a keyword reference if a lexical or top-level keyword binding for the identifier is visible; otherwise, it is a variable reference. After syntactic extensions have been expanded (see Chapter 8, no keyword references remain, so all remaining identifier expressions are variable references.

```
list  ⇒  #<procedure>
(define x 'a)
(list x x)  ⇒  (a a)
(let ((x 'b))
  (list x x))  ⇒  (b b)
(let ((let 'let)) let)  ⇒  let
```

It is an error to evaluate a top-level variable reference before the variable is defined at top-level, but it is not an error for such a reference to appear within a part of a that has not yet been evaluated. This permits mutually recursive procedures to be defined using top-level bindings.

```
i-am-not-defined  ⇒  error

(define f
  (lambda (x)
    (g x)))
(define g
  (lambda (x)
    (+ x x)))
(f 3)  ⇒  6
```

## 4.2. Lambda

(lambda *formals* *exp*$_1$ *exp*$_2$ ...)                                              **syntax**
**returns:** a procedure

The lambda syntactic form is used to create procedures. Any operation that creates
a procedure or establishes local variable bindings is ultimately defined in terms of
lambda.

The variables in *formals* are the formal parameters of the procedure, and the
sequence of expressions *exp*$_1$ *exp*$_2$ ... is its body.

The body may begin with a sequence of definitions, in which case the established
bindings are local to the procedure. If definitions are present, the body is replaced
by a letrec expression formed from the definitions and the remaining expressions.
Consult Section 3.5 or Section 4.4 for more details. The remainder of this discussion
of lambda assumes that this transformation has taken place, if necessary, so that
the body is a sequence of expressions without definitions.

When the procedure is created, the bindings of all variables occurring free within
the body, excluding the formal parameters, are retained with the procedure. Subsequently, whenever the procedure is applied to a sequence of actual parameters,
the formal parameters are bound to the actual parameters, the retained bindings
are restored, and the body is evaluated.

Upon application, the formal parameters defined by *formals* are bound to the
actual parameters as follows.

- If *formals* is a proper list of variables, e.g., (x y z), each variable is bound
  to the corresponding actual parameter. It is an error if too few or too many
  actual parameters are supplied.

- If *formals* is a single variable (not in a list), e.g., z, it is bound to a list of the
  actual parameters.

- If *formals* is an improper list of variables terminated by a variable, e.g.,
  (x y . z), each variable but the last is bound to the corresponding actual
  parameter. The last variable is bound to a list of the remaining actual parameters. It is an error if too few actual parameters are supplied.

When the body is evaluated, the expressions *exp*$_1$ *exp*$_2$ ... are evaluated in
sequence. The value of the last expression is the value of the procedure.

Procedures do not have a printed representation in the usual sense. Scheme systems print procedures in different ways; this book uses the notation #<procedure>.

```
(lambda (x) (+ x 3))  ⇒  #<procedure>
((lambda (x) (+ x 3)) 7)  ⇒  10
((lambda (x y) (* x (+ x y))) 7 13)  ⇒  140
((lambda (f x) (f x x)) + 11)  ⇒  22
((lambda () (+ 3 4)))  ⇒  7
```

```
((lambda (x . y) (list x y))
 28 37)  ⇒  (28 (37))
((lambda (x . y) (list x y))
 28 37 47 28)  ⇒  (28 (37 47 28))
((lambda (x y . z) (list x y z))
 1 2 3 4)  ⇒  (1 2 (3 4))
((lambda x x) 7 13)  ⇒  (7 13)
```

# 4.3. Local Binding

(let ((*var val*) ...) *exp*$_1$ *exp*$_2$ ...)                                     syntax
**returns:** the value of the final expression

let establishes local variable bindings. Each variable *var* is bound to the value of the corresponding expression *val*. The body of the let, in which the variables are bound, is the sequence of expressions *exp*$_1$ *exp*$_2$ ....

The forms let, let*, and letrec (let* and letrec are described after let) are similar but serve slightly different purposes. With let, in contrast with let* and letrec, the expressions *val* ... are all outside the scope of the variables *var* .... Also, in contrast with let*, no ordering is implied for the evaluation of the expressions *val* .... They may be evaluated from left to right, from right to left, or in any other order at the discretion of the implementation. Use let whenever the values are independent of the variables and the order of evaluation is unimportant.

The body of a let expression may begin with a sequence of definitions, which establish bindings local to the body of the let. See Section 3.5 or Section 4.4.

The following definition of let shows the typical derivation of let from lambda.

```
(define-syntax let
  (syntax-rules ()
    ((_ ((x v) ...) e1 e2 ...)
     ((lambda (x ...) e1 e2 ...) v ...))))
(let ((x (* 3.0 3.0)) (y (* 4.0 4.0)))
  (sqrt (+ x y)))  ⇒  5.0
(let ((x 'a) (y '(b c)))
  (cons x y))  ⇒  (a b c)
(let ((x 0) (y 1))
  (let ((x y) (y x))
    (list x y)))  ⇒  (1 0)
```

Another form of let, *named* let, is described in Section 5.4, and a definition of the full let can be found on page 201.

(let* ((*var val*) ...) *exp₁ exp₂* ...)                                          **syntax**
**returns:** the value of the final expression

let* is similar to let except that the expressions *val* ... are evaluated in sequence
from left to right, and each of these expressions is within the scope of the variables
to the left. Use let* when there is a linear dependency among the values or when
the order of evaluation is important.

Any let* expression may be converted to a set of nested let expressions. The
following definition of let* demonstrates the typical transformation.

```
(define-syntax let*
  (syntax-rules ()
    ((_ () e1 e2 ...)
     (let () e1 e2 ...))
    ((_ ((x1 v1) (x2 v2) ...) e1 e2 ...)
     (let ((x1 v1))
       (let* ((x2 v2) ...) e1 e2 ...)))))
(let* ((x (* 5.0 5.0))
       (y (- x (* 4.0 4.0))))
  (sqrt y))  ⇒  3.0
(let ((x 0) (y 1))
  (let* ((x y) (y x))
    (list x y)))  ⇒  (1 1)
```

(letrec ((*var val*) ...) *exp₁ exp₂* ...)                                        **syntax**
**returns:** the value of the final expression

letrec is similar to let and let*, except that all of the expressions *val* ... are
within the scope of all of the variables *var* .... letrec allows the definition of
mutually recursive procedures.

The order of evaluation of the expressions *val* ... is unspecified, so it is an error
to reference any of the variables bound by the letrec expression before all of the
values have been computed. (Occurrence of a variable within a lambda expression
does not count as a reference, unless the resulting procedure is applied before all of
the values have been computed.)

Choose letrec over let or let* when there is a circular dependency among the
variables and their values and when the order of evaluation is unimportant.

A letrec expression of the form

(letrec ((*var val*) ...) *body*)

may be expressed in terms of let and set! as

```
(let ((var #f) ...)
  (let ((temp val) ...)
    (set! var temp) ...
    (let () body)))
```

where *temp* ... are unique variables, one for each (*var val*) pair. The outer **let** expression establishes the variable bindings. The initial value given each variable is unimportant, so any value suffices in place of **#f**. The bindings are established first so that the values may contain occurrences of the variables, i.e., so that the values are computed within the scope of the variables. The middle **let** evaluates the values and binds them to the temporary variables, and the **set!** expressions assign each variable to the corresponding value. The inner **let** is present in case *body* contains internal definitions.

This transformation does not enforce the restriction that the values must not directly reference one of the variables. More elaborate transformations that enforce this restriction and produce more efficient code are possible [23].

A definition of **letrec** performing this transformation is shown on page 199.

```
(letrec ((sum (lambda (x)
                (if (zero? x)
                    0
                    (+ x (sum (- x 1)))))))
  (sum 5))  ⇒  15
```

## 4.4. Variable Definitions

| | |
|---|---|
| (define *var exp*) | syntax |
| (define (*var_0 var_1* ...) *exp_1 exp_2* ...) | syntax |
| (define (*var_0* . *var_r*) *exp_1 exp_2* ...) | syntax |
| (define (*var_0 var_1 var_2* ... . *var_r*) *exp_1 exp_2* ...) | syntax |

**returns:** unspecified

In the first form, **define** creates a new binding of *var* to the value of *exp*. The remaining are shorthand forms for binding variables to procedures; they are identical to the following definition in terms of **lambda**.

```
(define var
  (lambda formals
    exp_1 exp_2 ...))
```

where *formals* is (*var_1* ...), *var_r*, or (*var_1 var_2* ... . *var_r*) for the second, third, and fourth **define** formats.

Definitions often appear at "top level," i.e., outside the scope of any **lambda** or any form derived from **lambda**, such as **let**, **let***, or **letrec**. A variable bound at

top level is visible within any expression typed at the keyboard or loaded from a
file, except where shadowed by a local binding.

Definitions may also appear at the front of a lambda body or body of any form
derived from lambda. These *internal definitions* must precede the expressions in
the body. Any lambda expression whose body begins with definitions may be transformed into an equivalent lambda expression without such definitions, by rewriting
the body as a letrec expression. That is, a lambda expression of the form

```
(lambda formals
  (define var val) ...
  exp₁ exp₂ ...)
```

may be expressed in the equivalent form below.

```
(lambda formals
  (letrec ((var val) ...)
    exp₁ exp₂ ...))
```

Although this shows the transformation for the first and simpler form of definition,
either form may appear within a lambda body.

Syntax definitions may appear along with variable definitions wherever variable
definitions may appear; see Chapter 8.

```
(define x 3)
x  ⇒  3
(define f
  (lambda (x y)
    (* (+ x y) 2)))
(f 5 4)  ⇒  18
(define (sum-of-squares x y)
  (+ (* x x) (* y y)))
(sum-of-squares 3 4)  ⇒  25
(define f
  (lambda (x)
    (+ x 1)))
(let ((x 2))
  (define f
    (lambda (y)
      (+ y x)))
  (f 3))  ⇒  5
(f 3)  ⇒  4
```

A set of definitions may be grouped by enclosing them in a begin form. Definitions grouped in this manner may appear wherever ordinary variable and syntax
definitions may appear. They are treated as if written separately, i.e., without

the enclosing `begin` form. This feature allows syntactic extensions to expand into groups of definitions.

```
(define-syntax multi-define-syntax
  (syntax-rules ()
    ((_ (var exp) ...)
     (begin
       (define-syntax var exp)
       ...))))
(let ()
  (define plus
    (lambda (x y)
        (if (zero? x)
            y
            (plus (sub1 x) (add1 y)))))
  (multi-define-syntax
    (add1 (syntax-rules () ((_ e) (+ e 1))))
    (sub1 (syntax-rules () ((_ e) (- e 1)))))
  (plus 7 8))  ⇒  15
```

## 4.5. Assignment

(set! *var exp*)                                                    **syntax**
**returns:** unspecified

`set!` does not establish a new binding for *var* but rather alters the value of an existing binding. It first evaluates *exp*, then assigns *var* to the value of *exp*. Any subsequent reference to *var* within the scope of the altered binding evaluates to the new value.

It is an error to assign a top-level variable that has not yet been defined, although many implementations do not enforce this restriction.

Assignments are not employed as frequently in Scheme as in most traditional languages, but they are useful for implementing state changes.

```
(define flip-flop
  (let ((state #f))
    (lambda ()
      (set! state (not state))
      state)))

(flip-flop)  ⇒  #t
(flip-flop)  ⇒  #f
(flip-flop)  ⇒  #t
```

Assignments are also using for caching values. The example below uses a technique called *memoization*, in which a procedure records the values associated with old input values so it need not recompute them, to implement a fast version of the otherwise exponential doubly-recursive definition of the Fibonacci function (see page 66).

```
(define memoize
  (lambda (proc)
    (let ((cache '()))
      (lambda (x)
        (cond
          ((assq x cache) => cdr)
          (else (let ((ans (proc x)))
                  (set! cache (cons (cons x ans) cache))
                  ans)))))))
(define fibonacci
  (memoize
    (lambda (n)
      (if (< n 2)
          1
          (+ (fibonacci (- n 1)) (fibonacci (- n 2)))))))
(fibonacci 100)   ⇒   573147844013817084101
```

# CHAPTER 5

# Control Operations

*Three warped, two-armed spirals.*

This chapter introduces the syntactic forms and procedures that serve as control structures for Scheme programs, The first section covers the most basic control structure, procedure application, and the remaining sections cover sequencing, conditional evaluation, recursion, continuations, delayed evaluation, multiple values, and evaluation of constructed programs.

# 5.1. Procedure Application

(*procedure exp* ...)                                                   **syntax**
**returns:** result of applying the value of *procedure* to the values of *exp* ...

Procedure application is the most basic Scheme control structure. Any structured form without a syntax keyword in the first position is a procedure application. The expressions *procedure* and *exp* ... are evaluated and the value of *procedure* is applied to the values of *exp* ....

The order in which the procedure and argument expressions are evaluated is unspecified. It may be left to right, right to left, or any other order. The evaluation is guaranteed to be sequential, however; whatever order is chosen, each expression is fully evaluated before evaluation of the next is started.

```
(+ 3 4)  ⇒  7

((if (odd? 3) + -) 6 2)  ⇒  8

((lambda (x) x) 5)  ⇒  5

(let ((f (lambda (x) (+ x x))))
  (f 8))  ⇒  16
```

(apply *procedure obj* ... *list*)                                     **procedure**
**returns:** the result of applying *procedure* to *obj* ... and the elements of *list*

apply invokes *procedure*, passing the first *obj* as the first argument, the second *obj* as the second argument, and so on for each object in *obj* ..., and passing the elements of *list* in order as the remaining arguments. Thus, *procedure* is called with as many arguments as there are *objs* plus elements of *list*.

apply is useful when some or all of the arguments to be passed to a procedure are in a list, since it frees the programmer from explicitly destructuring the list.

```
(apply + '(4 5))  ⇒  9

(apply min '(6 8 3 2 5))  ⇒  2

(apply min  5 1 3 '(6 8 3 2 5))  ⇒  1

(apply vector 'a 'b '(c d e))  ⇒  #5(a b c d e)
```

```
(define first
  (lambda (l)
    (apply (lambda (x . y) x)
           l)))
(define rest
  (lambda (l)
    (apply (lambda (x . y) y) l)))
(first '(a b c d))  ⇒  a
(rest '(a b c d))  ⇒  (b c d)
```

## 5.2. Sequencing

(begin *exp₁* *exp₂* ...)                                              syntax
**returns:** the result of the last expression

The expressions *exp₁* *exp₂* ... are evaluated in sequence from left to right. begin
is used to sequence assignments, input/output, or other operations that cause side
effects.

```
(define x 3)
(begin
  (set! x (+ x 1))
  (+ x x))  ⇒  8
```

A begin form may contain zero or more definitions in place of the expressions
*exp₁* *exp₂* ..., in which case it is considered to be a definition and may appear
only where definitions are valid.

```
(let ()
  (begin (define x 3) (define y 4))
  (+ x y))  ⇒  7
```

This form of begin is primarily used by syntactic extensions that must expand into
multiple definitions. (See page 91.)

The bodies of many syntactic forms, including lambda, let, let*, and letrec,
as well as the result clauses of cond, case, and do, are treated as if they were inside
an implicit begin; that is, the expressions making up the body or result clause are
executed in sequence.

```
(define swap-pair!
  (lambda (x)
    (let ((temp (car x)))
      (set-car! x (cdr x))
      (set-cdr! x temp)
      x)))
(swap-pair! (cons 'a 'b))  ⇒  (b . a)
```

# 5.3. Conditionals

(if *test consequent alternative*)                           **syntax**
(if *test consequent*)                                       **syntax**
**returns:** the value of *consequent* or *alternative* depending on the value of *test*

*test*, *consequent*, and *alternative* are expressions. If no *alternative* is supplied and *test* evaluates to false, the result is unspecified.

```
(let ((l '(a b c)))
  (if (null? l)
      '()
      (cdr l)))  ⇒  (b c)
(let ((l '()))
  (if (null? l)
      '()
      (cdr l)))  ⇒  ()
(let ((abs
        (lambda (x)
          (if (< x 0)
              (- 0 x)
              x))))
  (abs -4))  ⇒  4
(let ((x -4))
  (if (< x 0)
      (list 'minus (- 0 x))
      (list 'plus 4)))  ⇒  (minus 4)
```

(not *obj*)                                                  **procedure**
**returns:** #t if *obj* is false, #f otherwise

not is equivalent to (lambda (x) (if x #f #t)).

```
(not #f)    ⇒  #t
(not #t)    ⇒  #f
(not '())   ⇒  #f
(not (< 4 5))  ⇒  #f
```

(and *exp* ...)                                              **syntax**
**returns:** see explanation

**and** evaluates its subexpressions in sequence from left to right and stops immediately (without evaluating the remaining expressions) if any expression evaluates to false. The value of the last expression evaluated is returned. A syntax definition of **and** appears on page 60.

```
(let ((x 3))
  (and (> x 2) (< x 4)))  ⇒  #t
(let ((x 5))
  (and (> x 2) (< x 4)))  ⇒  #f
(and #f '(a b) '(c d))  ⇒  #f
(and '(a b) '(c d) '(e f))  ⇒  (e f)
```

(or *exp* ...)                                                                    **syntax**
**returns:** see explanation

or evaluates its subexpressions in sequence from left to right and stops immediately
(without evaluating the remaining expressions) if any expression evaluates to a true
value. The value of the last expression evaluated is returned. A syntax definition
of **or** appears on page 61.

```
(let ((x 3))
  (or (< x 2) (> x 4)))  ⇒  #f
(let ((x 5))
  (or (< x 2) (> x 4)))  ⇒  #t
(or #f '(a b) '(c d))  ⇒  (a b)
```

(cond *clause*$_1$ *clause*$_2$ ...)                                              **syntax**
**returns:** see explanation

Each *clause* but the last must take one of the forms below.

(*test*)
(*test* *exp*$_1$ *exp*$_2$ ...)
(*test* => *exp*)

The last clause may be in any of the above forms or it may be an "else clause" of
the form

(else *exp*$_1$ *exp*$_2$ ...)

Each *test* is evaluated in order until one evaluates to a true value or until all of the
tests have been evaluated. If the first clause whose *test* evaluates to a true value is
in the first form given above, the value of *test* is returned.

If the first clause whose *test* evaluates to a true value is in the second form given
above, the expressions *exp*$_1$ *exp*$_2$... are evaluated in sequence and the value of the
last expression is returned.

If the first clause whose *test* evaluates to a true value is in the third form given
above, the expression *exp* is evaluated. The value should be a procedure of one

argument, which is applied to the value of *test*. The result of this application is returned.

If none of the tests evaluates to a true value and an `else` clause is present, the expressions $exp_1$ $exp_2$ ... of the `else` clause are evaluated in sequence and the value of the last expression is returned.

If none of the tests evaluates to a true value and no `else` clause is present, the value is unspecified.

See page 196 for a syntax definition of `cond`.

```
(let ((x 0))
  (cond
    ((< x 0) (list 'minus (abs x)))
    ((> x 0) (list 'plus x))
    (else (list 'zero x))))   ⇒   (zero 0)
(define select
  (lambda (x)
    (cond
      ((not (symbol? x)))
      ((assq x '((a . 1) (b . 2) (c . 3)))
       => cdr)
      (else 0))))
(select 3)   ⇒   #t
(select 'b)  ⇒   2
(select 'e)  ⇒   0
```

(case $exp_0$ *clause$_1$* *clause$_2$* ...)                                  **syntax**
**returns:** see explanation

Each clause but the last must take the form

((*key* ...) $exp_1$ $exp_2$ ...)

where each *key* is a datum distinct from the other keys. The last clause may be in the above form or it may be an `else` clause of the form

(else $exp_1$ $exp_2$ ...)

$exp_0$ is evaluated and the result is compared (using `eqv?`) against the keys of each clause in order. If a clause containing a matching key is found, the expressions $exp_1$ $exp_2$ ... are evaluated in sequence and the value of the last expression is returned.

If none of the clauses contains a matching key and an `else` clause is present, the expressions $exp_1$ $exp_2$ ... of the `else` clause are evaluated in sequence and the value of the last expression is returned.

If none of the clauses contains a matching key and no `else` clause is present, the value is unspecified.

See page 196 for a syntax definition of `case`

```
(let ((x 4) (y 5))
  (case (+ x y)
    ((1 3 5 7 9) 'odd)
    ((0 2 4 6 8) 'even)
    (else 'out-of-range)))   ⇒   odd
```

## 5.4. Recursion, Iteration, and Mapping

(let *name* ((*var val*) ...) *exp*$_1$ *exp*$_2$ ...)                             **syntax**
**returns:** value of the last expression

This form of `let`, called *named* `let`, is a general-purpose iteration and recursion construct. It is similar to the more common form of `let` (see Section 4.3) in the binding of the variables *var* ... to the values *val* ... within the body *exp*$_1$ *exp*$_2$ .... In addition, the variable *name* is bound within the body to a procedure that may be called to recur or iterate; the arguments to the procedure become the new values of the variables *var* ....

A named `let` expression of the form

(let *name* ((*var val*) ...)
  *exp*$_1$ *exp*$_2$ ...)

can be rewritten with `letrec` as follows.

((letrec ((*name* (lambda (*var* ...) *exp*$_1$ *exp*$_2$ ...)))
   *name*)
 *val* ...)

A syntax definition of `let` that implements this transformation and handles unnamed `let` as well can be found on page 201.

The procedure `divisors` defined below uses named `let` to compute the nontrivial divisors of a nonnegative integer.

```
(define divisors
  (lambda (n)
    (let f ((i 2))
      (cond
        ((>= i n) '())
        ((integer? (/ n i))
         (cons i (f (+ i 1))))
        (else (f (+ i 1)))))))
(divisors 5)   ⇒   ()
(divisors 32)   ⇒   (2 4 8 16)
```

The version above is non-tail-recursive when a divisor is found and tail-recursive when a divisor is not found. The version below is fully tail-recursive. It builds up the list in reverse order, but this is easy to remedy, either by reversing the list on exit or by starting at $n - 1$ and counting down to 1.

```
(define divisors
  (lambda (n)
    (let f ((i 2) (ls '()))
      (cond
        ((>= i n) ls)
        ((integer? (/ n i))
         (f (+ i 1) (cons i ls)))
        (else (f (+ i 1) ls))))))
```

(do ((*var val update*) ...) (*test res* ...) *exp* ...)                     **syntax**
**returns:** the value of the last *res*

**do** allows a common restricted form of iteration to be expressed succinctly. The variables *var* ... are bound initially to the values of *val* ... and are rebound on each subsequent iteration to the values of *update* .... The expressions *test*, *update* ..., *exp* ..., and *res* ... are all within the scope of the bindings established for *var* ....

On each step, the test expression *test* is evaluated. If the value of *test* is true, iteration ceases, the result expressions *res* ... are evaluated in sequence, and the value of the last expression is returned. If no result expressions are present, the value of the **do** expression is unspecified.

If the value of *test* is false, the expressions *exp* ... are evaluated in sequence, the expressions *update* ... are evaluated, new bindings for *var* ... to the values of *update* ... are created, and iteration continues.

The expressions *exp* ... are evaluated only for effect and are often omitted entirely. Any *update* expression may be omitted, in which case the effect is the same as if the *update* were simply the corresponding *var*.

Although looping constructs in most languages require that the loop iterands be updated via assignment, **do** requires the loop iterands *val* ... to be updated via rebinding. In fact, no side effects are involved in the evaluation of a **do** expression unless they are performed explicitly by its subexpressions.

See page 202 for a syntax definition of **do**.

The definitions of **factorial** and **fibonacci** below are straightforward translations of the tail-recursive named-**let** versions given in Section 3.2.

```
(define factorial
  (lambda (n)
    (do ((i n (- i 1)) (a 1 (* a i)))
        ((zero? i) a))))
```

```
(factorial 10)  ⇒  3628800
(define fibonacci
  (lambda (n)
    (if (= n 0)
        0
        (do ((i n (- i 1)) (a1 1 (+ a1 a2)) (a2 0 a1))
            ((= i 1) a1)))))
(fibonacci 6)  ⇒  8
```

The definition of **divisors** below is similar to the tail-recursive definition of **divisors** given with the description of named **let** above.

```
(define divisors
  (lambda (n)
    (do ((i 2 (+ i 1))
         (ls '()
             (if (integer? (/ n i))
                 (cons i ls)
                 ls)))
        ((>= i n) ls))))
```

The definition of **scale-vector!** below, which scales each element of a vector $v$ by a constant $k$, demonstrates a nonempty **do** body.

```
(define scale-vector!
  (lambda (v k)
    (let ((n (vector-length v)))
      (do ((i 0 (+ i 1)))
          ((= i n))
        (vector-set! v i (* (vector-ref v i) k))))))
(define vec (vector 1 2 3 4 5))
(scale-vector! vec 2)
vec  ⇒  #(2 4 6 8 10)
```

(**map** *procedure* *list*$_1$ *list*$_2$ ...)                                        **procedure**
**returns:** list of results

**map** applies *procedure* to corresponding elements of the lists *list*$_1$ *list*$_2$ ... and returns a list of the resulting values. The lists *list*$_1$ *list*$_2$ ... must be of the same length, and *procedure* must accept as many arguments as there are lists.

```
(map abs '(1 -2 3 -4 5 -6))  ⇒  (1 2 3 4 5 6)
(map (lambda (x y) (* x y))
     '(1 2 3 4)
     '(8 7 6 5))  ⇒  (8 14 18 20)
```

While the order in which the applications themselves occur is not specified, the order of the values in the output list is the same as that of the corresponding values in the input lists.

map might be defined as follows.

```
(define map
  (lambda (f ls . more)
    (if (null? more)
        (let map1 ((ls ls))
          (if (null? ls)
              '()
              (cons (f (car ls))
                    (map1 (cdr ls)))))
        (let map-more ((ls ls) (more more))
          (if (null? ls)
              '()
              (cons (apply f (car ls) (map car more))
                    (map-more (cdr ls)
                              (map cdr more)))))))))
```

No error checking is done by this version of map; f is assumed to be a procedure and the other arguments are assumed to be proper lists of the same length. An interesting feature of this definition is that map uses itself to pull out the cars and cdrs of the list of input lists; this works because of the special treatment of the single-list case.

(for-each *procedure list₁ list₂* ...)                                           **procedure**
**returns:** unspecified

for-each is similar to map except that for-each does not create and return a list of the resulting values, and for-each guarantees to perform the applications in sequence over the lists from left to right. for-each may be defined as follows.

```
(define for-each
  (lambda (f ls . more)
    (do ((ls ls (cdr ls)) (more more (map cdr more)))
        ((null? ls))
      (apply f (car ls) (map car more)))))
(let ((same-count 0))
  (for-each
    (lambda (x y)
      (if (= x y)
          (set! same-count (+ same-count 1))))
    '(1 2 3 4 5 6)
    '(2 3 3 4 7 6))
  same-count)  ⇒  3
```

# 5.5. Continuations

Continuations in Scheme are procedures that represent the remainder of a computation from a given point in the continuation. They may be obtained with `call-with-current-continuation`, which can be abbreviated `call/cc` in many Scheme implementations.

`(call-with-current-continuation` *procedure*`)`                    **procedure**
**returns:** the result of applying *procedure* to the current continuation

`call-with-current-continuation` is often abbreviated `call/cc` for the obvious reason that it requires fewer keystrokes to type. If the implementation you use does not have a binding for `call/cc`, you can define it or use the longer name in your code.

`(define call/cc call-with-current-continuation)`

`call/cc` obtains its continuation and passes it to *procedure*, which must accept one argument. The continuation itself is represented by a procedure of one argument. (In the context of multiple values, a continuation may actually accept zero or more than one argument; see Section 5.7.) Each time this procedure is applied to a value, it returns the value to the continuation of the `call/cc` application. That is, when the continuation procedure is given a value, it returns the value as the result of the application of `call/cc`.

If *procedure* returns normally when passed the continuation procedure, the value returned by `call/cc` is the value returned by *procedure*.

Continuations allow the implementation of nonlocal exits, backtracking [9, 21], coroutines [11], and multitasking [6, 24].

The example below illustrates the use of a continuation to perform a nonlocal exit from a loop.

```
(define member
  (lambda (x ls)
    (call/cc
      (lambda (break)
        (do ((ls ls (cdr ls)))
            ((null? ls) #f)
            (if (equal? x (car ls))
                (break ls)))))))
(member 'd '(a b c))  ⇒  #f
(member 'b '(a b c))  ⇒  (b c)
```

Additional examples are given in Sections 3.3 and 9.11.

The current continuation is typically represented internally as a stack of procedure activation records, and obtaining the continuation involves encapsulating the stack within a procedural object. Since an encapsulated stack has indefinite extent, some mechanism must be used to preserve the stack contents indefinitely. This can be done with surprising ease and efficiency and with no impact on programs that do not use continuations [12].

(**dynamic-wind** *in body out*)                                         **procedure**
**returns:** result of applying *body*

**dynamic-wind** offers "protection" from continuation invocation. It is useful for performing tasks that must be performed whenever control enters or leaves *body*, either normally or by continuation application.

The three arguments *in*, *body*, and *out* must be procedures of no arguments, i.e., *thunks*. Before applying *body*, and each time *body* is entered subsequently by the application of a continuation created within *body*, the *in* thunk is applied. Upon normal exit from *body* and each time *body* is exited by the application of a continuation created outside *body*, the *out* thunk is applied.

Thus, it is guaranteed that *in* is invoked at least once. In addition, if *body* ever returns, *out* is invoked at least once.

**dynamic-wind** appears in the Revised[5] Report but not in the ANSI/IEEE standard.

The following example demonstrates the use of **dynamic-wind** to be sure that an input port is closed after processing, regardless of whether the processing completes normally.

```
(let ((p (open-input-file "input-file")))
  (dynamic-wind
    (lambda () #f)
    (lambda () (process p))
    (lambda () (close-input-port p))))
```

Common Lisp provides a similar facility (**unwind-protect**) for protection from nonlocal exits. This is often sufficient. **unwind-protect** provides only the equivalent to *out*, however, since Common Lisp does not support fully general continuations. Here is how **unwind-protect** might be specified with **dynamic-wind**.

```
(define-syntax unwind-protect
  (syntax-rules ()
    ((_ body cleanup ...)
     (dynamic-wind
       (lambda () #f)
       (lambda () body)
       (lambda () cleanup ...)))))
```

```
((call/cc
   (let ((x 'a))
     (lambda (k)
       (unwind-protect
         (k (lambda () x))
         (set! x 'b))))))   ⇒  b
```

Some Scheme implementations support a controlled form of assignment known as *fluid binding*, in which a variable takes on a temporary value during a given computation and reverts to the old value after the computation has completed. The syntactic form `fluid-let` defined below in terms of `dynamic-wind` permits the fluid binding of a single variable `x` to a value `v` within a sequence of expressions `e1 e2 ...`.

```
(define-syntax fluid-let
  (syntax-rules ()
    ((_ ((x v)) e1 e2 ...)
     (let ((y v))
       (let ((swap (lambda () (let ((t x)) (set! x y) (set! y t)))))
         (dynamic-wind swap (lambda () e1 e2 ...) swap))))))
```

(Implementations that support `fluid-let` generally extend it to allow an indefinite number of `(x v)` pairs, as with `let`.)

If no continuations are invoked within the body of a `fluid-let`, the behavior is the same as if the variable were simply assigned the new value on entry and assigned the old value on return.

```
(let ((x 3))
  (+ (fluid-let ((x 5))
       x)
     x))   ⇒  8
```

A fluid-bound variable also reverts to the old value if a continuation created outside of the `fluid-let` is invoked.

```
(let ((x 'a))
  (let ((f (lambda () x)))
    (cons (call/cc
            (lambda (k)
              (fluid-let ((x 'b))
                (f))))
          (f))))   ⇒  (b . a)
```

If control has left a `fluid-let` body, either normally or by the invocation of a continuation, and control reenters the body by the invocation of a continuation, the temporary value of the fluid-bound variable is reinstated. Furthermore, any changes to the temporary value are maintained and reflected upon reentry.

```
(define reenter #f)
(define x 0)
(fluid-let ((x 1))
  (call/cc (lambda (k) (set! reenter k)))
  (set! x (+ x 1))
  x)  ⇒  2
x  ⇒  0
(reenter '*)  ⇒  3
(reenter '*)  ⇒  4
x  ⇒  0
```

An implementation of dynamic-wind is given below. In addition to defining dynamic-wind, the code redefines call/cc (call-with-current-continuation).

```
(define dynamic-wind #f)
(let ((winders '()))
  (define common-tail
    (lambda (x y)
      (let ((lx (length x)) (ly (length y)))
        (do ((x (if (> lx ly) (list-tail x (- lx ly)) x) (cdr x))
             (y (if (> ly lx) (list-tail y (- ly lx)) y) (cdr y)))
            ((eq? x y) x)))))
  (define do-wind
    (lambda (new)
      (let ((tail (common-tail new winders)))
        (let f ((l winders))
          (if (not (eq? l tail))
              (begin
                (set! winders (cdr l))
                ((cdar l))
                (f (cdr l)))))
        (let f ((l new))
          (if (not (eq? l tail))
              (begin
                (f (cdr l))
                ((caar l))
                (set! winders l)))))))
  (set! call/cc
    (let ((c call/cc))
      (lambda (f)
        (c (lambda (k)
             (f (let ((save winders))
                  (lambda (x)
                    (if (not (eq? save winders)) (do-wind save))
                    (k x)))))))))
  (set! call-with-current-continuation call/cc)
```

```
(set! dynamic-wind
  (lambda (in body out)
    (in)
    (set! winders (cons (cons in out) winders))
    (let ((ans (body)))
      (set! winders (cdr winders))
      (out)
      ans)))))
```

Together, dynamic-wind and call/cc manage a list of *winders*. A winder is a pair of *in* and *out* thunks established by a call to dynamic-wind. Whenever dynamic-wind is invoked, the *in* thunk is invoked, a new winder containing the *in* and *out* thunks is placed on the winders list, the *body* thunk is invoked, the winder is removed from the winders list, and the *out* thunk is invoked. This ordering ensures that the winder is on the winders list only when control has passed through *in* and not yet entered *out*. Whenever a continuation is obtained, the winders list is saved, and whenever the continuation is invoked, the saved winders list is reinstated. During reinstatement, the *out* thunk of each winder on the current winders list that is not also on the saved winders list is invoked, followed by the *in* thunk of each winder on the saved winders list that is not also on the current winders list. The winders list is updated incrementally, again to ensure that a winder is on the current winders list only if control has passed through its *in* thunk and not entered its *out* thunk.

The test (not (eq? save winders)) performed in call/cc is not strictly necessary but makes invoking a continuation less costly whenever the saved winders list is the same as the current winders list.

## 5.6. Delayed Evaluation

The syntactic form delay and the procedure force may be used in combination to implement *lazy evaluation*. An expression subject to lazy evaluation is not evaluated until its value is required and once evaluated is never reevaluated. delay and force appear in the Revised[5] Report but not in the ANSI/IEEE standard.

(delay *exp*)                                                                    **syntax**
**returns:** a promise

The first time the promise is *forced* (with force), it evaluates *exp*, "remembering" the resulting value. Thereafter, each time the promise is forced, it returns the remembered value instead of reevaluating *exp*. See the examples given for force below.

(force *promise*)                                                          **procedure**
**returns:** result of forcing *promise*

delay may be defined as

```
(define-syntax delay
  (syntax-rules ()
    ((_ exp) (make-promise (lambda () exp)))))
```

where make-promise is defined as

```
(define make-promise
  (lambda (p)
    (let ((val #f) (set? #f))
      (lambda ()
        (if (not set?)
            (let ((x (p)))
              (if (not set?)
                  (begin (set! val x)
                         (set! set? #t)))))
        val)))))
```

With this definition of delay, force simply invokes the promise to force evaluation
or to retrieve the saved value.

```
(define force
  (lambda (promise)
    (promise)))
```

The second test of the variable set? in make-promise is necessary in the unlikely
event that, as a result of applying $p$, the promise is recursively forced. Since a
promise must always return the same value, the result of the first application of $p$
to complete is returned.

delay and force are typically used only in the absence of side effects, e.g.,
assignments, so that the order of evaluation is unimportant.

The benefit of using delay and force is that some amount of computation might
be avoided altogether if it is delayed until absolutely required. Delayed evaluation
may be used to construct conceptually infinite lists, or *streams*. The example below
shows how a stream abstraction may be built with delay and force. A stream is a
promise that, when forced, returns a pair whose cdr is a stream.

```
(define stream-car
  (lambda (s)
    (car (force s))))
```

```
(define stream-cdr
  (lambda (s)
    (cdr (force s))))
```

```
(define counters
  (let next ((n 1))
    (delay (cons n (next (+ n 1))))))
(stream-car counters)   ⇒  1
(stream-car (stream-cdr counters))   ⇒  2
(define stream-add
  (lambda (s1 s2)
    (delay (cons
             (+ (stream-car s1) (stream-car s2))
             (stream-add (stream-cdr s1) (stream-cdr s2))))))
(define even-counters
  (stream-add counters counters))
(stream-car even-counters)   ⇒  2
(stream-car (stream-cdr even-counters))   ⇒  4
```

# 5.7. Multiple Values

While all Scheme primitives and most user-defined procedures return exactly one value, some programming problems are best solved by returning something other than one value. For example, a procedure that partitions a list of values into two sublists needs to return two values. While it is possible for the producer of multiple values to package them into a data structure and for the consumer to extract them, it is often cleaner to use the built in multiple-values interface. This interface consists of two procedures: **values** and **call-with-values**. The former produces multiple values and the latter links procedures that produce multiple-value values with procedures that consume them. The multiple values interface appears in the Revised[5] Report but not in the ANSI/IEEE standard.

(values *obj* ...)                                                 **procedure**
**returns:** see discussion following

The procedure **values** accepts any number of arguments and simply passes (returns) the arguments to its continuation.

```
(values)   ⇒
(values 1)   ⇒  1
(values 1 2 3)   ⇒  1
                    2
                    3
```

```
(define head&tail
  (lambda (ls)
    (values (car ls) (cdr ls))))
(head&tail '(a b c))   ⇒   a
                           (b c)
```

(call-with-values *producer* *consumer*)                    **procedure**
**returns:** see discussion following

*producer* and *consumer* must be procedures. `call-with-values` applies *consumer* to the values returned by invoking *producer* without arguments.

```
(call-with-values
  (lambda () (values 'bond 'james))
  (lambda (x y) (cons y x)))   ⇒   (james . bond)
(call-with-values values list)   ⇒   '()
```

In the second example, `values` itself serves as the producer. It receives no arguments and thus returns no values. `list` is thus applied to no arguments and so returns the empty list.

The procedure `dxdy` defined below computes the change in $x$ and $y$ coordinates for a pair of points whose coordinates are represented by $(x . y)$ pairs.

```
(define dxdy
  (lambda (p1 p2)
    (values (- (car p2) (car p1))
            (- (cdr p2) (cdr p1)))))
(dxdy '(0 . 0) '(0 . 5))   ⇸   0
                               5
```

`dxdy` can be used to compute the length and slope of a segment represented by two endpoints.

```
(define segment-length
  (lambda (p1 p2)
    (call-with-values
      (lambda () (dxdy p1 p2))
      (lambda (dx dy) (sqrt (+ (* dx dx) (* dy dy)))))))
(define segment-slope
  (lambda (p1 p2)
    (call-with-values
      (lambda () (dxdy p1 p2))
      (lambda (dx dy) (/ dy dx)))))
(segment-length '(1 . 4) '(4 . 8))   ⇒   5
(segment-slope '(1 . 4) '(4 . 8))   ⇒   4/3
```

We can of course combine these to form one procedure that returns two values.

```
(define describe-segment
  (lambda (p1 p2)
    (call-with-values
      (lambda () (dxdy p1 p2))
      (lambda (dx dy)
        (values
          (sqrt (+ (* dx dx) (* dy dy)))
          (/ dy dx))))))
(describe-segment '(1 . 4) '(4 . 8))   ⇒   5
                                       ⇒   4/3
```

The example below employs multiple values to divide a list nondestructively into two sublists of alternating elements.

```
(define split
  (lambda (ls)
    (if (or (null? ls) (null? (cdr ls)))
        (values ls '())
        (call-with-values
          (lambda () (split (cddr ls)))
          (lambda (odds evens)
            (values (cons (car ls) odds)
                    (cons (cadr ls) evens)))))))
(split '(a b c d e f))   ⇒   (a c e)
                             (b d f)
```

At each level of recursion, the procedure **split** returns two values: a list of the odd-numbered elements from the argument list and a list of the even-numbered elements.

The continuation of a call to **values** need not be one established by a call to **call-with-values**, nor must only **values** be used to return to a continuation established by **call-with-values**. In particular, (**values** $v$) and $v$ are equivalent in all situations. For example:

```
(+ (values 2) 4)   ⇒   6

(if (values #t) 1 2)   ⇒   1

(call-with-values
  (lambda () 4)
  (lambda (x) x))   ⇒   4
```

Similarly, **values** may be used to pass any number of values to a continuation that ignores the values, as in:

```
(begin (values 1 2 3) 4)   ⇒   4
```

Because a continuation may accept zero or more than one value, continuations obtained via `call-with-current-continuation` (`call/cc`) may accept zero or more than one argument.

```
(call-with-values
  (lambda ()
    (call/cc (lambda (k) (k 2 3))))
  (lambda (x y) (list x y)))  ⇒  (2 3)
```

Many Scheme operators pass along multiple values. Most of these are "automatic," in the sense that nothing special must be done by the implementation to make this happen. The usual expansion of `let` into a direct `lambda` call automatically propagates multiple values produced by the body of the `let`. Other operators must be coded specially to pass along multiple values. For example, if the computation delayed by `delay` produces multiple values, all of the values must be retained so that `force` can return them. This is easily accomplished via `call-with-values`, `apply`, and `values`, as the following alternative definition of `make-promise` (see Section 5.6) demonstrates.

```
(define make-promise
  (lambda (p)
    (let ((vals #f) (set? #f))
      (lambda ()
        (if (not set?)
            (call-with-values p
              (lambda x
                (if (not set?)
                    (begin (set! vals x)
                           (set! set? #t))))))
        (apply values vals)))))
(define p (delay (values 1 2 3)))
(force p)  ⇒  1
               2
               3
(call-with-values (lambda () (force p)) +)  ⇒  6
```

Other operators that must be coded similarly to pass along multiple return values include `call-with-input-file`, `call-with-output-file`, `with-input-from-file`, `with-output-to-file`, and `dynamic-wind`.

The behavior is unspecified when a continuation expecting exactly one value receives zero values or more than one value. For example, the behavior of each of the following expressions is unspecified.

```
(if (values 1 2) 'x 'y)

(+ (values) 5)
```

Similarly, since there is no requirement to signal an error when the wrong number of arguments is passed to a procedure (although most implementations do so), the behavior of each of the following expressions is also unspecified.

```scheme
(call-with-values
  (lambda () (values 2 3 4))
  (lambda (x y) x))
```

```scheme
(call-with-values
  (lambda () (call/cc (lambda (k) (k 0))))
  (lambda (x y) x))
```

In the interests of catching possible coding errors and for consistency with the signaling of errors when procedures receive incorrect numbers of arguments, some implementations, including *Chez Scheme*, signal an error whenever an unexpected number of values is received. This includes the case where too few or too many are passed to the consumer of a `call-with-values` call and the case where zero or more than one value is passed to a single-value continuation, such as in the test part of an `if` expression. An implementation may, however, silently suppress additional values or supply defaults for missing values.

Programs that wish to force extra values to be ignored in particular contexts can do so easily by calling `call-with-values` explicitly. A syntactic form, which we might call `first`, can be defined to abstract the discarding of more than one value when only one is desired.

```scheme
(define-syntax first
  (syntax-rules ()
    ((_ expr)
     (call-with-values
       (lambda () expr)
       (lambda (x . y) x)))))
```

```scheme
(if (first (values #t #f)) 'a 'b)  ⇒  a
```

Since *producer* is most often a `lambda` expression, it is often convenient to use a syntactic extension that suppresses the lambda expression in the interest of readability.

```scheme
(define-syntax with-values
  (syntax-rules ()
    ((_ expr consumer)
     (call-with-values (lambda () expr) consumer))))
```

```scheme
(with-values (values 1 2) list)  ⇒  (1 2)
(with-values (split '(1 2 3 4))
  (lambda (odds evens)
    evens))  ⇒  (2 4)
```

If the *consumer* is also a `lambda` expression, the multiple-value variant of `let` defined below might be even more convenient.

```
(define-syntax let-values
  (syntax-rules ()
    ((_ ((fmls e0)) e1 e2 ...)
     (with-values e0
       (lambda fmls e1 e2 ...)))))
(let-values (((odds evens) (split '(1 2 3 4))))
  evens)   ⇒   (2 4)

(let-values ((ls (values 'a 'b 'c)))
  ls)   ⇒   (a b c)
```

This version of `let-values` is restricted to binding one set of variables to the values produced by one expression. A more general implementation of `let-values` that binds more than one set of variables to corresponding sets of values is given on page 200.

The definitions of `values` and `call-with-values` (and concomitant redefinition of `call/cc`) below demonstrate that the multiple return values interface can be implemented entirely in Scheme. No error checking can be done, however, for the case in which more than one value is returned to a single-value context such as the test part of an `if` expression.

```
(define call/cc call/cc)
(define values #f)
(define call-with-values #f)
(let ((magic (cons 'multiple 'values)))
  (define magic?
    (lambda (x)
      (and (pair? x) (eq? (car x) magic))))
  (set! call/cc
    (let ((primitive-call/cc call/cc))
      (lambda (p)
        (primitive-call/cc
          (lambda (k)
            (p (lambda args
                 (k (apply values args)))))))))
  (set! values
    (lambda args
      (if (and (not (null? args)) (null? (cdr args)))
          (car args)
          (cons magic args)))))
```

```
(set! call-with-values
  (lambda (producer consumer)
    (let ((x (producer)))
      (if (magic? x)
          (apply consumer (cdr x))
          (consumer x))))))
```

Multiple values can be implemented much more efficiently [1], but this code serves to illustrate the meanings of the operators and can be used to provide multiple values in implementations that do not support them.

## 5.8. Eval

Scheme's eval procedure allows programmers to write programs that construct and evaluate other programs. This ability to do *meta programming* should not be overused but is extremely handy when needed.

eval and the environment specifiers appear in the Revised[5] Report but not in the the ANSI/IEEE standard.

(eval *obj env-spec*)                                      **procedure**
**returns:** value of the Scheme form represented by *obj*

*env-spec* must be an environment specifier returned by interaction-environment, scheme-report-environment, or null-environment. eval treats *obj* as the representation of an expression. It evaluates the expression in the specified environment and returns its value.

```
(define cons 'not-cons)
(eval '(let ((x 3)) (cons x 4))
      (scheme-report-environment 5))  ⇒  (x . 4)

(define lambda 'not-lambda)
(eval '(lambda (x) x) (null-environment))  ⇒  #<procedure>

(eval '(cons 3 4) (null-environment))  ⇒  error
```

An implementation may extend eval to support other environments. An implementation may also permit *obj* to be the representation of a definition, but eval must not allow the creation of new bindings in a null or scheme-report environment. The effect of assigning (through the use of *eval*) a variable bound in a scheme-report environment is unspecified; thus, the environment may be immutable.

(scheme-report-environment *version*)                    **procedure**
(null-environment *version*)                             **procedure**
**returns:** see below

*version* must be an exact integer. This integer specifies a revision of the Revised Report on Scheme, i.e., the Revised$^v$ Report on Scheme for version $v$.

scheme-report-environment returns a specifier for an environment that is empty except for all bindings defined in the specified report that are either required or both optional and supported by the implementation. null-environment returns a specifier for an environment that is empty except for the bindings for all syntactic keywords defined in the specified report that are either required or both optional and supported by the implementation.

scheme-report-environment and null-environment must accept the value of *version* that corresponds to the most recent Revised Report that the implementation claims to support, starting with the Revised$^5$ Report. They may also accept other values of *version*. An error is signaled if the implementation does not support the given version.

(interaction-environment)                                **procedure**
**returns:** an environment specifier

interaction-environment returns an environment specifier that represents an environment containing implementation-dependent bindings. This environment is typically the one in which the implementation evaluates expressions dynamically typed by the user.

# CHAPTER 6

## *Operations on Objects*

*Three two-armed spirals.*

This chapter describes the operations on objects, including lists, numbers, characters, strings, vectors, and symbols. The first section covers constant objects and quotation. The second section describes generic equivalence predicates for comparing two objects and predicates for determining the *type* of an object. Later sections describe procedures that deal primarily with one of the object types mentioned above. There is no section treating operations on procedures, since the only operation defined specifically for procedures is application, and this is described in Chapter 5. Operations on ports are covered in the more general discussion of input and output in Chapter 7.

## 6.1. Constants and Quotation

*constant*            syntax
**returns:** *constant*

*constant* is any self-evaluating constant, i.e., a number, boolean, character, or string. Constants are immutable; see the note in the description of **quote** below.

```
3.2  ⇒  3.2
#f  ⇒  #f
#\c  ⇒  #\c
"hi"  ⇒  "hi"
```

(**quote** *obj*)            syntax
'*obj*            syntax
**returns:** *obj*

'*obj* is equivalent to (**quote** *obj*). The abbreviated form is converted into the longer form by the Scheme reader (see **read**).

    **quote** inhibits the normal evaluation rule for *obj*, allowing *obj* to be employed as data. Although any Scheme object may be quoted, quotation is not necessary for self-evaluating constants, i.e., numbers, booleans, characters, and strings.

    Quoted and self-evaluating constants are immutable. That is, it is an error to alter a constant via **set-car!**, **string-set!**, etc. An implementation may choose to share storage among different constants to save space.

```
(+ 2 3)  ⇒  5
'(+ 2 3)  ⇒  (+ 2 3)
(quote (+ 2 3))  ⇒  (+ 2 3)
'a  ⇒  a
'cons  ⇒  cons
'()  ⇒  ()
'7  ⇒  7
```

(quasiquote *obj*)                                                                    **syntax**
`*obj*                                                                                **syntax**
(unquote *obj*)                                                                       **syntax**
,*obj*                                                                                **syntax**
(unquote-splicing *obj*)                                                              **syntax**
,@*obj*                                                                               **syntax**
**returns:** see explanation

`*obj* is equivalent to (quasiquote *obj*), ,*obj* is equivalent to (unquote *obj*), and
,@*obj* is equivalent to (unquote-splicing *obj*). The abbreviated forms are converted into the longer forms by the Scheme reader (see **read**).

quasiquote is similar to **quote**, but it allows parts of the quoted text to be "unquoted." Within a quasiquote expression, subforms of unquote and unquote-splicing forms are evaluated, and everything else is quoted, i.e., left unevaluated. The value of each unquote subform is inserted into the output in place of the unquote form, while the value of each unquote-splicing subform is spliced into the surrounding list or vector structure. unquote and unquote-splicing are valid only within quasiquote expressions.

quasiquote expressions may be nested, with each quasiquote introducing a new level of quotation and each unquote or unquote-splicing taking away a level of quotation. An expression nested within *n* quasiquote expressions must be within *n* unquote or unquote-splicing expressions to be evaluated.

```
`(+ 2 3)  ⇒  (+ 2 3)

`(+ 2 ,(* 3 4))  ⇒  (+ 2 12)
`(a b (,(+ 2 3) c) d)  ⇒  (a b (5 c) d)
`(a b ,(reverse '(c d e)) f g)  ⇒  (a b (e d c) f g)
(let ((a 1) (b 2))
  `(,a . ,b))  ⇒  (1 . 2)

`(+ ,@(cdr '(* 2 3)))  ⇒  (+ 2 3)
`(a b ,@(reverse '(c d e)) f g)  ⇒  (a b e d c f g)
(let ((a 1) (b 2))
  `(,a ,@b))  ⇒  (1 . 2)
`#(,@(list 1 2 3))  ⇒  #(1 2 3)

``,(cons 'a 'b)  ⇒  `,(cons 'a 'b)
``,(cons 'a 'b)  ⇒  '(a . b)
```

# 6.2. Generic Equivalence and Type Predicates

This section describes the basic Scheme predicates (procedures returning one of the boolean values #t or #f) for determining the type of an object or the equivalence of two objects. The equivalence predicates `eq?`, `eqv?`, and `equal?` are discussed first, followed by the type predicates.

(`eq?` *obj*₁ *obj*₂)                                                                          **procedure**

**returns:** `#t` if *obj*₁ and *obj*₂ are identical, `#f` otherwise

In most Scheme systems, two objects are considered identical if they are represented internally by the same pointer value and distinct (not identical) if they are represented internally by different pointer values, although other criteria, such as time-stamping, are possible.

Although the particular rules for object identity vary somewhat from system to system, the following rules always hold.

- Two objects of different types (booleans, the empty list, pairs, numbers, characters, strings, vectors, symbols, and procedures) are distinct.

- Two objects of the same type with different contents or values are distinct.

- The boolean object `#t` is identical to itself wherever it appears, and `#f` is identical to itself wherever it appears, but `#t` and `#f` are distinct.

- The empty list `()` is identical to itself wherever it appears.

- Two symbols (created by `read` or by `string->symbol`) are identical if and only if they have the same name (by `string=?`).

- A quoted pair, vector, or string is identical to itself, as is a pair, vector, or string created by an application of `cons`, `vector`, `string`, etc. Two pairs, vectors, or strings created by different applications of `cons`, `vector`, `string`, etc., are distinct. One consequence is that `cons`, for example, may be used to create a unique object distinct from all other objects.

- Two procedures that may behave differently are distinct. A procedure created by an evaluation of a `lambda` expression is identical to itself. Two procedures created by the same `lambda` expression at different times, or by similar `lambda` expressions, may or may not be identical.

`eq?` cannot be used to compare numbers and characters reliably. Although every inexact number is distinct from every exact number, two exact numbers, two inexact numbers, or two characters with the same value may or may not be identical.

Since constant objects are immutable, i.e., it is an error to modify one, all or portions of different quoted constants or self-evaluating literals may be represented internally by the same object. Thus, `eq?` may return `#t` when applied to equal parts of different immutable constants.

```
(eq? 'a 3)  ⇒  #f
(eq? #t 't)  ⇒  #f
(eq? "abc" 'abc)  ⇒  #f
(eq? "hi" '(hi))  ⇒  #f
(eq? #f '())  ⇒  #f

(eq? 9/2 7/2)  ⇒  #f
(eq? 3.4 53344)  ⇒  #f
(eq? 3 3.0)  ⇒  #f
(eq? 1/3 #i1/3)  ⇒  #f

(eq? 9/2 9/2)  ⇒  unspecified
(eq? 3.4 (+ 3.0 .4))  ⇒  unspecified
(let ((x (* 12345678987654321 2)))
  (eq? x x))  ⇒  unspecified

(eq? #\a #\b)  ⇒  #f
(eq? #\a #\a)  ⇒  unspecified
(let ((x (string-ref "hi" 0)))
  (eq? x x))  ⇒  unspecified

(eq? #t #t)  ⇒  #t
(eq? #f #f)  ⇒  #t
(eq? #t #f)  ⇒  #f
(eq? (null? '()) #t)  ⇒  #t
(eq? (null? '(a)) #f)  ⇒  #t

(eq? (cdr '(a)) '())  ⇒  #t

(eq? 'a 'a)  ⇒  #t
(eq? 'a 'b)  ⇒  #f
(eq? 'a (string->symbol "a"))  ⇒  #t

(eq? '(a) '(b))  ⇒  #f
(eq? '(a) '(a))  ⇒  unspecified
(let ((x '(a . b))) (eq? x x))  ⇒  #t
(let ((x (cons 'a 'b)))
  (eq? x x))  ⇒  #t
(eq? (cons 'a 'b) (cons 'a 'b))  ⇒  #f

(eq? "abc" "cba")  ⇒  #f
(eq? "abc" "abc")  ⇒  unspecified
(let ((x "hi")) (eq? x x))  ⇒  #t
(let ((x (string #\h #\i))) (eq? x x))  ⇒  #t
(eq? (string #\h #\i)
     (string #\h #\i))  ⇒  #f
```

```
(eq? '#(a) '#(b))  ⇒  #f
(eq? '#(a) '#(a))  ⇒  unspecified
(let ((x '#(a))) (eq? x x))  ⇒  #t
(let ((x (vector 'a)))
  (eq? x x))  ⇒  #t
(eq? (vector 'a) (vector 'a))  ⇒  #f

(eq? car car)  ⇒  #t
(eq? car cdr)  ⇒  #f
(let ((f (lambda (x) x)))
  (eq? f f))  ⇒  #t
(let ((f (lambda () (lambda (x) x))))
  (eq? (f) (f)))  ⇒  unspecified
(eq? (lambda (x) x) (lambda (y) y))  ⇒  unspecified

(let ((f (lambda (x)
           (lambda ()
             (set! x (+ x 1))
             x))))
  (eq? (f 0) (f 0)))  ⇒  #f
```

(eqv? *obj₁* *obj₂*)                                         **procedure**
**returns:** #t if $obj_1$ and $obj_2$ are equivalent, #f otherwise

eqv? is similar to eq? except that eqv? is guaranteed to return #t for two exact numbers, two inexact numbers, or two characters with the same value (by = or char=?). eqv? is less implementation-dependent but generally more expensive than eq?. eqv? might be defined as follows.

```
(define eqv?
  (lambda (x y)
    (cond
      ((eq? x y))
      ((number? x)
       (and (number? y)
            (if (exact? x)
                (and (exact? y) (= x y))
                (and (inexact? y) (= x y)))))
      ((char? x) (and (char? y) (char=? x y)))
      (else #f))))

(eqv? 'a 3)  ⇒  #f
(eqv? #t 't)  ⇒  #f
(eqv? "abc" 'abc)  ⇒  #f
(eqv? "hi" '(hi))  ⇒  #f
(eqv? #f '())  ⇒  #f
```

```
(eqv? 9/2 7/2)  ⇒  #f
(eqv? 3.4 53344)  ⇒  #f
(eqv? 3 3.0)  ⇒  #f
(eqv? 1/3 #i1/3)  ⇒  #f

(eqv? 9/2 9/2)  ⇒  #t
(eqv? 3.4 (+ 3.0 .4))  ⇒  #t
(let ((x (* 12345678987654321 2)))
  (eqv? x x))  ⇒  #t

(eqv? #\a #\b)  ⇒  #f
(eqv? #\a #\a)  ⇒  #t
(let ((x (string-ref "hi" 0)))
  (eqv? x x))  ⇒  #t

(eqv? #t #t)  ⇒  #t
(eqv? #f #f)  ⇒  #t
(eqv? #t #f)  ⇒  #f
(eqv? (null? '()) #t)  ⇒  #t
(eqv? (null? '(a)) #f)  ⇒  #t

(eqv? (cdr '(a)) '())  ⇒  #t

(eqv? 'a 'a)  ⇒  #t
(eqv? 'a 'b)  ⇒  #f
(eqv? 'a (string->symbol "a"))  ⇒  #t

(eqv? '(a) '(b))  ⇒  #f
(eqv? '(a) '(a))  ⇒  unspecified
(let ((x '(a . b))) (eqv? x x))  ⇒  #t
(let ((x (cons 'a 'b)))
  (eqv? x x))  ⇒  #t
(eqv? (cons 'a 'b) (cons 'a 'b))  ⇒  #f

(eqv? "abc" "cba")  ⇒  #f
(eqv? "abc" "abc")  ⇒  unspecified
(let ((x "hi")) (eqv? x x))  ⇒  #t
(let ((x (string #\h #\i))) (eqv? x x))  ⇒  #t
(eqv? (string #\h #\i)
      (string #\h #\i))  ⇒  #f

(eqv? '#(a) '#(b))  ⇒  #f
(eqv? '#(a) '#(a))  ⇒  unspecified
(let ((x '#(a))) (eqv? x x))  ⇒  #t
(let ((x (vector 'a)))
  (eqv? x x))  ⇒  #t
(eqv? (vector 'a) (vector 'a))  ⇒  #f
```

```
(eqv? car car)   ⇒   #t
(eqv? car cdr)   ⇒   #f
(let ((f (lambda (x) x)))
  (eqv? f f))   ⇒   #t
(let ((f (lambda () (lambda (x) x))))
  (eqv? (f) (f)))   ⇒   unspecified
(eqv? (lambda (x) x) (lambda (y) y))   ⇒   unspecified

(let ((f (lambda (x)
           (lambda ()
             (set! x (+ x 1))
             x))))
  (eqv? (f 0) (f 0)))   ⇒   #f
```

(equal? $obj_1$ $obj_2$)                                              **procedure**
**returns:** #t if $obj_1$ and $obj_2$ have the same structure and contents, #f otherwise

Two objects are equal if they are equivalent according to eqv? or if they are strings
that are string=?, pairs whose cars and cdrs are equal, or vectors of the same
length whose corresponding elements are equal.

   equal? is recursively defined and must compare not only numbers and characters
for equivalence but also pairs, strings, and vectors. The result is that equal? is less
discriminating than either eq? or eqv?. It is also likely to be more expensive.

   equal? might be defined as follows.

```
(define equal?
  (lambda (x y)
    (cond
      ((eqv? x y))
      ((pair? x)
       (and (pair? y)
            (equal? (car x) (car y))
            (equal? (cdr x) (cdr y))))
      ((string? x) (and (string? y) (string=? x y)))
      ((vector? x)
       (and (vector? y)
            (let ((n (vector-length x)))
              (and (= (vector-length y) n)
                   (let loop ((i 0))
                     (or (= i n)
                         (and (equal? (vector-ref x i) (vector-ref y i))
                              (loop (+ i 1)))))))))
      (else #f))))
```

```
(equal? 'a 3)  ⇒  #f
(equal? #t 't)  ⇒  #f
(equal? "abc" 'abc)  ⇒  #f
(equal? "hi" '(hi))  ⇒  #f
(equal? #f '())  ⇒  #f

(equal? 9/2 7/2)  ⇒  #f
(equal? 3.4 53344)  ⇒  #f
(equal? 3 3.0)  ⇒  #f
(equal? 1/3 #i1/3)  ⇒  #f

(equal? 9/2 9/2)  ⇒  #t
(equal? 3.4 (+ 3.0 .4))  ⇒  #t
(let ((x (* 12345678987654321 2)))
  (equal? x x))  ⇒  #t

(equal? #\a #\b)  ⇒  #f
(equal? #\a #\a)  ⇒  #t
(let ((x (string-ref "hi" 0)))
  (equal? x x))  ⇒  #t

(equal? #t #t)  ⇒  #t
(equal? #f #f)  ⇒  #t
(equal? #t #f)  ⇒  #f
(equal? (null? '()) #t)  ⇒  #t
(equal? (null? '(a)) #f)  ⇒  #t

(equal? (cdr '(a)) '())  ⇒  #t

(equal? 'a 'a)  ⇒  #t
(equal? 'a 'b)  ⇒  #f
(equal? 'a (string->symbol "a"))  ⇒  #t

(equal? '(a) '(b))  ⇒  #f
(equal? '(a) '(a))  ⇒  #t
(let ((x '(a . b))) (equal? x x))  ⇒  #t
(let ((x (cons 'a 'b)))
  (equal? x x))  ⇒  #t
(equal? (cons 'a 'b) (cons 'a 'b))  ⇒  #t

(equal? "abc" "cba")  ⇒  #f
(equal? "abc" "abc")  ⇒  #t
(let ((x "hi")) (equal? x x))  ⇒  #t
(let ((x (string #\h #\i))) (equal? x x))  ⇒  #t
(equal? (string #\h #\i)
        (string #\h #\i))  ⇒  #t
```

```
(equal? '#(a) '#(b))  ⇒  #f
(equal? '#(a) '#(a))  ⇒  #t
(let ((x '#(a))) (equal? x x))  ⇒  #t
(let ((x (vector 'a)))
  (equal? x x))  ⇒  #t
(equal? (vector 'a) (vector 'a))  ⇒  #t

(equal? car car)  ⇒  #t
(equal? car cdr)  ⇒  #f
(let ((f (lambda (x) x)))
  (equal? f f))  ⇒  #t
(let ((f (lambda () (lambda (x) x))))
  (equal? (f) (f)))  ⇒  unspecified
(equal? (lambda (x) x) (lambda (y) y))  →  unspecified

(let ((f (lambda (x)
           (lambda ()
             (set! x (+ x 1))
             x))))
  (equal? (f 0) (f 0)))  ⇒  #f
```

**(boolean?** *obj***)**                                        **procedure**
**returns:** #t if *obj* is either #t or #f, #f otherwise

boolean? is equivalent to (lambda (x) (or (eq? x #t) (eq? x #f))).

```
(boolean? #t)  ⇒  #t
(boolean? #f)  ⇒  #t
(boolean? 't)  ⇒  #f
(boolean? '())  ⇒  #f
```

**(null?** *obj***)**                                          **procedure**
**returns:** #t if *obj* is the empty list, #f otherwise

null? is equivalent to (lambda (x) (eq? x '())).

```
(null? '())  ⇒  #t
(null? '(a))  ⇒  #f
(null? (cdr '(a)))  ⇒  #t
(null? 3)  ⇒  #f
(null? #f)  ⇒  #f
```

(pair? *obj*)                                                          **procedure**
**returns:** #t if *obj* is a pair, #f otherwise

```
(pair? '(a b c))  ⇒  #t
(pair? '(3 . 4))  ⇒  #t
(pair? '())  ⇒  #f
(pair? '#(a b))  ⇒  #f
(pair? 3)  ⇒  #f
```

(number? *obj*)                                                        **procedure**
**returns:** #t if *obj* is a number, #f otherwise
(complex? *obj*)                                                       **procedure**
**returns:** #t if *obj* is a complex number, #f otherwise
(real? *obj*)                                                          **procedure**
**returns:** #t if *obj* is a real number, #f otherwise
(rational? *obj*)                                                      **procedure**
**returns:** #t if *obj* is a rational number, #f otherwise
(integer? *obj*)                                                       **procedure**
**returns:** #t if *obj* is an integer, #f otherwise

These predicates form a hierarchy: any integer is rational, any rational is real, any real is complex, and any complex is numeric. Most implementations do not provide internal representations for irrational numbers, so all real numbers are typically rational as well.

```
(integer? 1901)  ⇒  #t
(rational? 1901)  ⇒  #t
(real? 1901)  ⇒  #t
(complex? 1901)  ⇒  #t
(number? 1901)  ⇒  #t

(integer? -3.0)  ⇒  #t
(rational? -3.0)  ⇒  #t
(real? -3.0)  ⇒  #t
(complex? -3.0)  ⇒  #t
(number? -3.0)  ⇒  #t

(integer? 7.0+0.0i)  ⇒  #t
(rational? 7.0+0.0i)  ⇒  #t
(real? 7.0+0.0i)  ⇒  #t
(complex? 7.0+0.0i)  ⇒  #t
(number? 7.0+0.0i)  ⇒  #t
```

```
(integer? -2/3)   ⇒   #f
(rational? -2/3)   ⇒   #t
(real? -2/3)   ⇒   #t
(complex? -2/3)   ⇒   #t
(number? -2/3)   ⇒   #t

(integer? -2.345)   ⇒   #f
(rational? -2.345)   ⇒   #t
(real? -2.345)   ⇒   #t
(complex? -2.345)   ⇒   #t
(number? -2.345)   ⇒   #t

(integer? 3.2-2.01i)   ⇒   #f
(rational? 3.2-2.01i)   ⇒   #f
(real? 3.2-2.01i)   ⇒   #f
(complex? 3.2-2.01i)   ⇒   #t
(number? 3.2-2.01i)   ⇒   #t

(integer? 'a)   ⇒   #f
(rational? '(a b c))   ⇒   #f
(real? "3")   ⇒   #f
(complex? #(1 2))   ⇒   #f
(number? #\a)   ⇒   #f
```

(char? *obj*)                                          **procedure**
returns: #t if *obj* is a character, #f otherwise

```
(char? 'a)   ⇒   #f
(char? 97)   ⇒   #f
(char? #\a)   ⇒   #t
(char? "a")   ⇒   #f
(char? (string-ref (make-string 1) 0))   ⇒   #t
```

(string? *obj*)                                        **procedure**
returns: #t if *obj* is a string, #f otherwise

```
(string? "hi")   ⇒   #t
(string? 'hi)   ⇒   #f
(string? #\h)   ⇒   #f
```

(vector? *obj*)                                                              **procedure**
**returns:** #t if *obj* is a vector, #f otherwise

```
(vector? '#())  ⇒  #t
(vector? '#(a b c))  ⇒  #t
(vector? (vector 'a 'b 'c))  ⇒  #t
(vector? '())  ⇒  #f
(vector? '(a b c))  ⇒  #f
(vector? "abc")  ⇒  #f
```

(symbol? *obj*)                                                             **procedure**
**returns:** #t if *obj* is a symbol, #f otherwise

```
(symbol? 't)  ⇒  #t
(symbol? "t")  ⇒  #f
(symbol? '(t))  ⇒  #f
(symbol? #\t)  ⇒  #f
(symbol? 3)  ⇒  #f
(symbol? #t)  ⇒  #f
```

(procedure? *obj*)                                                          **procedure**
**returns:** #t if *obj* is a procedure, #f otherwise

```
(procedure? car)  ⇒  #t
(procedure? 'car)  ⇒  #f
(procedure? (lambda (x) x))  ⇒  #t
(procedure? '(lambda (x) x))  ⇒  #f
(call/cc procedure?)  ⇒  #t
```

## 6.3. Lists and Pairs

The pair, or *cons cell*, is the most fundamental of Scheme's structured object types. The most common use for pairs is to build lists, which are ordered sequences of pairs linked one to the next by the *cdr* field. The elements of the list occupy the *car* fields of the pairs. The cdr of the last pair in a *proper list* is the empty list, (); the cdr of the last pair in an *improper list* can be anything other than ().

Pairs may be used to construct binary trees. Each pair in the tree structure is an internal node of the binary tree; its car and cdr are the children of the node.

Proper lists are printed as sequences of objects separated by whitespace (that is, blanks, tabs, and newlines) and enclosed in parentheses. Brackets ( [ ] ) may also be used in some Scheme systems. For example, (1 2 3) and (a (nested list)) are proper lists. The empty list is written as ().

Improper lists and trees require a slightly more complex syntax. A single pair is written as two objects separated by whitespace and a dot, e.g., (a . b). This is referred to as *dotted-pair notation*. Improper lists and trees are also written in dotted-pair notation; the dot appears wherever necessary, e.g., (1 2 3 . 4) or ((1 . 2) . 3). Proper lists may be written in dotted-pair notation as well. For example, (1 2 3) may be written as (1 . (2 . (3 . ()))).

Unless otherwise stated, it is an error to pass an improper list to a procedure requiring a list argument.

It is possible to create a circular list or a cyclic graph by destructively altering the car or cdr field of a pair, using set-car! or set-cdr!. Some of the procedures listed in this section may loop indefinitely when handed a cyclic structure.

(cons $obj_1$ $obj_2$)                                           **procedure**
**returns:** a new pair whose car and cdr are $obj_1$ and $obj_2$

cons is the pair constructor procedure. $obj_1$ becomes the car and $obj_2$ becomes the cdr of the new pair.

```
(cons 'a '())    ⇒  (a)
(cons 'a '(b c)) ⇒  (a b c)
(cons 3 4)  ⇒  (3 . 4)
```

(car *pair*)                                                    **procedure**
**returns:** the car of *pair*

It is an error to ask for the car of the empty list.

```
(car '(a))   ⇒  a
(car '(a b c))  ⇒  a
(car (cons 3 4))  ⇒  3
```

(cdr *pair*)                                                    **procedure**
**returns:** the cdr of *pair*

It is an error to ask for the cdr of the empty list.

```
(cdr '(a))   ⇒  ()
(cdr '(a b c))  ⇒  (b c)
(cdr (cons 3 4))  ⇒  4
```

(set-car! *pair obj*)                                           **procedure**
**returns:** unspecified

set-car! changes the car of *pair* to *obj*.

```
(let ((x '(a b c)))
  (set-car! x 1)
  x)  ⇒  (1 b c)
```

(set-cdr! *pair obj*)                                          **procedure**
**returns:** unspecified

set-cdr! changes the cdr of *pair* to *obj*.

```
(let ((x '(a b c)))
  (set-cdr! x 1)
  x)  ⇒  (a . 1)
```

(caar *pair*)                                                  **procedure**
(cadr *pair*)                                                  **procedure**

⋮

(cddddr *pair*)                                                **procedure**
**returns:** the caar, cadr, ..., or cddddr of *pair*

These procedures are defined as the composition of up to four cars and cdrs. The a's and d's between the c and r represent the application of car or cdr in order from right to left. For example, the procedure cadr applied to a pair yields the car of the cdr of the pair and is equivalent to (lambda (x) (car (cdr x))).

```
(caar '((a)))  ⇒  a
(cadr '(a b c))  ⇒  b
(cdddr '(a b c d))  ⇒  (d)
(cadadr '(a (b c)))  ⇒  c
```

(list *obj* ...)                                               **procedure**
**returns:** a list of *obj* ...

list is equivalent to (lambda x x).

```
(list)  ⇒  ()
(list 1 2 3)  ⇒  (1 2 3)
(list 3 2 1)  ⇒  (3 2 1)
```

(list? *obj*)                                                  **procedure**
**returns:** #t if *obj* is a proper list, #f otherwise

list? must return #f for all improper lists, including cyclic lists. A definition of list? is shown on page 64.

```
(list? '())  ⇒  #t
(list? '(a b c))  ⇒  #t
(list? 'a)  ⇒  #f
(list? '(3 . 4))  ⇒  #f
(list? 3)  ⇒  #f
(let ((x (list 'a 'b 'c)))
  (set-cdr! (cddr x) x)
  (list? x))  ⇒  #f
```

(length *list*)                                                      **procedure**
**returns:** the number of elements in *list*

length may be defined as follows.

```
(define length
  (lambda (ls)
    (let loop ((ls ls) (n 0))
      (if (null? ls)
          n
          (loop (cdr ls) (+ n 1))))))
(length '())  ⇒  0
(length '(a b c))  ⇒  3
```

(list-ref *list n*)                                                  **procedure**
**returns:** the $n$th element (zero-based) of *list*

$n$ must be an exact nonnegative integer strictly less than the length of *list*. list-ref
may be defined as follows.

```
(define list-ref
  (lambda (ls n)
    (if (= n 0)
        (car ls)
        (list-ref (cdr ls) (- n 1)))))
(list-ref '(a b c) 0)  ⇒  a
(list-ref '(a b c) 1)  ⇒  b
(list-ref '(a b c) 2)  ⇒  c
```

(list-tail *list n*)                                                 **procedure**
**returns:** the $n$th tail (zero-based) of *list*

$n$ must be an exact nonnegative integer less than or equal to the length of *list*. The
result is not a copy; the tail is **eq?** to the $n$th cdr of *list* (or to *list* itself, if $n$ is
zero).

list-tail appears in the Revised[5] Report but not in the ANSI/IEEE standard. It may be defined as follows.

```
(define list-tail
  (lambda (ls n)
    (if (= n 0)
        ls
        (list-tail (cdr ls) (- n 1)))))
```

```
(list-tail '(a b c) 0)  ⇒  (a b c)
(list-tail '(a b c) 2)  ⇒  (c)
(list-tail '(a b c) 3)  ⇒  ()
(list-tail '(a b c . d) 2)  ⇒  (c . d)
(list-tail '(a b c . d) 3)  ⇒  d
(let ((x (list 1 2 3)))
  (eq? (list-tail x 2)
       (cddr x)))  ⇒  #t
```

(append *list* ...)                                           **procedure**
**returns:** the concatenation of the input lists

**append** returns a new list consisting of the elements of the first list followed by the elements of the second list, the elements of the third list, and so on. The new list is made from new pairs for all arguments but the last; the last (which need not actually be a list) is merely placed at the end of the new structure. **append** may be defined as follows.

```
(define append
  (lambda args
    (let f ((ls '()) (args args))
      (if (null? args)
          ls
          (let g ((ls ls))
            (if (null? ls)
                (f (car args) (cdr args))
                (cons (car ls) (g (cdr ls)))))))))
```

```
(append '(a b c) '())  ⇒  (a b c)
(append '() '(a b c))  ⇒  (a b c)
(append '(a b) '(c d))  ⇒  (a b c d)
(append '(a b) 'c)  ⇒  (a b . c)
(let ((x (list 'b)))
  (eq? x (cdr (append '(a) x))))  ⇒  #t
```

(**reverse** *list*)                                                                procedure
**returns:** a new list containing the elements of *list* in reverse order

**reverse** may be defined as follows.

```
(define reverse
  (lambda (ls)
    (let rev ((ls ls) (new '()))
      (if (null? ls)
          new
          (rev (cdr ls) (cons (car ls) new)))))))
(reverse '())  ⇒  ()
(reverse '(a b c))  ⇒  (c b a)
```

(**memq** *obj list*)                                                              procedure
(**memv** *obj list*)                                                              procedure
(**member** *obj list*)                                                            procedure
**returns:** the first tail of *list* whose car is equivalent to *obj*, or #f

These procedures traverse the argument *list* in order, comparing the elements of *list* against *obj*. If an object equivalent to *obj* is found, the tail of the list whose first element is that object is returned. If the list contains more than one object equivalent to *obj*, the first tail whose first element is equivalent to *obj* is returned. If no object equivalent to *obj* is found, #f is returned. The equivalence test for **memq** is eq?, for **memv** is eqv?, and for **member** is equal?.

These procedures are most often used as predicates, but their names do not end with a question mark because they return a useful true value in place of #t. **memq** may be defined as follows.

```
(define memq
  (lambda (x ls)
    (cond
      ((null? ls) #f)
      ((eq? (car ls) x) ls)
      (else (memq x (cdr ls)))))))
```

**memv** and **member** may be defined similarly, with eqv? and equal? in place of eq?.

```
(memq 'a '(b c a d e))  ⇒  (a d e)
(memq 'a '(b c d e g))  ⇒  #f
(memq 'a '(b a c a d a))  ⇒  (a c a d a)

(memv 3.4 '(1.2 2.3 3.4 4.5))  ⇒  (3.4 4.5)
(memv 3.4 '(1.3 2.5 3.7 4.9))  ⇒  #f
(let ((ls (list 'a 'b 'c)))
  (set-car! (memv 'b ls) 'z)
  ls)  ⇒  (a z c)
```

```
(member '(b) '((a) (b) (c)))  ⇒  ((b) (c))
(member '(d) '((a) (b) (c)))  ⇒  #f
(member "b" '("a" "b" "c"))  ⇒  ("b" "c")
(define count-occurrences
  (lambda (x ls)
    (cond
      ((memq x ls) =>
       (lambda (ls)
         (+ (count-occurrences x (cdr ls)) 1)))
      (else 0))))

(count-occurrences 'a '(a b c d a))
```

(assq *obj alist*)                                                procedure
(assv *obj alist*)                                                procedure
(assoc *obj alist*)                                               procedure
**returns:** first element of *alist* whose car is equivalent to *obj*, or **#f**

The argument *alist* must be an *association list*. An association list is a proper list whose elements are key-value pairs of the form (**key . value**). Associations are useful for storing information (values) associated with certain objects (keys).

These procedures traverse the association list, testing each key for equivalence with *obj*. If an equivalent key is found, the key-value pair is returned. Otherwise, **#f** is returned.

The equivalence test for **assq** is **eq?**, for **assv** is **eqv?**, and for **assoc** is **equal?**. **assq** may be defined as follows.

```
(define assq
  (lambda (x ls)
    (cond
      ((null? ls) #f)
      ((eq? (caar ls) x) (car ls))
      (else (assq x (cdr ls))))))
```

**assv** and **assoc** may be defined similarly, with **eqv?** and **equal?** in place of **eq?**.

```
(assq 'b '((a . 1) (b . 2)))  ⇒  (b . 2)
(cdr (assq 'b '((a . 1) (b . 2))))  ⇒  2
(assq 'c '((a . 1) (b . 2)))  ⇒  #f

(assv 2/3 '((1/3 . 1) (2/3 . 2)))  ⇒  (2/3 . 2)
(assv 2/3 '((1/3 . a) (3/4 . b)))  ⇒  #f

(assoc '(a) '(((a) . a) (-1 . b)))  ⇒  ((a) . a)
(assoc '(a) '(((b) . b) (a . c)))  ⇒  #f
```

```
(let ((alist '((2 . a) (3 . b))))
  (set-cdr! (assv 3 alist) 'c)
  alist)  ⇒  ((2 . a) (3 . c))
```

The interpreter given in Section 9.7 represents environments as association lists and uses `assq` for both variable lookup and assignment.

## 6.4. Numbers

Scheme numbers may be classified as integers, rational numbers, real numbers, or complex numbers, although an implementation may support only a subset of these numeric classes. This classification is hierarchical, in that all integers are rational, all rational numbers are real, and all real numbers are complex. The predicates `integer?`, `rational?`, `real?`, and `complex?` described in Section 6.2 are used to determine into which of these classes a number falls.

A Scheme number may also be classified as *exact* or *inexact*, depending upon the quality of operations used to derive the number and the inputs to these operations. The predicates `exact?` and `inexact?` may be used to determine the exactness of a number. Most operations on numbers in Scheme are *exactness preserving*: if given exact operands they return exact values, and if given inexact operands or a combination of exact and inexact operands they return inexact values.

Exact integer and rational arithmetic is typically supported to arbitrary precision; the size of an integer or of the denominator or numerator of a ratio is limited only by system storage constraints. Although other representations are possible, inexact numbers are typically represented by *floating-point* numbers supported by the host computer's hardware or by system software. Complex numbers are typically represented as ordered pairs (*real-part*, *imag-part*), where *real-part* and *imag-part* are exact integers, exact rationals, or floating-point numbers.

Scheme numbers are written in a straightforward manner not much different from ordinary conventions for writing numbers. An exact integer is normally written as a sequence of numerals preceded by an optional sign. For example, 3, +19, -100000, and 208423089237489374 all represent exact integers.

An exact rational number is normally written as two sequences of numerals separated by a slash (/) and preceded by an optional sign. For example, 3/4, -6/5, and 1/1208203823 are all exact rational numbers. A ratio is reduced immediately when it is read and may in fact reduce to an exact integer.

Inexact integers and rational numbers are normally written in either floating-point or scientific notation. Floating-point notation consists of a sequence of numerals followed by a decimal point and another sequence of numerals, all preceded by an optional sign. Scientific notation consists of an optional sign, a sequence of numerals, an optional decimal point followed by a second string of numerals, and an exponent; an exponent is written as the letter e followed by an optional sign and a sequence of numerals. For example, `1.0` and `-200.0` are valid inexact integers, and `1.5`, `0.034`, `-10e-10` and `1.5e-5` are valid inexact rational numbers. The exponent is the power of ten by which the number preceding the exponent should be scaled, so that `2e3` is equivalent to `2000.0`.

The special digit `#` (hash) may be used in place of a normal digit in certain contexts to signify that the value of the digit is unknown. Numbers that include hash digits are naturally inexact, even if they are written in the style of exact integers or rational numbers. Hash digits may appear after one or more nonhash digits to signify an inexact integer; after one or more nonhash digits in the first or second part of a ratio to specify an inexact rational number; or after one or more nonhash digits before or after the decimal point of an inexact number written in floating-point or scientific notation. No significant (known) digit may follow a hash digit. For example, `1####`, `-1#/2#`, `.123###` and `1#.###` all specify inexact quantities.

Exact and inexact real numbers are written as exact or inexact integers or rational numbers; no provision is made in the syntax of Scheme numbers for nonrational real numbers, i.e., irrational numbers.

Complex numbers may be written in either rectangular or polar form. In rectangular form, a complex number is written as $x+yi$ or $x-yi$, where $x$ is an integer, rational, or real number and $y$ is an unsigned integer, rational, or real number. The real part, $x$, may be omitted, in which case it is assumed to be zero. For example, `3+4i`, `3.2-3/4i`, `+i`, and `-3e-5i` are complex numbers written in rectangular form. In polar form, a complex number is written as $x@y$, where $x$ and $y$ are integer, rational, or real numbers. For example, `1.1@1.764` and `-1@-1/2` are complex numbers written in polar form.

The exactness of a numeric representation may be overridden by preceding the representation by either `#e` or `#i`. `#e` forces the number to be exact, and `#i` forces it to be inexact. For example, `1`, `#e1`, `1/1`, `#e1/1`, `#e1.0`, `#e1e0`, and `#e1.##` all represent the exact integer 1, and `#i3/10`, `3#/100`, `0.3`, `#i0.3`, and `3e-1` all represent the inexact rational 0.3.

Numbers are written by default in base 10, although the special prefixes `#b` (binary), `#o` (octal), `#d` (decimal), and `#x` (hexadecimal) can be used to specify base 2, base 8, base 10, or base 16. For radix 16, the letters `a` through `f` or `A` through `F` serve as the additional numerals required to express digit values 10 through 15. For example, `#b10101` is the binary equivalent of $21_{10}$, `#o72` is the octal equivalent of $58_{10}$, and `#xC7` is the hexadecimal equivalent of $199_{10}$. Numbers written in floating-point and scientific notations are always written in base 10.

If both are present, radix and exactness prefixes may appear in either order.

A Scheme implementation may support more than one size of internal representation for inexact quantities. The exponent markers `s` (*short*), `f` (*single*), `d` (*double*), and `l` (*long*) may appear in place of the default exponent marker `e` to override the default size for numbers written in scientific notation. In implementations that support multiple representations, the default size has at least as much precision as *double*.

A precise grammar for Scheme numbers is included in the description of the formal syntax of Scheme starting on page 277.

Any number can be written in a variety of different ways, but the system printer (see **write** and **display**) and **number->string** express numbers in a compact form, using the fewest number of digits possible while retaining the property that, when read, the printed number is identical to the original number.

The remainder of this section describes procedures that operate on numbers. The type of numeric arguments accepted by these procedures is implied by the name given to the arguments: *num* for complex numbers (that is, all numbers), *real* for real numbers, *rat* for rational numbers, and *int* for integers.

---

(**exact?** *num*)  **procedure**

**returns:** #t if *num* is exact, #f otherwise

```
(exact? 1)   ⇒   #t
(exact? -15/16)   ⇒   #t
(exact? 2.01)   ⇒   #f
(exact? #i77)   ⇒   #f
(exact? #i2/3)   ⇒   #f
(exact? 1.0-2i)   ⇒   #f
(exact? -1#i)   ⇒   #f
```

---

(**inexact?** *num*)  **procedure**

**returns:** #t if *num* is inexact, #f otherwise

```
(inexact? -123)   ⇒   #f
(inexact? #i123)   ⇒   #t
(inexact? 1e23)   ⇒   #t
(inexact? 1###)   ⇒   #t
(inexact? 1#/2#)   ⇒   #t
(inexact? #e1#/2#)   ⇒   #f
(inexact? +i)   ⇒   #f
```

---

(= $num_1$ $num_2$ $num_3$ ...)  **procedure**
(< $real_1$ $real_2$ $real_3$ ...)  **procedure**
(> $real_1$ $real_2$ $real_3$ ...)  **procedure**
(<= $real_1$ $real_2$ $real_3$ ...)  **procedure**
(>= $real_1$ $real_2$ $real_3$ ...)  **procedure**

**returns:** #t if the relation holds, #f otherwise

The predicate = returns #t if its arguments are equal. The predicate < returns #t if its arguments are monotonically increasing, i.e., each argument is greater than the preceding ones, while > returns #t if its arguments are monotonically decreasing. The predicate <= returns #t if its arguments are monotonically nondecreasing, i.e., each argument is not less than the preceding ones, while >= returns #t if its arguments are monotonically nonincreasing.

As implied by the names of the arguments, = is defined for complex arguments while the other relational predicates are defined only for real arguments. Two complex numbers are considered equal if their real and imaginary parts are equal.

```
(= 7 7)  ⇒  #t
(= 7 9)  ⇒  #f

(< 2e3 3e2)  ⇒  #f
(<= 1 2 3 3 4 5)  ⇒  #t
(<= 1 2 3 4 5)  ⇒  #t

(> 1 2 2 3 3 4)  ⇒  #f
(>= 1 2 2 3 3 4)  ⇒  #f

(= -1/2 -0.5)  ⇒  #t
(= 2/3 .667)  ⇒  #f
(= 7.2+0i 7.2)  ⇒  #t
(= 7.2-3i 7)  ⇒  #f

(< 1/2 2/3 3/4)  ⇒  #t
(> 8 4.102 2/3 -5)  ⇒  #t

(let ((x 0.218723452))
  (< 0.210 x 0.220))  ⇒  #t

(let ((i 1) (v (vector 'a 'b 'c)))
  (< -1 i (vector-length v)))  ⇒  #t

(apply < '(1 2 3 4))  ⇒  #t
(apply > '(4 3 3 2))  ⇒  #f
```

(+ *num* ...)                                                    **procedure**
**returns:** the sum of the arguments *num*  ...

When called with no arguments, + returns 0.

```
(+)  ⇒  0
(+ 1 2)  ⇒  3
(+ 1/2 2/3)  ⇒  7/6
(+ 3 4 5)  ⇒  12
(+ 3.0 4)  ⇒  7.0
(+ 3+4i 4+3i)  ⇒  7+7i
(apply + '(1 2 3 4 5))  ⇒  15
```

(- *num₁*)                                                                   **procedure**
(- *num₁ num₂ num₃* ...)                                                      **procedure**
**returns:** see explanation

When called with one argument, - returns the negative of *num₁*. Thus, (- *num₁*)
is an idiom for (- 0 *num₁*).

   When called with two or more arguments, - returns the result of subtracting
the sum of the numbers *num₂* ... from *num₁*.

   The ANSI/IEEE standard includes only one- and two-argument variants. The
more general form is included in the Revised[5] Report.

```
(- 3)   ⇒   -3
(- -2/3)   →   2/3
(- 4 3.0)   →   1.0
(- 3.25+4.25i 1/4+1/4i)   ⇒   3.0+4.0i
(- 4 3 2 1)   ⇒   -2
```

(* *num* ...)                                                                 **procedure**
**returns:** the product of the arguments *num* ...

When called with no arguments, * returns 1.

```
(*)   ⇒   1
(* 3.4)   ⇒   3.4
(* 1 1/2)   ⇒   1/2
(* 3 4 5.5)   ⇒   66.0
(* 1+2i 3+4i)   ⇒   -5+10i
(apply * '(1 2 3 4 5))   ⇒   120
```

(/ *num₁*)                                                                   **procedure**
(/ *num₁ num₂ num₃* ...)                                                     **procedure**
**returns:** see explanation

When called with one argument, / returns the reciprocal of *num₁*. That is,
(/ *num₁*) is an idiom for (/ 1 *num₁*).

   When called with two or more arguments, / returns the result of dividing *num₁*
by the product of the remaining arguments *num₂* ....

   The ANSI/IEEE standard includes only one- and two-argument variants. The
more general form is included in the Revised[5] Report.

```
(/ -17)  ⇒  -1/17
(/ 1/2)  ⇒  2
(/ .5)  ⇒  2.0
(/ 3 4)  ⇒  3/4
(/ 3.0 4)  ⇒  .75
(/ -5+10i 3+4i)  ⇒  1+2i
(/ 60 5 4 3 2)  ⇒  1/2
```

**(zero?** *num***)**                                                                      **procedure**
**returns:** #t if *num* is zero, #f otherwise

**zero?** is equivalent to (**lambda** (x) (= x 0)).

```
(zero? 0)  ⇒  #t
(zero? 1)  ⇒  #f
(zero? (- 3.0 3.0))  ⇒  #t
(zero? (+ 1/2 1/2))  ⇒  #f
(zero? 0+0i)  ⇒  #t
(zero? 0.0-0.0i)  ⇒  #t
```

**(positive?** *real***)**                                                                 **procedure**
**returns:** #t if *real* is greater than zero, #f otherwise

**positive?** is equivalent to (**lambda** (x) (> x 0)).

```
(positive? 128)  ⇒  #t
(positive? 0.0)  ⇒  #f
(positive? 1.8e-15)  ⇒  #t
(positive? -2/3)  ⇒  #f
(positive? .001-0.0i)  ⇒  #t
```

**(negative?** *real***)**                                                                 **procedure**
**returns:** #t if *real* is less than zero, #f otherwise

**negative?** is equivalent to (**lambda** (x) (< x 0)).

```
(negative? -65)  ⇒  #t
(negative? 0)  ⇒  #f
(negative? -0.0121)  ⇒  #t
(negative? 15/16)  ⇒  #f
(negative? -7.0+0.0i)  ⇒  #t
```

(even? *int*)                                                              **procedure**
**returns:** #t if *int* is even, #f otherwise

```
(even? 0)  ⇒  #t
(even? 1)  ⇒  #f
(even? 2.0)  ⇒  #t
(even? -120762398465)  ⇒  #f
(even? 2.0+0.0i)  ⇒  #t
```

(odd? *int*)                                                              **procedure**
**returns:** #t if *int* is odd, #f otherwise

```
(odd? 0)  ⇒  #f
(odd? 1)  ⇒  #t
(odd? 2.0)  ⇒  #f
(odd? -120762398465)  ⇒  #t
(odd? 2.0+0.0i)  ⇒  #f
```

(quotient *int$_1$* *int$_2$*)                                            **procedure**
**returns:** the integer quotient of *int$_1$* and *int$_2$*

```
(quotient 45 6)  ⇒  7
(quotient 6.0 2.0)  ⇒  3.0
(quotient 3.0 -2)  ⇒  -1.0
```

(remainder *int$_1$* *int$_2$*)                                           **procedure**
**returns:** the integer remainder of *int$_1$* and *int$_2$*

The result of **remainder** has the same sign as *int$_1$*.

```
(remainder 16 4)  ⇒  0
(remainder 5 2)  ⇒  1
(remainder -45.0 7)  ⇒  -3.0
(remainder 10.0 -3.0)  ⇒  1.0
(remainder -17 -9)  ⇒  -8
```

(modulo *int$_1$* *int$_2$*)                                              **procedure**
**returns:** the integer modulus of *int$_1$* and *int$_2$*

The result of **modulo** has the same sign as *int$_2$*.

```
(modulo 16 4)  ⇒  0
(modulo 5 2)  ⇒  1
(modulo -45.0 7)  ⇒  4.0
(modulo 10.0 -3.0)  ⇒  -2.0
(modulo -17 -9)  ⇒  -8
```

(truncate *real*)                                                 **procedure**
**returns:** the integer closest to *real* toward zero

```
(truncate 19)   ⇒   19
(truncate 2/3)   ⇒   0
(truncate -2/3)   ⇒   0
(truncate 17.3)   ⇒   17.0
(truncate -17/2)   ⇒   -8
```

(floor *real*)                                                   **procedure**
**returns:** the integer closest to *real* toward $-\infty$

```
(floor 19)   ⇒   19
(floor 2/3)   ⇒   0
(floor -2/3)   ⇒   -1
(floor 17.3)   ⇒   17.0
(floor -17/2)   ⇒   -9
```

(ceiling *real*)                                                 **procedure**
**returns:** the integer closest to *real* toward $+\infty$

```
(ceiling 19)   ⇒   19
(ceiling 2/3)   ⇒   1
(ceiling -2/3)   ⇒   0
(ceiling 17.3)   ⇒   18.0
(ceiling -17/2)   ⇒   -8
```

(round *real*)                                                   **procedure**
**returns:** the integer closest to *real*

If *real* is exactly between two integers, the closest even integer is returned.

```
(round 19)   ⇒   19
(round 2/3)   ⇒   1
(round -2/3)   ⇒   -1
(round 17.3)   ⇒   17.0
(round -17/2)   ⇒   -8
(round 2.5)   ⇒   2.0
(round 3.5)   ⇒   4.0
```

(abs *real*)                                                     **procedure**
**returns:** the absolute value of *real*

abs is equivalent to (lambda (x) (if (< x 0) (- x) x)). abs and magnitude (see page 150) are identical for real inputs.

```
(abs 1)  ⇒  1
(abs -3/4)  ⇒  3/4
(abs 1.83)  ⇒  1.83
(abs -0.093)  ⇒  0.093
```

(max *real₁ real₂ ...*)                                                procedure
**returns:** the maximum of *real₁ real₂ ...*

```
(max 4 -7 2 0 -6)  ⇒  4
(max 1/2 3/4 4/5 5/6 6/7)  ⇒  6/7
(max 1.5 1.3 -0.3 0.4 2.0 1.8)  ⇒  2.0
(max 5 2.0)  ⇒  5.0
(max -5 -2.0)  ⇒  -2.0
(let ((ls '(7 3 5 2 9 8)))
  (apply max ls))  ⇒  9
```

(min *real₁ real₂ ...*)                                                procedure
**returns:** the minimum of *real₁ real₂ ...*

```
(min 4 -7 2 0 -6)  ⇒  -7
(min 1/2 3/4 4/5 5/6 6/7)  ⇒  1/2
(min 1.5 1.3 -0.3 0.4 2.0 1.8)  ⇒  -0.3
(min 5 2.0)  ⇒  2.0
(min -5 -2.0)  ⇒  -5.0
(let ((ls '(7 3 5 2 9 8)))
  (apply min ls))  ⇒  2
```

(gcd *int ...*)                                                procedure
**returns:** the greatest common divisor of its arguments *int ...*

The result is always nonnegative, i.e., factors of −1 are ignored. When called with no arguments, gcd returns 0.

```
(gcd)  ⇒  0
(gcd 34)  ⇒  34
(gcd 33.0 15.0)  ⇒  3.0
(gcd 70 -42 28)  ⇒  14
```

(lcm *int ...*)                                                procedure
**returns:** the least common multiple of its arguments *int ...*

The result is always nonnegative, i.e., common multiples of −1 are ignored. Although lcm should probably return ∞ when called with no arguments, it is defined to return 1. If one or more of the arguments is 0, lcm returns 0.

```
(lcm)  ⇒  1
(lcm 34)  ⇒  34
(lcm 33.0 15.0)  ⇒  165.0
(lcm 70 -42 28)  ⇒  420
(lcm 17.0 0)  ⇒  0
```

(expt $num_1$ $num_2$)                                                      **procedure**
**returns:** $num_1$ raised to the $num_2$ power

If both arguments are 0, **expt** returns 1.

```
(expt 2 10)  ⇒  1024
(expt 2 -10)  ⇒  1/1024
(expt 2 -10.0)  ⇒  9.765625e-4
(expt -1/2 5)  ⇒  -1/32
(expt 3.0 3)  ⇒  27.0
(expt +i 2)  ⇒  -1
```

(exact->inexact $num$)                                                      **procedure**
**returns:** an inexact representation for $num$

If $num$ is already inexact, it is returned unchanged. If no inexact representation
for $num$ is supported by the implementation, an error may be signaled.

```
(exact->inexact 3)  ⇒  3.0
(exact->inexact 3.0)  ⇒  3.0
(exact->inexact -1/4)  ⇒  -.25
(exact->inexact 3+4i)  ⇒  3.0+4.0i
(exact->inexact (expt 10 20))  ⇒  1e20
```

(inexact->exact $num$)                                                      **procedure**
**returns:** an exact representation for $num$

If $num$ is already exact, it is returned unchanged. If no exact representation for
$num$ is supported by the implementation, an error may be signaled.

```
(inexact->exact 3.0)  ⇒  3
(inexact->exact 3)  ⇒  3
(inexact->exact -.25)  ⇒  -1/4
(inexact->exact 3.0+4.0i)  ⇒  3+4i
(inexact->exact 1e20)  ⇒  100000000000000000000
```

(rationalize $real_1$  $real_2$)                                    **procedure**
**returns:** see below

rationalize returns the simplest rational number that differs from $real_1$ by no more than $real_2$. A rational number $q_1 = n_1/m_1$ is simpler than another rational number $q_2 = n_2/m_2$ if $|n_1| \leq |n_2|$ and $|m_1| \leq |m_2|$ and either $|n_1| < |n_2|$ or $|m_1| < |m_2|$.

```
(rationalize 3/10 1/10)  ⇒  1/3
(rationalize .3 1/10)  ⇒  0.3333333333333333
(eqv? (rationalize .3 1/10) #i1/3)  ⇒  #t
```

(numerator $rat$)                                                  **procedure**
returns. the numerator of $rat$

If $rat$ is an integer, the numerator is $rat$.

```
(numerator 9)  ⇒  9
(numerator 9.0)  ⇒  9.0
(numerator 2/3)  ⇒  2
(numerator -9/4)  ⇒  -9
(numerator -2.25)  ⇒  -9.0
```

(denominator $rat$)                                                **procedure**
**returns:** the denominator of $rat$

If $rat$ is an integer, the denominator is 1.

```
(denominator 9)  ⇒  1
(denominator 9.0)  ⇒  1.0
(denominator 2/3)  ⇒  3
(denominator -9/4)  ⇒  4
(denominator -2.25)  ⇒  4.0
```

(real-part $num$)                                                  **procedure**
**returns:** the real component of $num$

If $num$ is real, real-part returns $num$.

```
(real-part 3+4i)  ⇒  3
(real-part -2.3+0.7i)  ⇒  -2.3
(real-part -i)  ⇒  0
(real-part 17.2)  ⇒  17.2
(real-part -17/100)  ⇒  -17/100
```

(imag-part *num*)                                                                      **procedure**
**returns:** the imaginary component of *num*

If *num* is real, imag-part returns zero.

```
(imag-part 3+4i)  ⇒  4
(imag-part -2.3+0.7i)  ⇒  0.7
(imag-part -i)  ⇒  -1
(imag-part 17.2)  ⇒  0.0
(imag-part -17/100)  ⇒  0
```

(make-rectangular *real₁ real₂*)                                                       **procedure**
**returns:** a complex number with real component $real_1$ and imaginary component $real_2$

```
(make-rectangular -2 7)  ⇒  -2+7i
(make-rectangular 2/3 -1/2)  ⇒  2/3-1/2i
(make-rectangular 3.2 5.3)  ⇒  3.2+5.3i
```

(make-polar *real₁ real₂*)                                                             **procedure**
**returns:** a complex number with magnitude $real_1$ and angle $real_2$

```
(make-polar 2 0)  ⇒  2
(make-polar 2.0 0.0)  ⇒  2.0+0.0i
(make-polar 1.0 (asin -1.0))  ⇒  0.0-1.0i
(eqv? (make-polar 7.2 -0.588) 7.2@-0.588)  ⇒  #t
```

(angle *num*)                                                                          **procedure**
**returns:** the angle part of the polar representation of *num*

The range of the result is $-\pi$ (exclusive) to $+\pi$ (inclusive).

```
(angle 7.3@1.5708)  ⇒  1.5708
(angle 5.2)  ⇒  0.0
```

(magnitude *num*)                                                                      **procedure**
**returns:** the magnitude of *num*

magnitude and abs (see page 146) are identical for real arguments. The magnitude
of a complex number $x + yi$ is $+\sqrt{x^2 + y^2}$.

```
(magnitude 1)  ⇒  1
(magnitude -3/4)  ⇒  3/4
(magnitude 1.83)  ⇒  1.83
(magnitude -0.093)  ⇒  0.093
(magnitude 3+4i)  ⇒  5
(magnitude 7.25@1.5708)  ⇒  7.25
```

(sqrt *num*)                                                          **procedure**
**returns:** the principal square root of *num*

Implementations are encouraged, but not required, to return exact results for exact
inputs to sqrt whenever feasible.

```
(sqrt 16)  ⇒  4
(sqrt 1/4)  ⇒  1/2
(sqrt 4.84)  ⇒  2.2
(sqrt -4.84)  ⇒  0.0+2.2i
(sqrt 3+4i)  ⇒  2+1i
(sqrt -3.0-4.0i)  ⇒  1.0-2.0i
```

(exp *num*)                                                          **procedure**
**returns:** *e* to the *num* power

```
(exp 0.0)  ⇒  1.0
(exp 1.0)  ⇒  2.7182818284590455
(exp -.5)  ⇒  0.6065306597126334
```

(log *num*)                                                          **procedure**
**returns:** the natural log of *num*

The log of a complex number $z$ is defined as follows.

$$\log(z) = \log(\text{magnitude}(z)) + i\,\text{angle}(z)$$

```
(log 1.0)  ⇒  0.0
(log (exp 1.0))  ⇒  1.0
(/ (log 100) (log 10))  ⇒  2.0
(log (make-polar (exp 2.0) 1.0))  ⇒  2.0+1.0i
```

**(sin** *num***)**                                                         procedure
**(cos** *num***)**                                                         procedure
**(tan** *num***)**                                                         procedure
**returns:** the sine, cosine, or tangent of *num*

The argument is specified in radians.


**(asin** *num***)**                                                        procedure
**(acos** *num***)**                                                        procedure
**returns:** the arc sine or the arc cosine of *num*

The result is in radians. The arc sine and arc cosine of a complex number $z$ are defined as follows.

$$\sin^{-1}(z) = -i \log(iz + \sqrt{1 - z^2})$$
$$\cos^{-1}(z) = \pi/2 - \sin^{-1}(z)$$


**(atan** *num***)**                                                        procedure
**(atan** *real$_1$  real$_2$***)**                                         procedure
**returns:** see explanation

When passed a single complex argument *num* (the first form), **atan** returns the arc tangent of *num*. The arc tangent of a complex number $z$ is defined as follows.

$$\tan^{-1}(z) = (\log(1 + iz) - \log(1 - iz))/(2i)$$

When passed two real arguments (the second form), **atan** is equivalent to **(lambda (x y) (angle (make-rectangular x y)))**.


**(string->number** *string***)**                                          procedure
**(string->number** *string radix***)**                                    procedure
**returns:** the number represented by *string*, or **#f**

If *string* is a valid representation of a number, that number is returned, otherwise **#f** is returned. The number is interpreted in radix *radix*, which must be an exact integer in the set $\{2, 8, 10, 16\}$. If not specified, *radix* defaults to 10. Any radix specifier within *string*, e.g., **#x**, overrides the *radix* argument.

```
(string->number "0")  ⇒  0
(string->number "3.4e3")  ⇒  3400.0
(string->number "#x#e-2e2")  ⇒  -738
(string->number "#e-2e2" 16)  ⇒  -738
(string->number "#i15/16")  ⇒  0.9375
(string->number "10" 16)  ⇒  16
```

(number->string *num*)             **procedure**
(number->string *num radix*)          **procedure**
**returns:** an external representation of *num* as a string

The num is expressed in radix *radix*, which must be an exact integer in the set $\{2, 8, 10, 16\}$. If not specified, *radix* defaults to 10. In any case, no radix specifier appears in the resulting string.

The external representation is such that, when converted back into a number using **string->number**, the resulting numeric value is equivalent to *num*. That is, for all inputs:

```
(eqv? (string->number
         (number->string num radix)
         radix)
      num)
```

returns **#t**. Inexact results are expressed using the fewest number of significant digits possible without violating the above restriction.

```
(number->string 3.4)   ⇒  "3.4"
(number->string 1e2)   ⇒  "100.0"
(number->string 1e23)  ⇒  "1e23"
(number->string -7/2)  ⇒  "-7/2"
(number->string 220/9 16)  ⇒  "DC/9"
```

# 6.5. Characters

Characters are atomic objects representing letters, digits, special symbols such as $ or -, and certain nongraphic control characters such as space and newline. Characters are written with a #\ prefix. For most characters, the prefix is followed by the character itself. The written character representation of the letter A, for example, is #\A. The characters newline and space may be written in this manner as well, but they can also be written as #\newline or #\space.

This section describes the operations that deal primarily with characters. See also the following section on strings and Chapter 7 on input and output for other operations relating to characters.

(char=? *char₁ char₂ char₃* ...)      **procedure**
(char<? *char₁ char₂ char₃* ...)      **procedure**
(char>? *char₁ char₂ char₃* ...)      **procedure**
(char<=? *char₁ char₂ char₃* ...)      **procedure**
(char>=? *char₁ char₂ char₃* ...)      **procedure**
**returns:** **#t** if the relation holds, **#f** otherwise

These predicates behave in a similar manner to the numeric predicates =, <, >,

<=, and >=. For example, `char=?` returns #t when its arguments are equivalent characters, and `char<?` returns #t when its arguments are monotonically increasing character values.

Independent of the particular representation employed, the following relationships are guaranteed to hold.

- The lower-case letters #\a through #\z are in order from low to high; e.g., #\d is less than #\e.

- The upper-case letters #\A through #\Z are in order from low to high; e.g., #\Q is less than #\R.

- The digits #\0 through #\9 are in order from low to high; e.g., #\3 is less than #\4.

- All digits precede all lower-case letters, or all lower-case letters precede all digits.

- All digits precede all upper-case letters, or all upper-case letters precede all digits.

The tests performed by `char=?`, `char<?`, `char>?`, `char<=?`, and `char>=?` are case-sensitive. That is, the character #\A is not equivalent to the character #\a according to these predicates.

The ANSI/IEEE standard includes only two-argument versions of these procedures. The more general versions are mentioned in the Revised[5] Report.

```
(char>? #\a #\b)   ⇒   #f
(char<? #\a #\b)   ⇒   #t
(char<? #\a #\b #\c)   ⇒   #t
(let ((c #\r))
  (char<=? #\a c #\z))   ⇒   #t
(char<=? #\Z #\W)   ⇒   #f
(char=? #\+ #\+)   ⇒   #t
(or (char<? #\a #\0)
    (char<? #\0 #\a))   ⇒   #t
```

| | |
|---|---|
| (char-ci=? $char_1$ $char_2$ $char_3$ ...) | procedure |
| (char-ci<? $char_1$ $char_2$ $char_3$ ...) | procedure |
| (char-ci>? $char_1$ $char_2$ $char_3$ ...) | procedure |
| (char-ci<=? $char_1$ $char_2$ $char_3$ ...) | procedure |
| (char-ci>=? $char_1$ $char_2$ $char_3$ ...) | procedure |

**returns:** #t if the relation holds, #f otherwise

These predicates are identical to the predicates `char=?`, `char<?`, `char>?`, `char<=?`, and `char>=?` except that they are case-insensitive. This means that when two letters are compared, case is unimportant. For example, `char=?` considers `#\a` and `#\A` to be distinct values; `char-ci=?` does not.

The ANSI/IEEE standard includes only two-argument versions of these procedures. The more general versions are mentioned in the Revised[5] Report.

```
(char-ci<? #\a #\B)   ⇒   #t
(char-ci=? #\W #\w)   ⇒   #t
(char-ci=? #\= #\+)   ⇒   #f
(let ((c #\R))
  (list (char<=? #\a c #\z)
        (char-ci<=? #\a c #\z)))   ⇒   (#f #t)
```

**(char-alphabetic? *char*)**        **procedure**
**returns:** #t if *char* is a letter, #f otherwise

```
(char-alphabetic? #\a)   ⇒   #t
(char-alphabetic? #\T)   ⇒   #t
(char-alphabetic? #\8)   ⇒   #f
(char-alphabetic? #\$)   ⇒   #f
```

**(char-numeric? *char*)**        **procedure**
**returns:** #t if *char* is a digit, #f otherwise

```
(char-numeric? #\7)       ⇒   #t
(char-numeric? #\2)       ⇒   #t
(char-numeric? #\X)       ⇒   #f
(char-numeric? #\space)   ⇒   #f
```

**(char-lower-case? *letter*)**        **procedure**
**returns:** #t if *letter* is lower-case, #f otherwise

If *letter* is not alphabetic, the result is unspecified.

```
(char-lower-case? #\r)   ⇒   #t
(char-lower-case? #\R)   ⇒   #f
(char-lower-case? #\8)   ⇒   unspecified
```

**(char-upper-case? *letter*)**        **procedure**
**returns:** #t if *letter* is upper-case, #f otherwise

If *letter* is not alphabetic, the result is unspecified.

```
(char-upper-case? #\r)   ⇒   #f
(char-upper-case? #\R)   ⇒   #t
(char-upper-case? #\8)   ⇒   unspecified
```

(char-whitespace? *char*)                                                procedure
**returns:** #t if *char* is whitespace, #f otherwise

Whitespace consists of spaces and newlines and possibly other nongraphic characters, depending upon the Scheme implementation and the underlying operating system.

```
(char-whitespace? #\space)   ⇒  #t
(char-whitespace? #\newline) ⇒  #t
(char-whitespace? #\Z)       ⇒  #f
```

(char-upcase *char*)                                                     procedure
**returns:** the upper-case character equivalent to *char*

If *char* is a lower-case character, char-upcase returns the upper-case equivalent. If *char* is not a lower-case character, char-upcase returns char.

```
(char-upcase #\g)  ⇒  #\G
(char-upcase #\Y)  ⇒  #\Y
(char-upcase #\7)  ⇒  #\7
```

(char-downcase *char*)                                                   procedure
**returns:** the lower-case character equivalent to *char*

If *char* is an upper-case character, char-downcase returns the lower-case equivalent. If *char* is not an upper-case character, char-downcase returns char.

```
(char-downcase #\g)  ⇒  #\g
(char-downcase #\Y)  ⇒  #\y
(char-downcase #\7)  ⇒  #\7
```

(char->integer *char*)                                                   procedure
**returns:** an exact integer representation for *char*

char->integer is useful for performing table lookups, with the integer representation of *char* employed as an index into a table. The integer representation of a character is typically the integer code supported by the operating system for character input and output.

Although the particular representation employed depends on the Scheme implementation and the underlying operating system, the rules regarding the relationship between character objects stated above under the description of char=? and its relatives holds for the integer representations of characters as well.

The following examples assume that the integer representation is the ASCII code for the character.

```
(char->integer #\h)  ⇒  104
(char->integer #\newline)  ⇒  10
```

The definition of `make-dispatch-table` below shows how the integer codes returned by `char->integer` may be used portably to associate values with characters in vector-based dispatch tables, even though the exact correspondence between characters and their integer codes is unspecified.

`make-dispatch-table` accepts two arguments: an association list (see **assv** in Section 6.3) associating characters with values and a default value for characters without associations. It returns a lookup procedure that accepts a character and returns the associated (or default) value. `make-dispatch-table` builds a vector that is used by the lookup procedure. This vector is indexed by the integer codes for the characters and contains the associated values. Slots in the vector between indices for characters with defined values are filled with the default value. The code works even if `char->integer` returns negative values or both negative and nonnegative values, although the table can get large if the character codes are not tightly packed.

```
(define make-dispatch-table
  (lambda (alist default)
    (let ((codes (map char->integer (map car alist))))
      (let ((first-index (apply min codes))
            (last-index (apply max codes)))
        (let ((n (+ (- last-index first-index) 1)))
          (let ((v (make-vector n default)))
            (for-each
              (lambda (i x) (vector-set! v (- i first-index) x))
              codes
              (map cdr alist))
            ;; table is built; return the table lookup procedure
            (lambda (c)
              (let ((i (char->integer c)))
                (if (<= first-index i last-index)
                    (vector-ref v (- i first-index))
                    default)))))))))

(define-syntax define-dispatch-table
  ;; define-dispatch-table associates sets of characters in strings
  ;; with values in a call to make-dispatch-table.
  (syntax-rules ()
    ((_ default (str val) ...)
     (make-dispatch-table
       (append (map (lambda (c) (cons c 'val))
                    (string->list str))
               ...)
       'default))))
```

```
(define t
  (define-dispatch-table
    unknown
    ("abcdefghijklmnopqrstuvwxyz" letter)
    ("ABCDEFGHIJKLMNOPQRSTUVWXYZ" letter)
    ("0123456789" digit)))
(t #\m)  ⇒  letter
(t #\0)  ⇒  digit
(t #\*)  ⇒  unknown
```

(integer->char *int*)                                              **procedure**
**returns:** the character object corresponding to the exact integer *int*

This procedure is the functional inverse of `char->integer`. It is an error for *int* to be outside the range of valid integer character codes.

The following examples assume that the integer representation is the ASCII code for the character.

```
(integer->char 48)   ⇒  #\0
(integer->char 101)  ⇒  #\e
```

## 6.6. Strings

Strings are sequences of characters and are typically used as messages or character buffers. Scheme provides operations for creating strings, extracting characters from strings, obtaining substrings, concatenating strings, and altering the contents of strings.

A string is written as a sequence of characters enclosed in double quotes, e.g., `"hi there"`. A double quote may be introduced into a string by preceding it by a backward slash, e.g., `"two \"quotes\" within"`. A backward slash may also be included by preceding it with a backward slash, e.g., `"a \\slash"`.

Strings are indexed by exact nonnegative integers, and the index of the first element of any string is 0. The highest valid index for a given string is one less than its length.

(string=? *string₁* *string₂* *string₃* ...)                       **procedure**
(string<? *string₁* *string₂* *string₃* ...)                       **procedure**
(string>? *string₁* *string₂* *string₃* ...)                       **procedure**
(string<=? *string₁* *string₂* *string₃* ...)                      **procedure**
(string>=? *string₁* *string₂* *string₃* ...)                      **procedure**
**returns:** #t if the relation holds, #f otherwise

As with =, <, >, <=, and >=, these predicates express relationships among all of the arguments. For example, `string>?` determines if the lexicographic ordering of its arguments is monotonically decreasing.

The comparisons are based on the character predicates `char=?`, `char<?`, `char>?`, `char<=?`, and `char>=?`. Two strings are lexicographically equivalent if they are the same length and consist of the same sequence of characters according to `char=?`. If two strings differ only in length, the shorter string is considered to be lexicographically less than the longer string. Otherwise, the first character position at which the strings differ determines which string is lexicographically less than the other, according to `char<?`.

The ANSI/IEEE standard includes only two-argument versions of these procedures. The more general versions are mentioned in the Revised[5] Report.

Two-argument `string=?` may be defined as follows.

```
(define string=?
  (lambda (s1 s2)
    (let ((n (string-length s1)))
      (and (= (string-length s2) n)
           (let loop ((i 0))
             (or (= i n)
                 (and (char=? (string-ref s1 i) (string-ref s2 i))
                      (loop (+ i 1)))))))))
```

Two-argument `string<?` may be defined as follows.

```
(define string<?
  (lambda (s1 s2)
    (let ((n1 (string-length s1)) (n2 (string-length s2)))
      (let loop ((i 0))
        (and (not (= i n2))
             (or (= i n1)
                 (let ((c1 (string-ref s1 i)) (c2 (string-ref s2 i)))
                   (or (char<? c1 c2)
                       (and (char=? c1 c2)
                            (loop (+ i 1)))))))))))
```

These definitions may be extended straightforwardly to support three or more arguments. `string<=?`, `string>?`, and `string>=?` may be defined similarly.

```
(string=? "mom" "mom")  ⇒  #t
(string<? "mom" "mommy")  ⇒  #t
(string>? "Dad" "Dad")  ⇒  #f
(string=? "Mom and Dad" "mom and dad")  ⇒  #f
(string<? "a" "b" "c")  ⇒  #t
```

(string-ci=? *string$_1$  string$_2$  string$_3$ ...*)                                procedure
(string-ci<? *string$_1$  string$_2$  string$_3$ ...*)                                procedure
(string-ci>? *string$_1$  string$_2$  string$_3$ ...*)                                procedure
(string-ci<=? *string$_1$  string$_2$  string$_3$ ...*)                               procedure
(string-ci>=? *string$_1$  string$_2$  string$_3$ ...*)                               procedure
**returns:** #t if the relation holds, #f otherwise

These predicates are case-insensitive versions of string=?, string<?, string>?, string<=?, and string>=?. That is, the comparisons are based on the character predicates char-ci=?, char-ci<?, char-ci>?, char-ci<=?, and char-ci>=?.

The ANSI/IEEE standard includes only two-argument versions of these procedures. The more general versions are mentioned in the Revised[5] Report.

Two-argument versions of these procedures may be defined in a manner similar to string=? and string<? above.

(string-ci=? "Mom and Dad" "mom and dad")  ⇒  #t
(string-ci<=? "say what" "Say What!?")  ⇒  #t
(string-ci>? "N" "m" "L" "k")  ⇒  #t


(string *char* ...)                                                                   procedure
**returns:** a string containing the characters *char* ...

(string)  ⇒  ""
(string #\a #\b #\c)  ⇒  "abc"
(string #\H #\E #\Y #\!)  ⇒  "HEY!"


(make-string *n*)                                                                     procedure
(make-string *n  char*)                                                               procedure
**returns:** a string of length *n*

*n* must be an exact nonnegative integer. If *char* is supplied, the string is filled with *char*, otherwise the characters contained in the string are unspecified.

(make-string 0)  ⇒  ""
(make-string 0 #\x)  ⇒  ""
(make-string 5 #\x)  ⇒  "xxxxx"


(string-length *string*)                                                              procedure
**returns:** the number of characters in *string*

The length of a string is always an exact nonnegative integer.

```
(string-length "abc")  ⇒  3
(string-length "")  ⇒  0
(string-length "hi there")  ⇒  8
(string-length (make-string 1000000))  ⇒  1000000
```

(string-ref *string n*)                                               **procedure**
**returns:** the *n*th character (zero-based) of *string*

*n* must be an exact nonnegative integer strictly less than the length of *string*.

```
(string-ref "hi there" 0)  ⇒  #\h
(string-ref "hi there" 5)  ⇒  #\e
```

(string-set! *string n char*)                                         **procedure**
**returns:** unspecified

*n* must be an exact nonnegative integer strictly less than the length of *string*.
string-set! changes the *n*th element of *string* to *char*.

```
(let ((str "hi three"))
  (string-set! str 5 #\e)
  (string-set! str 6 #\r)
  str)  ⇒  "hi there"
```

(string-copy *string*)                                                **procedure**
**returns:** a new copy of *string*

string-copy is equivalent to (lambda (s) (string-append s)). string-copy appears in the Revised[5] Report but not in the ANSI/IEEE standard.

```
(string-copy "abc")  ⇒  "abc"
(let ((str "abc"))
  (eq? str (string-copy str)))  ⇒  #f
```

(string-append *string* ...)                                          **procedure**
**returns:** a new string formed by concatenating the strings *string* ...

```
(string-append)  ⇒  ""
(string-append "abc" "def")  ⇒  "abcdef"
(string-append "Hey " "you " "there!")  ⇒  "Hey you there!"
```

The following implementation of **string-append** recurs down the list of strings to compute the total length, then allocates the new string and fills it up as it unwinds the recursion.

```
(define string-append
  (lambda args
    (let f ((ls args) (n 0))
      (if (null? ls)
          (make-string n)
          (let* ((s1 (car ls))
                 (m (string-length s1))
                 (s2 (f (cdr ls) (+ n m))))
            (do ((i 0 (+ i 1)) (j n (+ j 1)))
                ((= i m) s2)
              (string-set! s2 j (string-ref s1 i))))))))
```

(substring *string start end*)                                          **procedure**
**returns:** a copy of *string* from *start* (inclusive) to *end* (exclusive)

*start* and *end* must be exact nonnegative integers; *start* must be strictly less than
the length of *string*, while *end* may be less than or equal to the length of *string*.
If *end* $\leq$ *start*, a string of length zero is returned. **substring** may be defined as
follows.

```
(define substring
  (lambda (s1 m n)
    (let ((s2 (make-string (- n m))))
      (do ((j 0 (+ j 1)) (i m (+ i 1)))
          ((= i n) s2)
        (string-set! s2 j (string-ref s1 i))))))
```

```
(substring "hi there" 0 1)  ⇒  "h"
(substring "hi there" 3 6)  ⇒  "the"
(substring "hi there" 5 5)  ⇒  ""
```

```
(let ((str "hi there"))
  (let ((end (string-length str)))
    (substring str 0 end)))  ⇒  "hi there"
```

(string-fill! *string char*)                                            **procedure**
**returns:** unspecified

**string-fill!** sets every character in *string* to *char*. **string-fill!** appears in the
Revised[5] Report but not in the ANSI/IEEE standard. It may be defined as follows.

```
(define string-fill!
  (lambda (s c)
    (let ((n (string-length s)))
      (do ((i 0 (+ i 1)))
          ((= i n))
          (string-set! s i c)))))
(let ((str (string-copy "sleepy")))
  (string-fill! str #\Z)
  str)  ⇒  "ZZZZZZ"
```

(string->list *string*)                                  **procedure**
returns: a list of the characters in *string*

string->list allows a string to be converted into a list, so that Scheme's list-processing operations may be applied to the processing of strings. string->list appears in the Revised[5] Report but not in the ANSI/IEEE standard. It may be defined as follows.

```
(define string->list
  (lambda (s)
    (do ((i (- (string-length s) 1) (- i 1))
         (ls '() (cons (string-ref s i) ls)))
        ((< i 0) ls))))
(string->list "")  ⇒  ()
(string->list "abc")  ⇒  (#\a #\b #\c)
(apply char<? (string->list "abc"))  ⇒  #t
(map char-upcase (string->list "abc"))  ⇒  (#\A #\B #\C)
```

(list->string *list*)                                    **procedure**
returns: a string of the characters in *list*

*list* must consist entirely of characters.

list->string is the functional inverse of string->list. A program might use both procedures together, first converting a string into a list, then operating on this list to produce a new list, and finally converting the new list back into a string.

list->string appears in the Revised[5] Report but not in the ANSI/IEEE standard. It may be defined as follows.

```
(define list->string
  (lambda (ls)
    (let ((s (make-string (length ls))))
      (do ((ls ls (cdr ls)) (i 0 (+ i 1)))
          ((null? ls) s)
          (string-set! s i (car ls))))))
```

```
(list->string '()) ⇒ ""
(list->string '(#\a #\b #\c)) ⇒ "abc"
(list->string
  (map char-upcase
      (string->list "abc"))) ⇒ "ABC"
```

## 6.7. Vectors

Vectors are more convenient and efficient than lists for some applications. Whereas accessing an arbitrary element in a list requires a linear traversal of the list up to the selected element, arbitrary vector elements are accessed in constant time. The *length* of a vector in Scheme is the number of elements it contains. Vectors are indexed by exact nonnegative integers, and the index of the first element of any vector is 0. The highest valid index for a given vector is one less than its length.

As with lists, the elements of a vector may be of any type; a single vector may even hold more than one type of object.

A vector is written as a sequence of objects separated by whitespace, preceded by the prefix #( and followed by ). For example, a vector consisting of the elements a, b, and c would be written #(a b c).

---

(vector *obj* ...)                                                    **procedure**
**returns:** a vector of the objects *obj* ...

```
(vector) ⇒ #()
(vector 'a 'b 'c) ⇒ #(a b c)
```

---

(make-vector *n*)                                                    **procedure**
(make-vector *n* *obj*)                                              **procedure**
**returns:** a vector of length *n*

*n* must be an exact nonnegative integer. If *obj* is supplied, each element of the vector is filled with *obj*; otherwise, the elements are unspecified.

```
(make-vector 0) ⇒ #()
(make-vector 0 'a) ⇒ #()
(make-vector 5 'a) ⇒ #(a a a a a)
```

---

(vector-length *vector*)                                             **procedure**
**returns:** the number of elements in *vector*

The length of a vector is always an exact nonnegative integer.

```
(vector-length '#())  ⇒  0
(vector-length '#(a b c))  ⇒  3
(vector-length (vector 1 2 3 4))  ⇒  4
(vector-length (make-vector 300))  ⇒  300
```

(vector-ref *vector n*)                                              **procedure**
**returns:** the *n*th element (zero-based) of *vector*

*n* must be an exact nonnegative integer strictly less than the length of *vector*.

```
(vector-ref '#(a b c) 0)  ⇒  a
(vector-ref '#(a b c) 1)  ⇒  b
(vector ref '#(x y z w) 3)  ⇒  w
```

(vector-set! *vector n obj*)                                        **procedure**
**returns:** unspecified

*n* must be an exact nonnegative integer strictly less than the length of *vector*.
vector-set! changes the *n*th element of *vector* to *obj*.

```
(let ((v (vector 'a 'b 'c 'd 'e)))
  (vector-set! v 2 'x)
  v)  ⇒  #(a b x d e)
```

(vector-fill! *vector obj*)                                          **procedure**
**returns:** unspecified

vector-fill! replaces each element of *vector* with *obj*. vector-fill! appears in
the Revised[5] Report but not in the ANSI/IEEE standard. It may be defined as
follows.

```
(define vector-fill!
  (lambda (v x)
    (let ((n (vector-length v)))
      (do ((i 0 (+ i 1)))
          ((= i n))
          (vector-set! v i x)))))
(let ((v (vector 1 2 3)))
  (vector-fill! v 0)
  v)  ⇒  #(0 0 0)
```

(vector->list *vector*)                                                          **procedure**
**returns:** a list of the elements of *vector*

vector->list provides a convenient method for applying list-processing operations to vectors. vector->list appears in the Revised[5] Report but not in the
ANSI/IEEE standard. It may be defined as follows.

```
(define vector->list
  (lambda (s)
    (do ((i (- (vector-length s) 1) (- i 1))
         (ls '() (cons (vector-ref s i) ls)))
        ((< i 0) ls))))
```

```
(vector->list (vector))  ⇒  ()
(vector->list '#(a b c))  ⇒  (a b c)
```

```
(let ((v '#(1 2 3 4 5)))
  (apply * (vector->list v)))  ⇒  120
```

(list->vector *list*)                                                            **procedure**
**returns:** a vector of the elements of *list*

list->vector is the functional inverse of vector->list. The two procedures are
often used in combination to take advantage of a list-processing operation. A vector
may be converted to a list with vector->list, this list processed in some manner to
produce a new list, and the new list converted back into a vector with list->vector.

list->vector appears in the Revised[5] Report but not in the ANSI/IEEE standard. It may be defined as follows.

```
(define list->vector
  (lambda (ls)
    (let ((s (make-vector (length ls))))
      (do ((ls ls (cdr ls)) (i 0 (+ i 1)))
          ((null? ls) s)
        (vector-set! s i (car ls))))))
```

```
(list->vector '())  ⇒  #()
(list->vector '(a b c))  ⇒  #(a b c)
```

```
(let ((v '#(1 2 3 4 5)))
  (let ((ls (vector->list v)))
    (list->vector (map * ls ls))))  ⇒  #(1 4 9 16 25)
```

# 6.8. Symbols

Symbols are used for a variety of purposes as symbolic names in Scheme programs.
Strings could be used for most of the same purposes, but an important charac-

teristic of symbols makes comparisons between symbols much more efficient. This characteristic is that two symbols with the same name are identical in the sense of **eq?**. The reason is that the Scheme reader (see **read** in Section 7.1) and the procedure **string->symbol** catalog symbols in an internal symbol table and always return the same symbol whenever the same name is encountered. Thus, no character-by-character comparison is needed, as would be needed to compare two strings.

The property that two symbols may be compared quickly for equivalence makes them ideally suited for use as identifiers in the representation of programs, allowing fast comparison of identifiers. This property also makes symbols useful for a variety of other purposes. For example, symbols might be used as messages passed between procedures, labels for list-structured records, or names for objects stored in an association list (see **assq** in Section 6.3).

Symbols are written without double quotes or other bracketing characters. Parentheses, double quotes, spaces, and most other characters with a special meaning to the Scheme reader are not allowed within the printed representation of a symbol. Some implementations, however, support the use of backward slashes to escape special characters occurring in symbols, in a manner similar to the use of backward slashes in strings.

Refer to Section 1.1 or the formal syntax of Scheme at the back of this book for a precise description of the syntax of symbols.

---

(string->symbol *string*)                                                **procedure**
**returns:** a symbol whose name is *string*

**string->symbol** records all symbols it creates in an internal table that it shares with the system reader, **read**. If a symbol whose name is equivalent to string (according to the predicate **string=?**) already exists in the table, this symbol is returned. Otherwise, a new symbol is created with *string* as its name; this symbol is entered into the table and returned.

The system reader arranges to convert all symbols to a single case (lower case is assumed in this book), before entering them into the internal table. **string->symbol** does not. Thus, it is possible to produce symbols in lower case, upper case, or even mixed case, using **string->symbol**. It is also possible to create symbols with names that contain special characters, such as spaces or parentheses.

```
(string->symbol "x")  ⇒  x

(eq? (string->symbol "x") 'x)  ⇒  #t
(eq? (string->symbol "X") 'x)  ⇒  #f

(eq? (string->symbol "x")
     (string->symbol "x"))  ⇒  #t
```

**(symbol->string** *symbol*)                                                      **procedure**
**returns:** a string, the name of *symbol*

The string returned by **symbol->string** for a symbol created by an earlier call to
**string->symbol** may or may not be the same string (by **eq?**) as the string passed
to **string->symbol**. That is, an implementation is free to copy or not to copy a
string it uses as the name of a symbol. Unpredictable behavior can result if a string
passed to **string->symbol** is altered with **string-set!** or by any other means.

```
(symbol->string 'xyz)  ⇒  "xyz"
(symbol->string (string->symbol "Hi"))  ⇒  "Hi"
(symbol->string (string->symbol "()"))  ⇒  "()"
```

# CHAPTER 7

# Input and Output

*A six-armed spiral.*

All input and output operations are performed through *ports*. A port is a pointer into a (possibly infinite) stream of characters (typically a file), an opening through which programs may draw characters or objects from the stream or place characters or objects into the stream.

Ports are first-class objects, like any other object in Scheme. Like procedures, ports do not have a printed representation the way strings and numbers do, so they are shown here with the notation #<port>. There are initially two ports in the system: the current input port and the current output port. In an interactive session, these ports usually point to the terminal input and output streams. Several ways to open new ports are provided.

An input port often points to a finite stream, e.g., an input file stored on disk. If one of the input operations (read, read-char, or peek-char) is asked to read from a port that has reached the end of a finite stream, it returns a special *eof* (end of file) *object*. The predicate eof-object? may be used to determine if an object returned from read, read-char, or peek-char is an eof object.

# 7.1. Input Operations

(input-port? *obj*)                                                    **procedure**
returns: #t if *obj* is an input port, #f otherwise

(input-port? '(a b c)))   $\Rightarrow$   *unspecified*
(input-port? (current-input-port))   $\Rightarrow$   #t
(input-port? (open-input-file "infile.ss"))   $\rightarrow$   #t

The last example assumes that the file named by "infile.ss" may be opened for input.

(current-input-port)                                                   **procedure**
returns: the current input port

Most procedures involving input ports may be called with or without an explicit port argument. If called without an explicit port argument, the current input port is used. For example, (read-char) and (read-char (current-input-port)) both return the next character from the current input port.

(open-input-file *filename*)                                           **procedure**
returns: a new input port

*filename* must be a string. open-input-file creates a new input port for the file named by *filename*. An error is signaled if the file does not exist or cannot be opened for input. See the example given for close-input-port.

(close-input-port *input-port*)                                  **procedure**
**returns:** unspecified

close-input-port closes an input port. Once an input port has been closed, no
more input operations may be performed on that port. Because the operating
system may place limits on the number of ports open at one time or restrict access
to an open port, it is a good practice to close any port that will no longer be used
for input or output. Some Scheme implementations close ports automatically after
they become inaccessible to the program or when the Scheme program exits, but
it is best to close ports explicitly whenever possible.

It is not an error to close a port that has already been closed; doing so has no
effect.

The following shows the use of open-input-file and close-input-port in an
expression that gathers a list of objects from the file named by "myfile.ss." It is
functionally equivalent to the example given for call-with-input-file below.

```
(let ((p (open-input-file "myfile.ss")))
  (let f ((x (read p)))
    (if (eof-object? x)
        (begin
          (close-input-port p)
          '())
        (cons x (f (read p))))))
```

(call-with-input-file *filename proc*)                           **procedure**
**returns:** the result of invoking *proc*

*filename* must be a string. *proc* must be a procedure of one argument.

call-with-input-file creates a new input port for the file named by *filename*
and passes this port to *proc*. An error is signaled if the file does not exist or cannot
be opened for input. If *proc* returns, call-with-input-file closes the input port
and returns the value returned by *proc*.

call-with-input-file does not automatically close the input port if a continuation created outside of *proc* is invoked, since it is possible that another continuation
created inside of *proc* will be invoked at a later time, returning control to *proc*. If
*proc* does not return, an implementation is free to close the input port only if
it can prove that the input port is no longer accessible. As shown in Section 5.5,
dynamic-wind may be used to ensure that the port is closed if a continuation created
outside of *proc* is invoked.

The following example shows the use of `call-with-input-file` in an expression that gathers a list of objects from the file named by "myfile.ss." It is functionally equivalent to the example given for `close-input-port` above.

```
(call-with-input-file "myfile.ss"
  (lambda (p)
    (let f ((x (read p)))
      (if (eof-object? x)
          '()
          (cons x (f (read p)))))))
```

`call-with-input-file` might be defined as follows.

```
(define call-with-input-file
  (lambda (filename proc)
    (let ((p (open-input-file filename)))
      (let ((v (proc p)))
        (close-input-port p)
        v))))
```

**(with-input-from-file** *filename thunk*) procedure
**returns:** the value returned by *thunk*

*filename* must be a string.

with-input-from-file temporarily changes the current input port to be the result of opening the file named by *filename* for input during the application of *thunk*. If *thunk* returns, the port is closed and the current input port is restored to its old value.

The behavior of `with-input-from-file` is unspecified if a continuation created outside of *thunk* is invoked before *thunk* returns. An implementation may close the port and restore the current input port to its old value—but it may not.

with-input-from-file appears in the Revised[5] Report but not the ANSI/IEEE standard.

**(read)** procedure
**(read** *input-port*) procedure
**returns:** the next object from *input-port*

If *input-port* is not supplied, it defaults to the current input port. If *input-port* is at end of file, an eof object is returned. See the examples given for `close-input-port` and `call-with-input-file`.

```
(read-char)                                                        procedure
(read-char input-port)                                             procedure
```
**returns:** the next character from *input-port*

If *input-port* is not supplied, it defaults to the current input port. If *input-port* is at end of file, an eof object is returned. See the examples given for **peek-char** and **write-char**.

```
(peek-char)                                                        procedure
(peek-char input-port)                                             procedure
```
**returns:** the next character from *input-port*

If *input-port* is not supplied, it defaults to the current input port. If *input-port* is at end of file, an eof object is returned.

In contrast to **read-char**, **peek-char** does not consume the character it reads from *input-port*; a subsequent call to **peek-char** or **read-char** returns the same character.

**peek-char** is provided for applications requiring one character of lookahead. The procedure **read-word** defined below returns the next word from an input port as a string, where a word is defined to be a sequence of alphabetic characters. Since **read-word** does not know until it sees one character beyond the word that it has read the entire word, it uses **peek-char** to determine the next character and **read-char** to consume the character.

```
(define read-word
  (lambda (p)
    (list->string
      (let f ()
        (let ((c (peek-char p)))
          (cond
            ((eof-object? c) '())
            ((char-alphabetic? c)
             (read-char p)
             (cons c (f)))
            (else '()))))))))
```

```
(eof-object? obj)                                                  procedure
```
**returns:** #t if *obj* is an eof object, #f otherwise

An end-of-file object is returned by **read**, **read-char**, or **peek-char** when an input port has reached the end of input. Although end-of-file objects need not be distinct from other object types, they are unique in the sense that they cannot be confused with objects that may be returned by **read**, **read-char**, or **peek-char** when the input port has not reached the end of input. For example, if (eof-object? x) is #t, (eq? x #\a) must be false but (char? x) may be true or false.

(char-ready?)                                                    **procedure**
(char-ready? *input-port*)                                       **procedure**
**returns:** #t if a character is available on *input-port*, #f otherwise

If *input-port* is not supplied, it defaults to the current input port.

char-ready? allows a program to look for character input on an interactive port without hanging. If char-ready? returns #t, the next peek-char or read-char operation on *input-port* will not be delayed. If *input-port* is at end of file, char-ready? returns #t. char-ready? appears in the Revised[5] Report but not in the ANSI/IEEE standard.

# 7.2. Output Operations

(output-port? *obj*)                                             **procedure**
**returns:** #t if *obj* is an output port, #f otherwise

Ports need not be distinct from other object types.

```
(output-port? '(a b c)))  ⇒  unspecified
(output-port? (current-output-port))  ⇒  #t
(output-port? (open-output-file "outfile.ss"))  ⇒  #t
```

The last example assumes that file named by "outfile.ss" may be opened for output.

(current-output-port)                                           **procedure**
**returns:** the current output port

Most procedures involving output ports may be called with or without an explicit port argument. If called without an explicit port argument, the current output port is used. For example, (write *obj*) and (write *obj* (current-output-port)) both write to the current output port.

(open-output-file *filename*)                                   **procedure**
**returns:** a new output port

*filename* must be a string. open-output-file creates a new output port for the file named by *filename*. An error is signaled if the file cannot be opened for output. See the example given for close-output-port.

(close-output-port *output-port*)                               **procedure**
**returns:** unspecified

close-output-port closes an output port. Once an output port has been closed, no more output operations may be performed on that port. Because the operating system may place limits on the number of ports open at one time or restrict access to an open port, it is a good practice to close any port that will no longer be used for input or output. Also, because the system may buffer output for efficiency, some of the output may not appear on the file until the file has been closed. Some Scheme implementations close ports automatically after they become inaccessible to the program or when the Scheme program exits, but it is best to close ports explicitly whenever possible.

It is not an error to close a port that has already been closed; doing so has no effect.

The following shows the use of `open-output-file` and `close-output-port` to write a list of objects (the value of `list-to-be-printed`), separated by newlines, to the file named by "myfile.ss." It is functionally equivalent to the example given for `call-with-output-file` below.

```
(let ((p (open-output-file "myfile.ss")))
  (let f ((ls list-to-be-printed))
    (if (not (null? ls))
        (begin
          (write (car ls) p)
          (newline p)
          (f (cdr ls)))))
  (close-output-port p))
```

(`call-with-output-file` *filename proc*)                                **procedure**
**returns:** the result of invoking *proc*

*filename* must be a string. *proc* must be a procedure of one argument.

`call-with-output-file` creates a new output port for the file named by *filename* and passes this port to *proc*. An error is signaled if the file cannot be opened for output. If *proc* returns, `call-with-output-file` closes the output port and returns the value returned by *proc*.

`call-with-output-file` does not automatically close the output port if a continuation created outside of *proc* is invoked, since it is possible that another continuation created inside of *proc* will be invoked at a later time, returning control to *proc*. If *proc* does not return, an implementation is free to close the output port only if it can prove that the output port is no longer accessible. As shown in Section 5.5, `dynamic-wind` may be used to ensure that the port is closed if a continuation created outside of *proc* is invoked.

The following shows the use of `call-with-output-file` to write a list of objects (the value of `list-to-be-printed`), separated by newlines, to the file

named by "myfile.ss." It is functionally equivalent to the example given for
`close-output-port` above.

```
(call-with-output-file "myfile.ss"
  (lambda (p)
    (let f ((ls list-to-be-printed))
      (if (not (null? ls))
          (begin
            (write (car ls) p)
            (newline p)
            (f (cdr ls)))))))
```

`call-with-output-file` might be defined as follows.

```
(define call-with-output-file
  (lambda (filename proc)
    (let ((p (open-output-file filename)))
      (let ((v (proc p)))
        (close-output-port p)
        v))))
```

(**with-output-to-file** *filename thunk*)                    **procedure**
**returns:** the value returned by *thunk*

*filename* must be a string.

   `with-output-to-file` temporarily rebinds the current output port to be the
result of opening the file named by *filename* for output during the application of
*thunk*. If *thunk* returns, the port is closed and the current output port is restored
to its old value.

   The behavior of `with-output-to-file` is unspecified if a continuation created
outside of *thunk* is invoked before *thunk* returns. An implementation may close the
port and restore the current output port to its old value—but it may not.

   `with-output-to-file` appears in the Revised[5] Report but not the ANSI/IEEE
standard.

(**write** *obj*)                                              **procedure**
(**write** *obj output-port*)                                 **procedure**
**returns:** unspecified

If *output-port* is not supplied, it defaults to the current output port.

   `write` prints *obj* to *output-port* in such a way that it can later be read by the
procedure `read`, unless it contains unprintable objects such as procedures, ports,
or symbols containing nonstandard characters. Strings are printed within quote
marks, using slashes where necessary, and characters are printed with the #\ notation. See Section 9.5 for an implementation of `write` and `display`.

```
(display obj)                                                    procedure
(display obj output-port)                                        procedure
returns: unspecified
```

If *output-port* is not supplied, it defaults to the current output port.

display is similar to write but prints strings and characters found within *obj* directly. Strings are printed without quotation marks or slashes, and characters are printed without the #\ notation. For example, both (display "(a b c)") and (display '("a b" c)) would print (a b c). Because of this, display should not be used to print objects that are intended to be read with read. display is useful primarily for printing messages, with *obj* most often being a string. See Section 9.5 for an implementation of write and display.

```
(write-char char)                                               procedure
(write-char char output-port)                                   procedure
returns: unspecified
```

If *output-port* is not supplied, it defaults to the current output port. write-char writes the single character *char* to *output-port*, without the #\ notation. The following example copies the contents of one file to another, one character at a time.

```
(call-with-input-file "infile"
  (lambda (ip)
    (call-with-output-file "outfile"
      (lambda (op)
        (do ((c (read-char ip) (read-char ip)))
            ((eof-object? c))
          (write-char c op))))))
```

```
(newline)                                                       procedure
(newline output-port)                                           procedure
returns: unspecified
```

If *output-port* is not supplied, it defaults to the current output port. newline sends a newline character to *output-port*. It may be defined as follows.

```
(define newline
  (lambda args
    (apply write-char #\newline args)))
```

# 7.3. Loading Programs

(**load** *filename*)                                                   **procedure**
**returns:** unspecified

*filename* must be a string. **load** reads and evaluates in sequence each expression in the file specified by *filename*. **load** appears in the Revised[5] Report but not in the ANSI/IEEE standard.

# 7.4. Transcript Files

A transcript file is a record of an interactive session. It is also useful as a "quick-and-dirty" alternative to opening an output file and using explicit output operations

    **transcript-on** and **transcript-off** appear in the Revised[5] Report but not in the ANSI/IEEE standard.

(**transcript-on** *filename*)                                        **procedure**
**returns:** unspecified

*filename* must be a string.

    **transcript-on** opens the file named by *filename* for output, and it copies to this file all input from the current input port and all output to the current output port. An error is signaled if the file cannot be opened for output.

(**transcript-off**)                                                   **procedure**
**returns:** unspecified

**transcript-off** ends transcription and closes the transcript file.

# CHAPTER 8

# *Syntactic Extension*

*A warped, two-armed spiral.*

*Syntactic extensions*, or *macros*, are used to simplify and regularize repeated patterns in a program, to introduce syntactic forms with new evaluation rules, and to perform transformations that help make programs more efficient.

A syntactic extension typically takes the form (*keyword subform* ...), where *keyword* is the identifier that names the syntactic extension. The syntax of each *subform* varies from one syntactic extension to another. Syntactic extensions can also take the form of improper lists (or even singleton identifiers; see Section 8.3), although this is less common.

New syntactic extensions are defined by associating keywords with transformation procedures, or *transformers*. Syntactic extensions are defined globally using top-level `define-syntax` forms or within the scope of particular expressions using `let-syntax`, `letrec-syntax`, and internal `define-syntax`. Transformers are created using `syntax-rules` or `syntax-case`, which allow transformations to be specified via pattern matching.

Syntactic extensions are expanded into core forms at the start of evaluation (before compilation or interpretation) by a syntax *expander*. The expander is invoked once for each top-level form in a program. If the expander encounters a syntactic extension, it invokes the associated transformer to expand the syntactic extension, then repeats the expansion process for the form returned by the transformer. If the expander encounters a core syntactic form, it recursively processes the subforms, if any, and reconstructs the form from the expanded subforms. Information about identifier bindings is maintained during expansion to enforce lexical scoping for variables and keywords.

The syntactic extension mechanisms described in this chapter are part of the "syntax-case" system that has become a de facto standard in the absence of a standard full-featured syntactic extension system. A portable implementation of the syntax-case system is available at *http://www.scheme.com/syntax-case/*. The syntax-case system also supports modules and several other features that are described in the *Chez Scheme User's Guide* [5]. A description of the motivations behind and implementation of the system can be found in the articles "Syntactic Abstraction in Scheme" [7] and "Extending the Scope of Syntactic Abstraction" [22].

The Revised[5] Report includes only `let-syntax`, `letrec-syntax`, top-level `define-syntax`, and `syntax-rules`. The pattern language supported by the Revised[5] Report version of `syntax-rules` is also more limited, with pattern ellipses allowed only at the end of list- or vector-structured patterns. (See page 187.) Furthermore, the bodies of `let-syntax` and `letrec-syntax` are treated like `lambda` bodies, i.e., they open up new scopes, which prevents them from being used in contexts where definitions are required. (See page 185.) Programmers desiring to write programs that are guaranteed to run to all Revised[5] Report implementations should stick with the Revised[5] Report subset and use `let-syntax` and `letrec-syntax` in a manner consistent with either interpretation. The ANSI/IEEE standard does not include any syntactic extension mechanism.

## 8.1. Keyword Bindings

This section describes forms that establish bindings between keywords and transformers. Keyword bindings may be established at top level, using **define-syntax**, or locally, using **let-syntax**, **letrec-syntax**, or internal **define-syntax**. Existing keyword bindings may be rebound temporarily with **fluid-let-syntax**.

(**define-syntax** *keyword exp*)                                   **syntax**
**returns:** unspecified

*exp* must evaluate to a transformer.

The following example defines **let\*** as a syntactic extension, specifying the transformer with **syntax-rules** (see Section 8.2).

```
(define-syntax let*
  (syntax-rules ()
    ((_ () e1 e2 ...) (let () e1 e2 ...))
    ((_ ((i1 v1) (i2 v2) ...) e1 e2 ...)
     (let ((i1 v1))
       (let* ((i2 v2) ...) e1 e2 ...)))))
```

**define-syntax** forms appearing at top level behave similarly to top-level variable definitions, and **define-syntax** forms appearing at the front of a **lambda** or other body behave similarly to internal variable definitions. That is, a binding established by a top-level **define-syntax** form is visible globally, whereas one established by an internal **define-syntax** form is visible only within the body in which the **define-syntax** form appears.

All bindings established by a set of internal definitions, whether keyword or variable definitions, are visible within the definitions themselves. For example, the expression

```
(let ()
  (define even?
    (lambda (x)
      (or (= x 0) (odd? (- x 1)))))
  (define-syntax odd?
    (syntax-rules ()
      ((_ x) (not (even? x)))))
  (even? 10))
```

is valid and should return #t. It must be possible for the expander to determine the set of syntax and variable definitions that appears at the front of a body without referring to any of the locally defined identifiers. It is not legal, therefore, for an internal definition to affect the status of a (potential) internal definition in the same sequence of forms. For example,

```
(let ()
  (define-syntax bind-to-zero
    (syntax-rules ()
      ((_ id) (define id 0))))
  (bind-to-zero x)
  x)
```

is not valid, since it would require the expander to expand (bind-to-zero x) in order to recognize it as a syntax definition. Rewritten as follows it returns 0.

```
(let ()
  (define-syntax bind-to-zero
    (syntax-rules ()
      ((_ id) (define id 0))))
  (let ()
    (bind-to-zero x)
    x))
```

A top-level syntactic definition must be established before its first use in order for that use to be recognized.

---

(let-syntax ((*keyword exp*) ...) *form₁ form₂* ...)                            **syntax**
(letrec-syntax ((*keyword exp*) ...) *form₁ form₂* ...)                         **syntax**
**returns:** see explanation

Each *exp* must evaluate to a transformer. For both let-syntax and letrec-syntax, each *keyword* is bound within the forms *form₁ form₂* .... For letrec-syntax the binding scope also includes each *exp*.

A let-syntax or letrec-syntax form may expand into one or more expressions anywhere expressions are permitted, in which case the resulting expressions are treated as if enclosed in a begin expression. This allows a let-syntax or letrec-syntax form to expand into a definition or sequence of definitions anywhere definitions are permitted, in which case the definitions are treated as if they appeared in place of the let-syntax or letrec-syntax form. (This differs from the Revised[5] Report treatment of these forms; see page 183.)

The following example highlights how `let-syntax` and `letrec-syntax` differ.

```
(let ((f (lambda (x) (+ x 1))))
  (let-syntax ((f (syntax-rules ()
                    ((_ x) x)))
               (g (syntax-rules ()
                    ((_ x) (f x)))))
    (list (f 1) (g 1))))  ⇒  (1 2)
(let ((f (lambda (x) (+ x 1))))
  (letrec-syntax ((f (syntax-rules ()
                       ((_ x) x)))
                  (g (syntax-rules ()
                       ((_ x) (f x)))))
    (list (f 1) (g 1))))  ⇒  (1 1)
```

The two expressions are identical except that the `let-syntax` form in the first expression is a `letrec-syntax` form in the second. In the first expression, the `f` occurring in `g` refers to the `let`-bound variable `f`, whereas in the second it refers to the keyword `f` whose binding is established by the `letrec-syntax` form.

**(fluid-let-syntax ((*keyword exp*) ...) *form₁ form₂* ...)**                       **syntax**
**returns:** see explanation

Each *exp* must evaluate to a transformer. `fluid-let-syntax` is similar to `let-syntax`, except that instead of introducing new bindings for the keywords *keyword* ..., `fluid-let-syntax` temporarily alters the existing bindings for the keywords during the expansion of its body. That is, during the expansion of *form₁ form₂* ..., the visible lexical (or top-level) binding for each `keyword` is temporarily replaced by a new association between the keyword and the corresponding transformer. This affects any references to the keyword that resolve to the same lexical (or top-level) binding whether the references occur in the text of the body or are introduced during its expansion. In contrast, `let-syntax` captures only those references that occur within the text of its body.

The following example shows how `fluid-let-syntax` differs from `let-syntax`.

```
(let ((f (lambda (x) (+ x 1))))
  (let-syntax ((g (syntax-rules ()
                    ((_ x) (f x)))))
    (let-syntax ((f (syntax-rules ()
                      ((_ x) x))))
      (g 1))))  ⇒  2
```

```
(let ((f (lambda (x) (+ x 1))))
  (let-syntax ((g (syntax-rules ()
                    ((_ x) (f x)))))
    (fluid-let-syntax ((f (syntax-rules ()
                           ((_ x) x))))
      (g 1))))  ⇒  1
```

The two expressions are identical except that the inner `let-syntax` form in the first expression is a `fluid-let-syntax` form in the second. In the first expression, the `f` occurring in the expansion of `(g 1)` refers to the `let`-bound variable `f`, whereas in the second it refers to the keyword `f` by virtue of the fluid syntax binding for `f`.

# 8.2. Syntax-Rules Transformers

The `syntax-rules` form described in this section permits simple transformers to be specified in a convenient manner. These transformers may be bound to keywords using the mechanisms described in Section 8.1. While it is much less expressive than the mechanism described in Section 8.3, it is sufficient for defining many common syntactic extensions.

**(syntax-rules** (*literal* ...) *clause* ...**)**                              **syntax**
**returns:** a transformer

Each *literal* must be an identifier. Each clause takes the form:

(*pattern  template*)

Each *pattern* specifies one possible syntax that the input form might take, and the corresponding *template* specifies how the output should appear in each case.

Patterns consist of list structure, vector structure, identifiers, and constants. Each identifier within a pattern is either a *literal*, a *pattern variable*, or an *ellipsis*. The identifier ... is an ellipsis. Any identifier other than ... is a literal if it appears in the list of literals (*literal* ...); otherwise, it is a pattern variable. Literals serve as auxiliary keywords, such as `else` in `case` and `cond` expressions. List and vector structure within a pattern specifies the basic structure required of the input, pattern variables specify arbitrary substructure, and literals and constants specify atomic pieces that must match exactly. Ellipses specify repeated occurrences of the subpatterns they follow.

An input form $F$ matches a pattern $P$ if and only if

- $P$ is a pattern variable,
- $P$ is a literal identifier and $F$ is an identifier with the same binding (see `free-identifier=?` in Section 8.3),

- $P$ is of the form $(P_1 \ldots P_n)$ and $F$ is a list of $n$ elements that match $P_1$ through $P_n$,

- $P$ is of the form $(P_1 \ldots P_n . P_x)$ and $F$ is a list or improper list of $n$ or more elements whose first $n$ elements match $P_1$ through $P_n$ and whose $n$th cdr matches $P_x$,

- $P$ is of the form $(P_1 \ldots P_k \ P_e \ ellipsis \ P_{m+1} \ldots P_n)$, where *ellipsis* is the identifier **...** and $F$ is a proper list of $n$ elements whose first $k$ elements match $P_1$ through $P_k$, whose next $m - k$ elements each match $P_e$, and whose remaining $n - m$ elements match $P_{m+1}$ through $P_n$,

- $P$ is of the form $(P_1 \ldots P_k \ P_e \ ellipsis \ P_{m+1} \ldots P_n . P_x)$, where *ellipsis* is the identifier **...** and $F$ is a list or improper list of $n$ or more elements whose first $k$ elements match $P_1$ through $P_k$, whose next $m - k$ elements each match $P_e$, whose next $n - m$ elements match $P_{m+1}$ through $P_n$, and whose $n$th cdr matches $P_x$,

- $P$ is of the form #$(P_1 \ldots P_n)$ and $F$ is a vector of $n$ elements that match $P_1$ through $P_n$,

- $P$ is of the form #$(P_1 \ldots P_k \ P_e \ ellipsis \ P_{m+1} \ldots P_n)$, where *ellipsis* is the identifier **...** and $F$ is a vector of $n$ or more elements whose first $k$ elements match $P_1$ through $P_k$, whose next $m - k$ elements each match $P_e$, and whose remaining $n - m$ elements match $P_{m+1}$ through $P_n$, or

- $P$ is a pattern datum (any nonlist, nonvector, nonsymbol object) and $F$ is equal to $P$ in the sense of the `equal?` procedure.

The outermost structure of a `syntax-rules` *pattern* must actually be in one of the list-structured forms above, although subpatterns of the pattern may be in any of the above forms. Furthermore, the first element of the outermost pattern is ignored, since it is always assumed to be the keyword naming the syntactic form. (These statements do not apply to `syntax-case`; see Section 8.3.)

If an input form passed to a `syntax-rules` transformer matches the pattern for a given clause, the clause is accepted and the form is transformed as specified by the associated template. As this transformation takes place, pattern variables appearing in the pattern are bound to the corresponding input subforms. Pattern variables appearing within a subpattern followed by one or more ellipses may be bound to a set or sets of zero or more input subforms.

A template is a pattern variable, an identifier that is not a pattern variable, a pattern datum, a list of subtemplates $(S_1 \ldots S_n)$, an improper list of subtemplates $(S_1 \ S_2 \ldots S_n . T)$, or a vector of subtemplates #$(S_1 \ldots S_n)$. Each subtemplate $S_i$ is either a template or a template followed by one or more ellipses. The final element $T$ of an improper subtemplate list is a template.

Pattern variables appearing within a template are replaced in the output by the input subforms to which they are bound. Pattern data and identifiers that are not pattern variables are inserted directly into the output. List and vector structure within the template remains list and vector structure in the output. A subtemplate followed by an ellipsis expands into zero or more occurrences of the subtemplate. The subtemplate must contain at least one pattern variable from a subpattern followed by an ellipsis. (Otherwise, the expander could not determine how many times the subform should be repeated in the output.) Pattern variables that occur in subpatterns followed by one or more ellipses may occur only in subtemplates that are followed by (at least) as many ellipses. These pattern variables are replaced in the output by the input subforms to which they are bound, distributed as specified. If a pattern variable is followed by more ellipses in the template than in the associated pattern, the input form is replicated as necessary.

A template of the form (... *template*) is identical to *template*, except that ellipses within the template have no special meaning. That is, any ellipses contained within *template* are treated as ordinary identifiers. In particular, the template (... ...) produces a single ellipsis, .... This allows syntactic extensions to expand into forms containing ellipses.

The definition of **or** below demonstrates the use of **syntax-rules**.

```
(define-syntax or
  (syntax-rules ()
    ((_) #f)
    ((_ e) e)
    ((_ e1 e2 e3 ...)
     (let ((t e1)) (if t t (or e2 e3 ...))))))
```

The input patterns specify that the input must consist of the keyword and zero or more subexpressions. An underscore ( _ ), which is an ordinary pattern variable, is used by convention for the keyword position to remind the programmer and anyone reading the definition that the keyword position never fails to contain the expected keyword and need not be matched. (In fact, as mentioned above, **syntax-rules** ignores what appears in the keyword position.) If more than one subexpression is present (third clause), the expanded code both tests the value of the first subexpression and returns the value if it is not false. To avoid evaluating the expression twice, the transformer introduces a binding for the temporary variable **t**.

The expansion algorithm maintains lexical scoping automatically by renaming local identifiers as necessary. Thus, the binding for **t** introduced by the transformer is visible only within code introduced by the transformer and not within subforms of the input. Similarly, the references to the identifiers **let** and **if** are unaffected by any bindings present in the context of the input.

```
(let ((if #f))
  (let ((t 'okay))
    (or if t)))  ⇒  okay
```

This expression is transformed during expansion to the equivalent of the expression below.

```
((lambda (if1)
   ((lambda (t1)
      ((lambda (t2)
         (if t2 t2 t1))
       if1))
    'okay))
 #f)  ⇒  okay
```

In this sample expansion, if1, t1, and t2 represent identifiers to which if and t in the original expression and t in the expansion of or have been renamed.

The definition of a simplified version of cond below (simplified because it requires at least one output expression per clause and does not support the auxiliary keyword =>) demonstrates how auxiliary keywords such as else are recognized in the input to a transformer, via inclusion in the list of literals.

```
(define-syntax cond
  (syntax-rules (else)
    ((_ (else e1 e2 ...)) (begin e1 e2 ...))
    ((_ (e0 e1 e2 ...)) (if e0 (begin e1 e2 ...)))
    ((_ (e0 e1 e2 ...) c1 c2 ...)
     (if e0 (begin e1 e2 ...) (cond c1 c2 ...)))))
```

## 8.3. Syntax-Case Transformers

This section describes a more expressive mechanism for creating transformers, based on syntax-case, a generalized version of syntax-rules. This mechanism permits more complex transformations to be specified, including transformations that "bend" lexical scoping in a controlled manner, allowing a much broader class of syntactic extensions to be defined. Any transformer that may be defined using syntax-rules may be rewritten easily to use syntax-case instead; in fact, syntax-rules itself may be defined as a syntactic extension in terms of syntax-case, as demonstrated within the description of syntax below.

With this mechanism, transformers are procedures of one argument. The argument is a *syntax object* representing the form to be processed. The return value is a syntax object representing the output form. A syntax object contains contextual information about a form in addition to its structure. This contextual information is used by the expander to maintain lexical scoping.

A syntax object representing an identifier is itself referred to as an identifier; thus, the term *identifier* may refer either to the syntactic entity (symbol, variable, or keyword) or to the concrete representation of the syntactic entity as a syntax object. It is rarely necessary to distinguish the two uses.

Transformers destructure their input with `syntax-case` and rebuild their output with `syntax`. These two forms alone are sufficient for defining many syntactic extensions, including any that can be defined using `syntax-rules`. They are described below along with a set of additional forms and procedures that provide added functionality.

(`syntax-case` *exp* (*literal* ...) *clause* ...)                                    **syntax**
**returns:** see below

Each *literal* must be an identifier. Each *clause* must take one of the following two forms.

(*pattern output-expression*)
(*pattern fender output-expression*)

`syntax-case` patterns may be in any of the forms described in Section 8.2.

`syntax-case` first evaluates *exp*, then attempts to match the resulting value against the pattern from the first *clause*. This value is usually a syntax object, but it may be any Scheme object. If the value matches the pattern and no *fender* is present, *output-expression* is evaluated and its value returned as the value of the `syntax-case` expression. If the value does not match the pattern, the value is compared against the next clause, and so on. An error is signaled if the value does not match any of the patterns.

If the optional *fender* is present, it serves as an additional constraint on acceptance of a clause. If the value of the `syntax-case` *exp* matches the pattern for a given clause, the corresponding *fender* is evaluated. If *fender* evaluates to a true value, the clause is accepted; otherwise, the clause is rejected as if the input had failed to match the pattern. Fenders are logically a part of the matching process, i.e., they specify additional matching constraints beyond the basic structure of an expression.

Pattern variables contained within a clause's `pattern` are bound to the corresponding pieces of the input value within the clause's `fender` (if present) and `output-expression`. Pattern variables occupy the same name space as program variables and keywords; pattern variable bindings created by `syntax-case` can shadow (and be shadowed by) program variable and keyword bindings as well as other pattern variable bindings. Pattern variables, however, can be referenced only within `syntax` expressions.

See the examples following the description of `syntax`.

(syntax *template*)                                                                          syntax
**returns:** see below

A **syntax** expression is like a **quote** expression except that the values of pattern variables appearing within *template* are inserted into *template*, and contextual information associated both with the input and with the template is retained in the output to support lexical scoping. List and vector structures within the template become true lists or vectors (suitable for direct application of list or vector operations, like **map** or **vector-ref**) to the extent that the list or vector structures must be copied to insert the values of pattern variables. A **syntax** *template* is identical to a **syntax-rules** *template* and is treated similarly.

The definition of **or** below is equivalent to the one given in Section 8.2 except that it employs **syntax-case** and **syntax** in place of **syntax-rules**.

```
(define-syntax or
  (lambda (x)
    (syntax-case x ()
      ((_) (syntax #f))
      ((_ e) (syntax e))
      ((_ e1 e2 e3 ...)
       (syntax (let ((t e1)) (if t t (or e2 e3 ...)))))))))
```

In this version, the **lambda** expression that produces the transformer is explicit, as are the **syntax** forms in the output part of each clause. Any **syntax-rules** form can be expressed with **syntax-case** by making the **lambda** expression and **syntax** expressions explicit. This observation leads to the following definition of **syntax-rules** in terms of **syntax-case**.

```
(define-syntax syntax-rules
  (lambda (x)
    (syntax-case x ()
      ((_ (i ...) ((keyword . pattern) template) ...)
       (syntax (lambda (x)
                 (syntax-case x (i ...)
                   ((dummy . pattern) (syntax template))
                   ...)))))))
```

The unreferenced pattern variable **dummy** is used in place of each **keyword** since the first position of each **syntax-rules** pattern is always ignored.

Since the **lambda** and **syntax** expressions are implicit in a **syntax-rules** form, definitions expressed with **syntax-rules** are often shorter than the equivalent definitions expressed with **syntax-case**. The choice of which to use when either suffices is a matter of taste, but many transformers that can be written easily with **syntax-case** cannot be written easily or at all with **syntax-rules** (see Section 8.4).

(identifier? *obj*)                                                    **procedure**
**returns:** #t if *obj* is an identifier, #f otherwise

identifier? is often used within fenders to verify that certain subforms of an input
form are identifiers, as in the definition of unnamed let below.

```
(define-syntax let
  (lambda (x)
    (define ids?
      (lambda (ls)
        (or (null? ls)
            (and (identifier? (car ls))
                 (ids? (cdr ls))))))
    (syntax-case x ()
      ((_ ((i v) ...) e1 e2 ...)
       (ids? (syntax (i ...)))
       (syntax ((lambda (i ...) e1 e2 ...) v ...))))))
```

Syntactic extensions ordinarily take the form (*keyword subform* ...), but the
syntax-case system permits them to take the form of singleton identifiers as well.
For example, the keyword pcar in the expression below may be used both as an
identifier (in which case it expands into a call to car) or as a structured form (in
which case it expands into a call to set-car!).

```
(let ((p (cons 0 #f)))
  (define-syntax pcar
    (lambda (x)
      (syntax-case x ()
        (_ (identifier? x) (syntax (car p)))
        ((_ v) (syntax (set-car! p v))))))
  (let ((a pcar))
    (pcar 1)
    (list a pcar)))   ⇒  (0 1)
```

The fender (identifier? x) is used to recognize the singleton identifier case.


(free-identifier=? *identifier$_1$ identifier$_2$*)                    **procedure**
(bound-identifier=? *identifier$_1$ identifier$_2$*)                   **procedure**
**returns:** see below

Symbolic names alone do not distinguish identifiers unless the identifiers are
to be used only as symbolic data. The predicates free-identifier=? and
bound-identifier=? are used to compare identifiers according to their *intended
use* as free references or bound identifiers in a given context.

`free-identifier=?` is used to determine whether two identifiers would be equivalent if they were to appear as free identifiers in the output of a transformer. Because identifier references are lexically scoped, this means that (`free-identifier=?` $id_1$ $id_2$) is true if and only if the identifiers $id_1$ and $id_2$ refer to the same lexical or top-level binding. (For this comparison, all variables are assumed to have top-level bindings, whether defined yet or not.) Literal identifiers (auxiliary keywords) appearing in `syntax-case` patterns (such as `else` in `case` and `cond`) are matched with `free-identifier=?`.

Similarly, `bound-identifier=?` is used to determine if two identifiers would be equivalent if they were to appear as bound identifiers in the output of a transformer. In other words, if `bound-identifier=?` returns true for two identifiers, a binding for one will capture references to the other within its scope. In general, two identifiers are `bound-identifier=?` only if both are present in the original program or both are introduced by the same transformer application (perhaps implicitly—see `datum->syntax-object`). `bound-identifier=?` can be used for detecting duplicate identifiers in a binding construct or for other preprocessing of a binding construct that requires detecting instances of the bound identifiers.

The definition below is equivalent to the earlier definition of a simplified version of `cond` with `syntax-rules`, except that `else` is recognized via an explicit call to `free-identifier?` within a fender rather than via inclusion in the literals list.

```
(define-syntax cond
  (lambda (x)
    (syntax-case x ()
      ((_ (e0 e1 e2 ...))
       (and (identifier? (syntax e0))
            (free-identifier=? (syntax e0) (syntax else)))
       (syntax (begin e1 e2 ...)))
      ((_ (e0 e1 e2 ...)) (syntax (if e0 (begin e1 e2 ...))))
      ((_ (e0 e1 e2 ...) c1 c2 ...)
       (syntax (if e0 (begin e1 e2 ...) (cond c1 c2 ...)))))))
```

With either definition of `cond`, `else` is not recognized as an auxiliary keyword if an enclosing lexical binding for `else` exists. For example,

```
(let ((else #f))
  (cond (else (write "oops"))))
```

does *not* write `"oops"`, since `else` is bound lexically and is therefore not the same `else` that appears in the definition of `cond`.

The following definition of unnamed `let` uses `bound-identifier=?` to detect duplicate identifiers.

```
(define-syntax let
  (lambda (x)
    (define ids?
      (lambda (ls)
        (or (null? ls)
            (and (identifier? (car ls))
                 (ids? (cdr ls))))))
    (define unique-ids?
      (lambda (ls)
        (or (null? ls)
            (and (let notmem? ((x (car ls)) (ls (cdr ls)))
                   (or (null? ls)
                       (and (not (bound-identifier=? x (car ls)))
                            (notmem? x (cdr ls)))))
                 (unique-ids? (cdr ls))))))
    (syntax-case x ()
      ((_ ((i v) ...) e1 e2 ...)
       (and (ids? (syntax (i ...)))
            (unique-ids? (syntax (i ...))))
       (syntax ((lambda (i ...) e1 e2 ...) v ...))))))
```

With the definition of let above, the expression

```
(let ((a 3) (a 4)) (+ a a))
```

results in a syntax error, whereas

```
(let-syntax ((dolet (lambda (x)
                      (syntax-case x ()
                        ((_ b)
                         (syntax (let ((a 3) (b 4))
                                   (+ a b)))))))
  (dolet a))
```

evaluates to 7 since the identifier a introduced by dolet and the identifier a extracted from the input form are not bound-identifier=?. Since both occurrences of a, however, if left as free references, would refer to the same (top-level) binding for a, free-identifier=? would not distinguish them.

Two identifiers that are free-identifier=? may not be bound-identifier=?. An identifier introduced by a transformer may refer to the same enclosing binding as an identifier not introduced by the transformer, but an introduced binding for one will not capture references to the other. On the other hand, identifiers that are bound-identifier=? are free-identifier=?, as long as the identifiers have valid bindings in the context where they are compared.

(**with-syntax** (($pattern$ $val$) ...) $exp_1$ $exp_2$ ...)                                    **syntax**
**returns:** the value of the last $exp_i$

It is sometimes useful to construct a transformer's output in separate pieces, then put the pieces together. **with-syntax** facilitates this by allowing the creation of local pattern bindings.

*pattern* is identical in form to a **syntax-case** pattern. The value of each *val* is computed and destructured according to the corresponding *pattern*, and pattern variables within the *pattern* are bound as with **syntax-case** to appropriate portions of the value within $exp_1$ $exp_2$ ....

**with-syntax** may be defined as a syntactic extension in terms of **syntax-case**.

```
(define-syntax with-syntax
  (lambda (x)
    (syntax-case x ()
      ((_ ((p e0) ...) e1 e2 ...)
       (syntax (syntax-case (list e0 ...) ()
                 ((p ...) (begin e1 e2 ...)))))))))
```

The following definitions of full **cond** and **case** demonstrate the use of **with-syntax** to support transformers that employ recursion internally to construct their output.

```
(define-syntax cond
  (lambda (x)
    (syntax-case x ()
      ((_ c1 c2 ...)
       (let f ((c1 (syntax c1)) (cmore (syntax (c2 ...))))
         (if (null? cmore)
             (syntax-case c1 (else =>)
               ((else e1 e2 ...) (syntax (begin e1 e2 ...)))
               ((e0) (syntax (let ((t e0)) (if t t))))
               ((e0 => e1) (syntax (let ((t e0)) (if t (e1 t)))))
               ((e0 e1 e2 ...) (syntax (if e0 (begin e1 e2 ...)))))
             (with-syntax ((rest (f (car cmore) (cdr cmore))))
               (syntax-case c1 (=>)
                 ((e0) (syntax (let ((t e0)) (if t t rest))))
                 ((e0 => e1) (syntax (let ((t e0)) (if t (e1 t) rest))))
                 ((e0 e1 e2 ...)
                  (syntax (if e0 (begin e1 e2 ...) rest)))))))))))
```

```
(define-syntax case
  (lambda (x)
    (syntax-case x ()
      ((_ e c1 c2 ...)
       (with-syntax ((body
           (let f ((c1 (syntax c1)) (cmore (syntax (c2 ...))))
             (if (null? cmore)
                 (syntax-case c1 (else)
                   ((else e1 e2 ...) (syntax (begin e1 e2 ...)))
                   (((k ...) e1 e2 ...)
                    (syntax (if (memv t '(k ...)) (begin e1 e2 ...)))))
                 (with-syntax ((rest (f (car cmore) (cdr cmore))))
                   (syntax-case c1 ()
                     (((k ...) e1 e2 ...)
                      (syntax (if (memv t '(k ...))
                                  (begin e1 e2 ...)
                                  rest)))))))))
         (syntax (let ((t e)) body)))))))
```

(syntax-object->datum *obj*)                               **procedure**
**returns:** *obj* stripped of syntactic information

The procedure `syntax-object->datum` strips all syntactic information from a syntax object and returns the corresponding Scheme "datum." Identifiers stripped in this manner are converted to their symbolic names, which can then be compared with eq?. Thus, a predicate `symbolic-identifier=?` might be defined as follows.

```
(define symbolic-identifier=?
  (lambda (x y)
    (eq? (syntax-object->datum x)
         (syntax-object->datum y))))
```

Two identifiers that are `free-identifier=?` are `symbolic-identifier=?`; in order to refer to the same binding, two identifiers must have the same name. The converse is not always true, since two identifiers may have the same name but different bindings.

(datum->syntax-object *template-identifier obj*)            **procedure**
**returns:** a syntax object

`datum->syntax-object` constructs a syntax object from *obj* that contains the same contextual information as *template-identifier*, with the effect that the syntax object behaves as if it were introduced into the code when *template-identifier* was introduced. The template identifier is often the keyword of an input form, extracted from the form, and the object is often a symbol naming an identifier to be constructed.

`datum->syntax-object` allows a transformer to "bend" lexical scoping rules by creating *implicit identifiers* that behave as if they were present in the input form, thus permitting the definition of syntactic extensions that introduce visible bindings for or references to identifiers that do not appear explicitly in the input form. For example, we can define a `loop` expression that binds the variable `break` to an escape procedure within the loop body.

```
(define-syntax loop
  (lambda (x)
    (syntax-case x ()
      ((k e ...)
       (with-syntax ((break (datum->syntax-object (syntax k) 'break)))
         (syntax (call-with-current-continuation
                   (lambda (break)
                     (let f () e ... (f)))))))))))
(let ((n 3) (ls '()))
  (loop
    (if (= n 0) (break ls))
    (set! ls (cons 'a ls))
    (set! n (- n 1))))   ⇒   (a a a)
```

Were we to define `loop` as

```
(define-syntax loop
  (lambda (x)
    (syntax-case x ()
      ((_ e ...)
       (syntax (call-with-current-continuation
                 (lambda (break)
                   (let f () e ... (f)))))))))
```

the variable `break` would not be visible in `e` ....

It is also useful for *obj* to represent an arbitrary Scheme form, as demonstrated by the following definition of `include`, an expand-time version of `load`.

```
(define-syntax include
  (lambda (x)
    (define read-file
      (lambda (fn k)
        (let ((p (open-input-file fn)))
          (let f ((x (read p)))
            (if (eof-object? x)
                (begin (close-input-port p) '())
                (cons (datum->syntax-object k x)
                      (f (read p))))))))
```

```
(syntax-case x ()
  ((k filename)
   (let ((fn (syntax-object->datum (syntax filename))))
     (with-syntax (((exp ...) (read-file fn (syntax k))))
       (syntax (begin exp ...)))))))))
```

(include "filename") expands into a begin expression containing the forms found in the file named by "filename". For example, if the file f-def.ss contains the expression (define f (lambda () x)), the expression

```
(let ((x "okay"))
  (include "f-def.ss")
  (f))
```

evaluates to "okay".

The definition of include uses datum->syntax-object to convert the objects read from the file into syntax objects in the proper lexical context, so that identifier references and definitions within those expressions are scoped where the include form appears.

---

(generate-temporaries *list*)                                                  **procedure**
**returns:** a list of distinct generated identifiers

Transformers can introduce a fixed number of identifiers into their output by naming each identifier. In some cases, however, the number of identifiers to be introduced depends upon some characteristic of the input expression. A straightforward definition of letrec, for example, requires as many temporary identifiers as there are binding pairs in the input expression. The procedure generate-temporaries is used to construct lists of temporary identifiers.

*list* may be any list; its contents are not important. The number of temporaries generated is the number of elements in *list*. Each temporary is guaranteed to be different from all other identifiers.

A definition of letrec that uses generate-temporaries is shown below.

```
(define-syntax letrec
  (lambda (x)
    (syntax-case x ()
      ((_ ((i v) ...) e1 e2 ...)
       (with-syntax (((t ...) (generate-temporaries (syntax (i ...)))))
         (syntax (let ((i #f) ...)
                   (let ((t v) ...)
                     (set! i t) ...
                     (let () e1 e2 ...)))))))))
```

Any transformer that uses `generate-temporaries` in this fashion can be rewritten to avoid using it, albeit with a loss of clarity. The trick is to use a recursively defined intermediate form that generates one temporary per expansion step and completes the expansion after enough temporaries have been generated. Here is a definition of `let-values` (see page 115) that uses this technique to support multiple sets of bindings.

```
(define-syntax let-values
  (syntax-rules ()
    ((_ () f1 f2 ...) (let () f1 f2 ...))
    ((_ ((fmls1 expr1) (fmls2 expr2) ...) f1 f2 ...)
     (lvhelp fmls1 () () expr1 ((fmls2 expr2) ...) (f1 f2 ...)))))
(define-syntax lvhelp
  (syntax-rules ()
    ((_ (x1 . fmls) (x ...) (t ...) e m b)
     (lvhelp fmls (x ... x1) (t ... tmp) e m b))
    ((_ () (x ...) (t ...) e m b)
     (call-with-values
       (lambda () e)
       (lambda (t ...)
         (let-values m (let ((x t) ...) . b)))))
    ((_ xr (x ...) (t ...) e m b)
     (call-with-values
       (lambda () e)
       (lambda (t ... . tmpr)
         (let-values m (let ((x t) ... (xr tmpr)) . b)))))))
```

The implementation of `lvhelp` is complicated by the need to evaluate all of the right-hand-side expressions before creating any of the bindings and by the need to support improper formals lists.

A definition of `letrec` that does not use `generate-temporaries` is left as an exercise for the reader.

## 8.4. Examples

This section presents a series of illustrative syntactic extensions defined with either `syntax-rules` or `syntax-case`, starting with a few simple but useful syntactic extensions and ending with a fairly complex mechanism for defining structures with automatically generated constructors, predicates, field accessors, and field setters.

The simplest example in this section is the following definition of `rec`. `rec` is a syntactic extension that permits internally recursive anonymous (not externally named) procedures to be created with minimal effort.

```
(define-syntax rec
  (syntax-rules ()
    ((_ x e) (letrec ((x e)) x))))
(map (rec sum
        (lambda (x)
          (if (= x 0)
              0
              (+ x (sum (- x 1))))))
     '(0 1 2 3 4 5))  ⇒  (0 1 3 6 10 15)
```

Using **rec**, we can define the full **let** (both unnamed and named) as follows.

```
(define-syntax let
  (syntax-rules ()
    ((_ ((x v) ...) e1 e2 ...)
     ((lambda (x ...) e1 e2 ...) v ...))
    ((_ f ((x v) ...) e1 e2 ...)
     ((rec f (lambda (x ...) e1 e2 ...)) v ...))))
```

Of course, we can also define **let** directly in terms of **letrec**, although the definition is a bit less clear.

```
(define-syntax let
  (syntax-rules ()
    ((_ ((x v) ...) e1 e2 ...)
     ((lambda (x ...) e1 e2 ...) v ...))
    ((_ f ((x v) ...) e1 e2 ...)
     ((letrec ((f (lambda (x ...) e1 e2 ...))) f) v ...))))
```

These definitions rely upon the fact that the first pattern cannot match a named **let**, since the first subform of a named **let** must be an identifier, not a list of bindings. The following definition uses a fender to make this check more robust.

```
(define-syntax let
  (lambda (x)
    (syntax-case x ()
      ((_ ((x v) ...) e1 e2 ...)
       (syntax ((lambda (x ...) e1 e2 ...) v ...)))
      ((_ f ((x v) ...) e1 e2 ...)
       (identifier? (syntax f))
       (syntax ((rec f (lambda (x ...) e1 e2 ...)) v ...))))))
```

Of course, to be completely robust, the **ids?** and **all-ids?** checks employed in the definition of unnamed **let** in Section 8.3 should be employed here as well.

Both variants of **let** are easily described by simple one-line patterns, but **do** requires a bit more work. The precise syntax of **do** cannot be expressed directly with a single pattern because some of the bindings in a **do** expression's binding list may take

the form (var val) while others take the form (var val update). The following
definition of do uses syntax-case internally to parse the bindings separately from
the overall form.

```
(define-syntax do
  (lambda (x)
    (syntax-case x ()
      ((_ (binding ...) (test res ...) exp ...)
       (with-syntax ((((var val update) ...)
                      (map (lambda (b)
                             (syntax-case b ()
                               ((var val)
                                (syntax (var val var)))
                               ((var val update)
                                (syntax (var val update)))))
                           (syntax (binding ...)))))
         (syntax (let doloop ((var val) ...)
                   (if test
                       (begin (if #f #f) res ...)
                       (begin exp ... (doloop update ...)))))))))))
```

The odd looking expression (if #f #f) is inserted before the result expressions
res ... in case no result expressions are provided, since begin requires at least one
subexpression. The value of (if #f #f) is unspecified, which is what we want since
the value of do is unspecified if no result expressions are provided. At the expense
of a bit more code, we could use syntax-case to determine whether any result
expressions are provided and to produce a loop with either a one- or two-armed
if as appropriate. The resulting expansion would be cleaner but semantically
equivalent.

As mentioned in Section 8.2, ellipses lose their special meaning within templates
of the form (... template), This fact allows syntactic extensions to expand into
syntax definitions containing ellipses. This usage is illustrated by the definition
below of be-like-begin.

```
(define-syntax be-like-begin
  (syntax-rules ()
    ((_ name)
     (define-syntax name
       (syntax-rules ()
         ((_ e0 e1 (... ...))
          (begin e0 e1 (... ...))))))))
```

With be-like-begin defined in this manner, (be-like-begin sequence) has the
same effect as the following definition of sequence.

```
(define-syntax sequence
  (syntax-rules ()
    ((_ e0 e1 ...)
     (begin e0 e1 ...))))
```

That is, a `sequence` form becomes equivalent to a `begin` form so that, for example:

```
(sequence
  (display "Say what?")
  (newline))
```

prints "Say what?" followed by a newline.

The following example shows how one might restrict `if` expressions within a given expression to require the "else" (alternative) subexpression by defining the local `if` in terms of the top-level `if`.

```
(let-syntax ((if (lambda (x)
                   (syntax-case x ()
                     ((_ e1 e2 e3)
                      (syntax (if e1 e2 e3)))))))
  (if 1 2 3))  ⇒  2
(let-syntax ((if (lambda (x)
                   (syntax-case x ()
                     ((_ e1 e2 e3)
                      (syntax (if e1 e2 e3)))))))
  (if 1 2))  ⇒  error
```

Although this local definition of `if` looks simple enough, there are a few subtle ways in which an attempt to write it might go wrong. If `letrec-syntax` were used in place of `let-syntax`, the identifier `if` inserted into the output would refer to the local `if` rather than the top-level `if`, and expansion would loop indefinitely.

Similarly, if the underscore were replaced with the identifier `if`, expansion would again loop indefinitely. The `if` appearing in the template (if e1 e2 e3) would be treated as a pattern variable bound to the corresponding identifier `if` from the input form, which denotes the local version of `if`.

Placing `if` in the list of literals in an attempt to patch up the latter version would not work either. This would cause `syntax-case` to compare the literal `if` in the pattern, which would be scoped outside the `let-syntax` expression, with the `if` in the input expression, which would be scoped inside the `let-syntax`. Since they would not refer to the same binding, they would not be `free-identifier=?`, and a syntax error would result.

The conventional use of underscore ( _ ) helps the programmer avoid situations like these in which the wrong identifier is matched against or inserted by accident.

It is an error to generate a reference to an identifier that is not present within the context of an input form, which can happen if the "closest enclosing lexical binding" for an identifier inserted into the output of a transformer does not also enclose the input form. For example,

```
(let-syntax ((divide (lambda (x)
                       (let ((/ +))
                         (syntax-case x ()
                           ((_ e1 e2)
                            (syntax (/ e1 e2)))))))))
  (let ((/ *)) (divide 2 1)))
```

results in an error to the effect that / is referenced in an invalid context, since the occurrence of / in the output of divide is a reference to the variable / bound by the let expression within the transformer.

As noted in the description of identifier? in Section 8.3, singleton identifiers can be treated as syntactic extensions and expanded into arbitrary forms. Often, it is necessary to treat the case where an identifier appears in the first position of a structured expression differently from the case where it appears elsewhere, as in the pcar example given in the description for identifier?. In other situations, both cases must or may be treated the same. The form identifier-syntax defined below can make doing so more convenient.

```
(define-syntax identifier-syntax
  (lambda (x)
    (syntax-case x ()
      ((_ e)
       (syntax
         (lambda (x)
           (syntax-case x ()
             (id
              (identifier? (syntax id))
              (syntax e))
             ((id x (... ...))
              (identifier? (syntax id))
              (syntax (e x (... ...)))))))))))
(let ((x 0))
  (define-syntax x++
    (identifier-syntax
      (let ((t x)) (set! x (+ t 1)) t)))
  (let ((a x++))
    (list a x)))   ⇒   (0 1)
```

The following example uses `identifier-syntax`, `datum->syntax-object`, and local syntax definitions to define a form of *method*, one of the basic building blocks of object-oriented programming (OOP) systems. A `method` expression is similar to a `lambda` expression, except that in addition to the formal parameters and body, a `method` expression also contains a list of instance variables (`ivar ...`). When a method is invoked, it is always passed an *object* (*instance*), represented as a vector of *fields* corresponding to the instance variables, and zero or more additional arguments. Within the method body, the object is bound implicitly to the identifier `self` and the additional arguments are bound to the formal parameters. The fields of the object may be accessed or altered within the method body via instance variable references or assignments.

```
(define-syntax method
  (lambda (x)
    (syntax-case x ()
      ((k (ivar ...) formals e1 e2 ...)
       (with-syntax (((index ...)
                      (let f ((i 0) (ls (syntax (ivar ...))))
                        (if (null? ls)
                            '()
                            (cons i (f (+ i 1) (cdr ls))))))
                     (self (datum->syntax-object (syntax k) 'self))
                     (set! (datum->syntax-object (syntax k) 'set!)))
         (syntax
           (lambda (self . formals)
             (let-syntax ((ivar (identifier-syntax
                                   (vector-ref self index)))
                          ...)
               (let-syntax ((set! (syntax-rules (ivar ...)
                                    ((_ ivar e)
                                     (vector-set! self index e))
                                    ...
                                    ((_ x e) (set! x e)))))
                 e1 e2 ...)))))))))
```

Local bindings for `ivar ...` and for `set!` make the fields of the object appear to be ordinary variables, with references and assignments translated into calls to `vector-ref` and `vector-set!`. `datum->syntax-object` is used to make the introduced bindings of `self` and `set!` visible in the method body. Nested `let-syntax` expressions are needed so that the identifiers `ivar ...` serving as auxiliary keywords for the local version of `set!` are scoped properly. The examples below demonstrate simple uses of `method`.

```
(let ((m (method (a) (x) (list a x self))))
  (m #(1) 2))  ⇒  (1 2 #(1))
```

```
(let ((m (method (a) (x)
           (set! a x)
           (set! x (+ a x))
           (list a x self)))))
  (m #(1) 2))  ⇒  (2 4 #(2))
```

In a complete OOP system based on `method`, the instance variables `ivar` ... would likely be drawn from class declarations, not listed explicitly in the `method` forms, although the same techniques would be used to make instance variables appear as ordinary variables within method bodies.

The next example defines a `define-integrable` form that is similar to `define` for procedure definitions except that it causes the code for the procedure to be *integrated*, or inserted, wherever a direct call to the procedure is found. No semantic difference is visible between procedures defined with `define-integrable` and those defined with `define`, except that a top-level `define-integrable` form must appear before the first reference to the defined identifier, and syntactic extensions within the body of the defined procedure are expanded at the point of call. Lexical scoping is preserved, the actual parameters in an integrated call are evaluated once and at the proper time, integrable procedures may be used as first-class values, and recursive procedures do not cause indefinite recursive expansion.

A `define-integrable` has the following form.

(`define-integrable` *name lambda-expression*)

A `define-integrable` form expands into a pair of definitions: a syntax definition of *name* and a variable definition of a generated name, `residual-`*name*. The transformer for *name* converts apparent calls to *name* into direct calls to *lambda-expression*. Since the resulting forms are merely direct `lambda` applications (the equivalent of `let` expressions), the actual parameters are evaluated exactly once and before evaluation of the procedure's body, as required. All other references to *name* are replaced with references to `residual-`*name*. The definition of `residual-`*name* binds it to the value of *lambda-expression*. This allows the procedure to be used as a first-class value. Within *lambda-expression*, wherever it appears, *name* is rebound to a transformer that expands all references into references to `residual-`*name*. The use of `fluid-let-syntax` for this purpose prevents indefinite expansion from indirect recursion among integrable procedures. This allows the procedure to be recursive without causing indefinite expansion. Nothing special is done by `define-integrable` to maintain lexical scoping, since lexical scoping is maintained automatically by the expander.

```
(define-syntax define-integrable
  (lambda (x)
    (define make-residual-name
      (lambda (name)
        (datum->syntax-object name
          (string->symbol
            (string-append "residual-"
              (symbol->string (syntax-object->datum name)))))))
    (syntax-case x (lambda)
      ((_ name (lambda formals form1 form2 ...))
       (identifier? (syntax name))
       (with-syntax ((xname (make-residual-name (syntax name))))
         (syntax
           (begin
             (define-syntax name
               (lambda (x)
                 (syntax-case x ()
                   (_ (identifier? x) (syntax xname))
                   ((_ arg (... ...))
                    (syntax
                      ((fluid-let-syntax
                         ((name (identifier-syntax xname)))
                         (lambda formals form1 form2 ...))
                       arg (... ...)))))))
             (define xname
               (fluid-let-syntax ((name (identifier-syntax xname)))
                 (lambda formals form1 form2 ...)))))))))))
```

Some Scheme compilers integrate procedures automatically when it is appropriate
to do so. Compilers cannot normally integrate procedures bound at top-level, however, since code that assigns top-level variables can be introduced into the system
(via **eval** or **load**) at any time. **define-integrable** can be used to force the integration of procedures bound at top-level, even if the integration of locally bound
procedures is left to the compiler.

The final example of this section defines a simple structure definition facility that
represents structures as vectors with named fields. Structures are defined with
**define-structure**, which takes the form:

(define-structure *name field* ...)

where *name* names the structure and *field* ... names its fields. **define-structure**
expands into a series of generated definitions: a constructor **make-***name*, a type
predicate *name*?, and one accessor *name-field* and setter **set-***name-field*! per field
name.

```
(define-syntax define-structure
  (lambda (x)
    (define gen-id
      (lambda (template-id . args)
        (datum->syntax-object template-id
          (string->symbol
            (apply string-append
                   (map (lambda (x)
                          (if (string? x)
                              x
                              (symbol->string
                                (syntax-object->datum x))))
                        args))))))
    (syntax-case x ()
      ((_ name field ...)
       (with-syntax
         ((constructor (gen-id (syntax name) "make-" (syntax name)))
          (predicate (gen-id (syntax name) (syntax name) "?"))
          ((access ...)
           (map (lambda (x) (gen-id x (syntax name) "-" x))
                (syntax (field ...))))
          ((assign ...)
           (map (lambda (x) (gen-id x "set-" (syntax name) "-" x "!"))
                (syntax (field ...))))
          (structure-length (+ (length (syntax (field ...))) 1))
          ((index ...) (let f ((i 1) (ids (syntax (field ...))))
                         (if (null? ids)
                             '()
                             (cons i (f (+ i 1) (cdr ids)))))))
         (syntax (begin
                   (define constructor
                     (lambda (field ...)
                       (vector 'name field ...)))
                   (define predicate
                     (lambda (x)
                       (and (vector? x)
                            (= (vector-length x) structure-length)
                            (eq? (vector-ref x 0) 'name))))
                   (define access (lambda (x) (vector-ref x index))) ...
                   (define assign
                     (lambda (x update)
                       (vector-set! x index update)))
                   ...)))))))
```

The constructor accepts as many arguments as there are fields in the structure and creates a vector whose first element is the symbol *name* and whose remaining elements are the argument values. The type predicate returns true if its argument is a vector of the expected length whose first element is *name*.

Since a `define-structure` form expands into a `begin` containing definitions, it is itself a definition and can be used wherever definitions are valid.

The generated identifiers are created with `datum->syntax-object` to allow the identifiers to be visible where the `define-structure` form appears.

The examples below demonstrate the use of `define-structure`.

```
(define-structure tree left right)
(define t
  (make-tree
    (make-tree 0 1)
    (make-tree 2 3)))
t  ⇒  #(tree #(tree 0 1) #(tree 2 3))
(tree? t)  ⇒  #t
(tree-left t)  ⇒  #(tree 0 1)
(tree-right t)  ⇒  #(tree 2 3)
(set-tree-left! t 0)
t  ⇒  #(tree 0 #(tree 2 3))
```

Since the bodies of the generated procedures are short and simple, it may be desirable to use `define-integrable` as defined above in place of `define` for some or all of the generated procedure definitions.

# CHAPTER 9

# Extended Examples

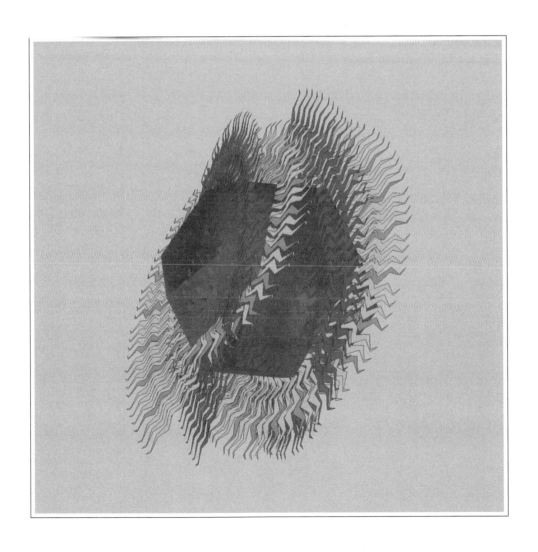

*Two warped, two-armed spirals and one polyhedron.*

This chapter presents a series of programs that perform more complicated tasks than most of the examples found throughout the earlier chapters of the book. They illustrate a variety of programming techniques and demonstrate a particular programming style.

Each section of this chapter describes one program in detail and gives examples of its use. This is followed by a listing of the code. At the end of each section are exercises intended to stimulate thought about the program and to suggest possible extensions. These exercises are generally more difficult than those found in Chapters 2 and 3, and a few are major projects.

Section 9.1 presents a simple matrix multiplication package. It demonstrates a set of procedures that could be written in almost any language. Its most interesting features are that all multiplication operations are performed by calling a single *generic* procedure, `mul`, which calls the appropriate help procedure depending upon the dimensions of its arguments, and that it dynamically allocates results of the proper size. Section 9.2 presents a useful merge sorting algorithm for ordering lists according to arbitrary predicates. Section 9.3 describes a syntactic form that is used to construct sets. It demonstrates a simple but efficient syntactic transformation from set notation to Scheme code. Section 9.4 presents a word counting program borrowed from *The C Programming Language* [15], translated from C into Scheme. It shows character and string manipulation, data structure creation and manipulation, and basic file input and output. Section 9.5 presents a basic Scheme printer that supports both `write` and `display` for all standard object types. Section 9.6 presents a simple formatted output facility similar to those found in many Scheme systems and in other languages. Section 9.7 presents a simple interpreter for Scheme that illustrates Scheme as a language implementation vehicle while giving an informal operational semantics for Scheme as well as a useful basis for investigating extensions to Scheme. Section 9.8 presents a small, extensible abstract object facility that could serve as the basis for an entire object-oriented subsystem. Section 9.9 presents a recursive algorithm for computing the Fourier transform of a sequence of input values. It highlights the use of Scheme's complex arithmetic. Section 9.10 presents a concise unification algorithm that shows how procedures can be used as continuations and as substitutions (unifiers) in Scheme. Section 9.11 describes a multitasking facility and its implementation in terms of continuations.

# 9.1. Matrix and Vector Multiplication

This example program involves mostly basic programming techniques. It demonstrates simple arithmetic and vector operations, looping with the `do` syntactic form, dispatching based on object type, and generating error messages.

Multiplication of scalar to scalar, scalar to matrix, or matrix to matrix is performed by a single *generic* procedure, called `mul`. `mul` is called with two arguments, and it decides based on the types of its arguments what operation to perform. Because scalar operations use Scheme's multiplication procedure, `*`, `mul` scalars can be any built-in numeric type (exact or inexact complex, real, rational, or integer).

The product of an $m \times n$ matrix $A$ and an $n \times p$ matrix $B$ is the $m \times p$ matrix $C$ whose entries are defined by

$$C_{ij} = \sum_{k=0}^{n-1} A_{ik} B_{kj}.$$

The product of a scalar $x$ and an $m \times n$ matrix $A$ is the $m \times n$ matrix $C$ whose entries are defined by the equation:

$$C_{ij} = x A_{ij}.$$

That is, each element of $C$ is the product of $x$ and the corresponding element of $A$. Vector-vector, vector-matrix, and matrix-vector multiplication may be considered special cases of matrix-matrix multiplication, where a vector is represented as a $1 \times n$ or $n \times 1$ matrix.

Here are a few examples, each preceded by the equivalent operation in standard mathematical notation.

- Scalar times scalar:

$$3 \times 4 = 12$$

```
(mul 3 4)   ⇒   12
```

- Scalar times vector ($1 \times 3$ matrix):

$$1/2 \times (1 \quad 2 \quad 3) = (1/2 \quad 1 \quad 3/2)$$

```
(mul 1/2 #(#(1 2 3)))   ⇒   #(#(1/2 1 3/2))
```

- Scalar times matrix:

$$-2 \times \begin{pmatrix} 3 & -2 & -1 \\ -3 & 0 & -5 \\ 7 & -1 & -1 \end{pmatrix} = \begin{pmatrix} -6 & 4 & 2 \\ 6 & 0 & 10 \\ -14 & 2 & 2 \end{pmatrix}$$

```
(mul -2
    #(#(3 -2 -1)
      #(-3 0 -5)
      #(7 -1 -1)))   ⇒   #(#(-6 4 2)
                            #(6 0 10)
                            #(-14 2 2))
```

- Vector times matrix:

$$(1 \quad 2 \quad 3) \times \begin{pmatrix} 2 & 3 \\ 3 & 4 \\ 4 & 5 \end{pmatrix} = (20 \quad 26)$$

```
(mul #(#(1 2 3))
     #(#(2 3)
       #(3 4)
       #(4 5)))   ⇒   #(#(20 26))
```

- Matrix times vector:

$$\begin{pmatrix} 2 & 3 & 4 \\ 3 & 4 & 5 \end{pmatrix} \times \begin{pmatrix} 1 \\ 2 \\ 3 \end{pmatrix} = \begin{pmatrix} 20 \\ 26 \end{pmatrix}$$

```
(mul #(#(2 3 4)
       #(3 4 5))
     #(#(1) #(2) #(3)))   ⇒   #(#(20) #(26))
```

- Matrix times matrix:

$$\begin{pmatrix} 1 & 2 & 3 \\ 4 & 5 & 6 \end{pmatrix} \times \begin{pmatrix} 1 & 2 & 3 & 4 \\ 2 & 3 & 4 & 5 \\ 3 & 4 & 5 & 6 \end{pmatrix} = \begin{pmatrix} 14 & 20 & 26 & 32 \\ 32 & 47 & 62 & 77 \end{pmatrix}$$

```
(mul #(#(1 2 3)
       #(4 5 6))
     #(#(1 2 3 4)
       #(2 3 4 5)
       #(3 4 5 6)))   ⇒   #(#(14 20 26 32)
                             #(32 47 62 77))
```

The code for mul and its helpers appears below. The first few definitions establish a set of procedures that support the matrix datatype. A matrix is a vector of vectors. Included are a procedure to create matrices, procedures to access and assign matrix elements, and a matrix predicate. Following these definitions is the definition of `mul` itself. Inside the `lambda` expression for `mul` are a set of definitions for help procedures that support `mul`.

   `mul` checks the types of its arguments and chooses the appropriate help procedure to do the work. Each helper operates on arguments of specific types. For example, `mat-sca-mul` multiplies a matrix by a scalar. If the type of either argument is invalid or the arguments are incompatible, e.g., rows or columns do not match up, `mul` or one of its helpers signals an error. Since no standard mechanism exists for signaling errors, we use the *Chez Scheme* `error` procedure briefly described in Section 2.7 to illustrate how errors might be reported.

```
;;; make-matrix creates a matrix (a vector of vectors).
(define make-matrix
  (lambda (rows columns)
    (do ((m (make-vector rows))
         (i 0 (+ i 1)))
        ((= i rows) m)
      (vector-set! m i (make-vector columns)))))

;;; matrix? checks to see if its argument is a matrix.
;;; It isn't foolproof, but it's generally good enough.
(define matrix?
  (lambda (x)
    (and (vector? x)
         (> (vector-length x) 0)
         (vector? (vector-ref x 0)))))

;; matrix-rows returns the number of rows in a matrix.
(define matrix-rows
  (lambda (x)
    (vector-length x)))

;; matrix-columns returns the number of columns in a matrix.
(define matrix-columns
  (lambda (x)
    (vector-length (vector-ref x 0))))

;;; matrix-ref returns the jth element of the ith row.
(define matrix-ref
  (lambda (m i j)
    (vector-ref (vector-ref m i) j)))

;;; matrix-set! changes the jth element of the ith row.
(define matrix-set!
  (lambda (m i j x)
    (vector-set! (vector-ref m i) j x)))
```

```
;;; mul is the generic matrix/scalar multiplication procedure
(define mul
  (lambda (x y)
    ;; mat-sca-mul multiplies a matrix by a scalar.
    (define mat-sca-mul
      (lambda (m x)
        (let* ((nr (matrix-rows m))
               (nc (matrix-columns m))
               (r  (make-matrix nr nc)))
          (do ((i 0 (+ i 1)))
              ((= i nr) r)
            (do ((j 0 (+ j 1)))
                ((= j nc))
              (matrix-set! r i j
                (* x (matrix-ref m i j)))))))
    ;; mat-mat-mul multiplies one matrix by another, after verifying
    ;; that the first matrix has as many columns as the second
    ;; matrix has rows.
    (define mat-mat-mul
      (lambda (m1 m2)
        (let* ((nr1 (matrix-rows m1))
               (nr2 (matrix-rows m2))
               (nc2 (matrix-columns m2))
               (r   (make-matrix nr1 nc2)))
          (if (not (= (matrix-columns m1) nr2))
              (match-error m1 m2))
          (do ((i 0 (+ i 1)))
              ((= i nr1) r)
            (do ((j 0 (+ j 1)))
                ((= j nc2))
              (do ((k 0 (+ k 1))
                   (a 0
                      (+ a
                         (* (matrix-ref m1 i k)
                            (matrix-ref m2 k j)))))
                  ((= k nr2)
                   (matrix-set! r i j a))))))))
    ;; type-error is called to complain when mul receives an invalid
    ;; type of argument.
    (define type-error
      (lambda (what)
        (error 'mul
          "~s is not a number or matrix"
          what)))
```

```
;; match-error is called to complain when mul receives a pair of
;; incompatible arguments.
(define match-error
   (lambda (what1 what2)
      (error 'mul
         "~s and ~s are incompatible operands"
         what1
         what2)))
;; body of mul; dispatch based on input types
(cond
   ((number? x)
    (cond
       ((number? y) (* x y))
       ((matrix? y) (mat-sca-mul y x))
       (else (type-error y))))
   ((matrix? x)
    (cond
       ((number? y) (mat-sca-mul x y))
       ((matrix? y) (mat-mat-mul x y))
       (else (type-error y))))
   (else (type-error x)))))
```

**Exercise 9.1.1.** Make the necessary changes to rename `mul` to `*`.

**Exercise 9.1.2.** The predicate `matrix?` is usually sufficient but not completely reliable, since it may return `#t` for objects that are not matrices. In particular, it does not verify that all of the matrix rows are vectors, that each row has the same number of elements, or that the elements themselves are numbers. Modify `matrix?` to perform each of these additional checks.

**Exercise 9.1.3.** Write similar generic procedures for addition and subtraction. Devise a generic `dispatch` procedure or syntactic form so that the type dispatching code need not be rewritten for each new operation.

**Exercise 9.1.4.** This version of `mul` uses vectors of vectors to represent matrices. Rewrite the system, using nested lists to represent matrices. What efficiency is gained or lost by this change?

# 9.2. Sorting

This section illustrates a list sorting algorithm based on a simple technique known as merge sorting. The procedure `sort` defined here accepts two arguments: a predicate and a list. It returns a list containing the elements of the old list sorted according to the predicate. The predicate should be a procedure that expects two arguments and returns #t if its first argument must precede its second in the sorted list and false otherwise. That is, if the predicate is applied to two elements $x$ and $y$, where $x$ appears after $y$ in the input list, it should return true only if $x$ should appear before $y$ in the output list. If this constraint is met, sort will perform a *stable sort*; with a stable sort, two elements that are already sorted with respect to each other will appear in the output in the same order in which they appeared in the input. Thus, sorting a list that is already sorted will result in no reordering, even if there are equivalent elements.

```
(sort < '(3 4 2 1 2 5))   ⇒   (1 2 2 3 4 5)
(sort > '(0.5 1/2))   ⇒   (0.5 1/2)
(sort > '(1/2 0.5))   ⇒   (1/2 0.5))
(list->string
  (sort char>?
        (string->list "coins")))   ⇒   "sonic"
```

A companion procedure, merge, is also defined by the code. merge accepts a predicate and two sorted lists and returns a merged list in sorted order of the elements of the two lists. With a properly defined predicate, merge is also stable in the sense that an item from the first list will appear before an item from the second list unless it is necessary that the item from the second list appear first.

```
(merge char<?
       '(#\a #\c)
       '(#\b #\c #\d))   ⇒   (#\a #\b #\c #\c #\d)
(merge <
       '(1/2 2/3 3/4)
       '(0.5 0.6 0.7))   ⇒   (1/2 0.5 0.6 2/3 0.7 3/4)
(list->string
  (merge char>?
    (string->list "old")
    (string->list "toe")))   ⇒   "tooled"
```

The merge sorting algorithm is simple and elegant. The input list is split into two approximately equal sublists. These sublists are sorted recursively, yielding two sorted lists. The sorted lists are then merged to form a single sorted list. The base case for the recursion is a list of one element, which is already sorted.

To reduce overhead, the implementation computes the length of the input list once, in sort, rather than at each step of the recursion, in dosort. This also allows dosort to isolate the first half of the list merely by halving the length, saving the cost of allocating a new list containing half of the elements. As a result, ls may contain more than n elements, but only the first n elements are considered part of the list.

```
(define sort #f)
(define merge #f)
(let ()
  (define dosort
    (lambda (pred? ls n)
      (if (= n 1)
          (list (car ls))
          (let ((i (quotient n 2)))
            (domerge pred?
                     (dosort pred? ls i)
                     (dosort pred? (list-tail ls i) (- n i)))))))
  (define domerge
    (lambda (pred? l1 l2)
      (cond
        ((null? l1) l2)
        ((null? l2) l1)
        ((pred? (car l2) (car l1))
         (cons (car l2) (domerge pred? l1 (cdr l2))))
        (else (cons (car l1) (domerge pred? (cdr l1) l2))))))
  (set! sort
    (lambda (pred? l)
      (if (null? l) l (dosort pred? l (length l)))))
  (set! merge
    (lambda (pred? l1 l2)
      (domerge pred? l1 l2))))
```

**Exercise 9.2.1.** In `dosort`, when n is 1, why is `(list (car ls))` returned instead of just `ls`? How much allocation would be saved overall by replacing `(list (car ls))` with `(if (null? (cdr ls)) ls (list (car ls)))`?

**Exercise 9.2.2.** How much work is actually saved by not copying the first part of the input list when splitting it in `dosort`?

**Exercise 9.2.3.** All or nearly all allocation could be saved if the algorithm were to work destructively, using `set-cdr!` to separate and join lists. Write destructive versions `sort!` and `merge!` of the `sort` and `merge`. Determine the difference between the two sets of procedures in terms of allocation and run time for various inputs.

## 9.3. A Set Constructor

This example describes a syntactic extension, `set-of`, that allows the construction of sets represented as lists with no repeated elements [17]. It uses `define-syntax` and `syntax-rules` to compile set expressions into recursion expressions. The expanded code is often as efficient as that which can be produced by hand.

A `set-of` expression takes the following form.

```
(set-of value exp ...)
```

*value* describes the elements of the set in terms of the bindings established by the expressions *exp* .... Each of the expressions *exp* ... can take one of three forms:

1. An expression of the form ($x$ `in` $s$) establishes a binding for $x$ to each element of the set $s$ in turn. This binding is visible within the remaining expressions *exp* ... and the expression *value*.

2. An expression of the form ($x$ `is` $e$) establishes a binding for $x$ to $e$. This binding is visible within the remaining expressions *exp* ... and the expression *value*. This form is essentially an abbreviation for ($x$ `in` (`list` $e$)).

3. An expression taking any other form is treated as a predicate; this is used to force refusal of certain elements as in the second of the examples below.

```
(set-of x
  (x in '(a b c)))  ⇒  (a b c)
(set-of x
  (x in '(1 2 3 4))
  (even? x))  ⇒  (2 4)
(set-of (cons x y)
  (x in '(1 2 3))
  (y is (* x x)))  ⇒  ((1 . 1) (2 . 4) (3 . 9))

(set-of (cons x y)
  (x in '(a b))
  (y in '(1 2)))  ⇒  ((a . 1) (a . 2) (b . 1) (b . 2))
```

A `set-of` expression is transformed into nested `let`, named `let`, and `if` expressions, corresponding to each `is`, `in`, or predicate subexpression. For example, the simple expression

```
(set-of x (x in '(a b c)))
```

is transformed into

```
(let loop ((set '(a b c)))
  (if (null? set)
      '()
      (let ((x (car set)))
        (set-cons x (loop (cdr set))))))
```

The expression

```
(set-of x (x in '(1 2 3 4)) (even? x))
```

is transformed into

```
(let loop ((set '(1 2 3 4)))
  (if (null? set)
      '()
      (let ((x (car set)))
        (if (even? x)
            (set-cons x (loop (cdr set)))
            (loop (cdr set))))))
```

The more complicated expression

```
(set-of (cons x y) (x in '(1 2 3)) (y is (* x x)))
```

is transformed into

```
(let loop ((set '(1 2 3)))
  (if (null? set)
      '()
      (let ((x (car set)))
        (let ((y (* x x)))
          (set-cons (cons x y)
                    (loop (cdr set)))))))
```

Finally, the expression

```
(set-of (cons x y) (x in '(a b)) (y in '(1 2)))
```

is transformed into nested named `let` expressions:

```
(let loop1 ((set1 '(a b)))
  (if (null? set1)
      '()
      (let ((x (car set1)))
        (let loop2 ((set2 '(1 2)))
          (if (null? set2)
              (loop1 (cdr set1))
              (let ((y (car set2)))
                (set-cons (cons x y)
                          (loop2 (cdr set2)))))))))
```

These are fairly straightforward transformations, except that the base case for the recursion on nested named `let` expressions varies depending upon the level. The base case for the outermost named `let` is always the empty list (), while the base case for an internal named `let` is the recursion step for the next outer named `let`. In order to handle this, the definition of `set-of` employs a help syntactic extension `set-of-help`. `set-of-help` takes an additional expression, `base`, which is the base case for recursion at the current level.

```
;;; set-of uses helper syntactic extension set-of-help, passing it
;;; an initial base expression of '()
(define-syntax set-of
  (syntax-rules ()
    ((_ e m ...)
     (set-of-help e '() m ...))))
```

```
;;; set-of-help recognizes in, is, and predicate expressions and
;;; changes them into nested named let, let, and if expressions.
(define-syntax set-of-help
  (syntax-rules (in is)
    ((_ e base)
     (set-cons e base))
    ((_ e base (x in s) m ...)
     (let loop ((set s))
       (if (null? set)
           base
           (let ((x (car set)))
             (set-of-help e (loop (cdr set)) m ...)))))
    ((_ e base (x is y) m ...)
     (let ((x y)) (set-of-help e base m ...)))
    ((_ e base p m ...)
     (if p (set-of-help e base m ...) base))))
```

```
;;; set-cons returns the original set y if x is already in y.
(define set-cons
  (lambda (x y)
    (if (memv x y)
        y
        (cons x y))))
```

**Exercise 9.3.1.** Write a procedure, union, that takes an arbitrary number of sets (lists) as arguments and returns the union of the sets, using only the set-of syntactic form. For example:

```
(union)  ⇒  ()
(union '(a b c))  ⇒  (a b c)
(union '(2 5 4) '(9 4 3))  ⇒  (2 5 9 4 3)
(union '(1 2) '(2 4) '(4 8))  ⇒  (1 2 4 8)
```

**Exercise 9.3.2.** A single-list version of map can (almost) be defined as follows.

```
(define map1
  (lambda (f ls)
    (set-of (f x) (x in ls))))
```

```
(map1 - '(1 2 3 2))   ⇒   (-1 -3 -2)
```

Why does this not work? What could be changed to make it work?

**Exercise 9.3.3.** Devise a different definition of `set-cons` that maintains sets in some sorted order, making the test for set membership, and hence `set-cons` itself, potentially more efficient.

# 9.4. Word Frequency Counting

This program demonstrates several basic programming techniques, including string and character manipulation, file input/output, data structure manipulation, and recursion. The program is adapted from Chapter 6 of *The C Programming Language* [15]. One reason for using this particular example is to show how a C program might look when converted almost literally into Scheme.

A few differences between the Scheme program and the original C program are worth noting. First, the Scheme version employs a different protocol for file input and output. Rather than implicitly using the standard input and output ports, it requires that filenames be passed in, thus demonstrating the opening and closing of files. Second, the procedure `get-word` returns one of three values: a string (the word), a nonalphabetic character, or an eof value. The original C version returned a flag for letter (to say that a word was read) or a nonalphabetic character. Furthermore, the C version passed in a string to fill and a limit on the number of characters in the string; the Scheme version builds a new string of whatever length is required (the characters in the word are held in a list until the end of the word has been found, then converted into a string with `list->string`). Finally, `char-type` uses the primitive Scheme character predicates `char-alphabetic?` and `char-numeric?` to determine whether a character is a letter or digit.

The main program, `frequency`, takes an input filename and an output filename as arguments, e.g., (`frequency "pickle" "freq.out"`) prints the frequency count for each word in the file "pickle" to the file "freq.out." As `frequency` reads words from the input file, it inserts them into a binary tree structure (using a binary sorting algorithm). Duplicate entries are recorded by incrementing the count associated with each word. Once end of file is reached, the program traverses the tree, printing each word with its count.

Assume that the file "pickle" contains the following text.

```
Peter Piper picked a peck of pickled peppers;
A peck of pickled peppers Peter Piper picked.
If Peter Piper picked a peck of pickled peppers,
Where's the peck of pickled peppers Peter Piper picked?
```

Then, after typing (frequency "pickle" "freq.out"), the file "freq.out" should
contain the following.

```
1 A
1 If
4 Peter
4 Piper
1 Where
2 a
4 of
4 peck
4 peppers
4 picked
4 pickled
1 s
1 the
```

(On some systems, the capitalized words may appear after the others.)

---

```
;;; If the next character on p is a letter, get-word reads a word
;;; from p and returns it in a string.  If the character is not a
;;; letter, get-word returns the character (on eof, the eof-object).
(define get-word
  (lambda (p)
    (let ((c (read-char p)))
      (if (eq? (char-type c) 'letter)
          (list->string
            (let loop ((c c))
              (cons c
                (if (memq (char-type (peek-char p)) '(letter digit))
                    (loop (read-char p))
                    '()))))
          c))))

;;; char-type tests for the eof-object first, since the eof-object
;;; may not be a valid argument to char-alphabetic? or char-numeric?
;;; It returns the eof-object, the symbol letter, the symbol digit,
;;; or the argument itself if it is not a letter or digit.
(define char-type
  (lambda (c)
    (cond
      ((eof-object? c) c)
      ((char-alphabetic? c) 'letter)
      ((char-numeric? c) 'digit)
      (else c))))
```

```
;;; Trees are represented as vectors with four fields: word, left,
;;; right, and count. Only one field, word, is initialized by an
;;; argument to the constructor procedure make-tree. The remaining
;;; fields are explicitly initialized and changed by subsequent
;;; operations. Most Scheme systems provide structure definition
;;; facilities that automate creation of structure manipulation
;;; procedures, but we simply define the procedures by hand here.
(define make-tree
  (lambda (word)
    (vector word '() '() 1)))

(define tree-word (lambda (tree) (vector-ref tree 0)))

(define tree-left (lambda (tree) (vector-ref tree 1)))
(define set-tree-left!
  (lambda (tree new-left)
    (vector-set! tree 1 new-left)))

(define tree-right (lambda (tree) (vector-ref tree 2)))
(define set-tree-right!
  (lambda (tree new-right)
    (vector-set! tree 2 new-right)))

(define tree-count (lambda (tree) (vector-ref tree 3)))
(define set-tree-count!
  (lambda (tree new-count)
    (vector-set! tree 3 new-count)))

;;; If the word already exists in the tree, tree increments its
;;; count. Otherwise, a new tree node is created and put into the
;;; tree. In any case, the new or modified tree is returned.
(define tree
  (lambda (node word)
    (cond
      ((null? node) (make-tree word))
      ((string=? word (tree-word node))
       (set-tree-count! node (+ (tree-count node) 1))
       node)
      ((string<? word (tree-word node))
       (set-tree-left! node (tree (tree-left node) word))
       node)
      (else
       (set-tree-right! node (tree (tree-right node) word))
       node))))
```

```
;;; tree-print prints the tree in "in-order," i.e., left subtree,
;;; then node, then right subtree.  For each word, the count and the
;;; word are printed on a single line.
(define tree-print
  (lambda (node p)
    (if (not (null? node))
        (begin
          (tree-print (tree-left node) p)
          (write (tree-count node) p)
          (write-char #\space p)
          (display (tree-word node) p)
          (newline p)
          (tree-print (tree-right node) p)))))
;;; frequency is the driver routine.  It opens the files, reads the
;;; words, and enters them into the tree.  When the input port
;;; reaches end-of-file, it prints the tree and closes the ports.
(define frequency
  (lambda (infn outfn)
    (let ((ip (open-input-file infn))
          (op (open-output-file outfn)))
      (let loop ((root '()))
        (let ((w (get-word ip)))
          (cond
            ((eof-object? w) (tree-print root op))
            ((string? w) (loop (tree root w)))
            (else (loop root)))))
      (close-input-port ip)
      (close-output-port op))))
```

**Exercise 9.4.1.** Replace the procedures used to implement the tree datatype with a record or structure definition, using the facilities provided by the Scheme system you are using or define-structure from Section 8.4.

**Exercise 9.4.2.** In the output file shown earlier, the capitalized words appeared before the others in the output file, and the capital A was not recognized as the same word as the lower-case a. Modify tree to use the case-insensitive versions of the string comparisons so that this does not happen.

**Exercise 9.4.3.** The "word" s appears in the file "freq.out," although it is really just a part of the contraction Where's. Adjust get-word to allow embedded single quote marks.

**Exercise 9.4.4.** Modify this program to "weed out" certain common words such as a, an, the, is, of, etc., in order to reduce the amount of output for long input files. Try to devise other ways to cut down on useless output.

**Exercise 9.4.5.** get-word buffers characters in a list, allocating a new pair (with cons) for each character. Make it more efficient by using a string to buffer the characters. Devise a way to allow the string to grow if necessary. [*Hint*: Use string-append.]

**Exercise 9.4.6.** This tree algorithm works by creating trees and later filling in its left and right fields. This requires many unnecessary assignments. Rewrite the tree procedure to avoid set-tree-left! and set-tree-right! entirely.

# 9.5. Scheme Printer

Printing Scheme objects may seem like a complicated process, but in fact a rudimentary printer is quite straightforward, as this example demonstrates. Both write and display are supported by the same code. Sophisticated Scheme implementations often support various printer controls and handle printing of cyclic objects, but the one given here is completely basic.

The main driver for the program is a procedure wr, which takes an object to print x, a flag d?, and a port p. The flag d? is #t if the code is to *display* the object, #f if it is to *write* the object. The d? flag is important only for characters and strings. Recall from Section 7.2 that display prints strings without the enclosing quote marks and characters without the #\ syntax.

The entry points write and display handle the optionality of the second (port) argument, passing the value of current-output-port when no port argument is provided.

Procedures, ports, and end-of-file objects are printed as #<procedure>, #<port>, and #<eof>. The tests for the end-of-file objects and ports are made early, since implementations are permitted to implement these object types as special cases of other object types. Objects of types not recognized by the printer are printed as #<unknown>; this can occur if the Scheme implementation provides extensions to the standard set of object types.

The code follows the module structure outlined in Section 3.5.

```
(define write #f)
(define display #f)
```

```
(let ()
  ;; wr is the driver, dispatching on the type of x
  (define wr
    (lambda (x d? p)
      (cond
        ((eof-object? x) (write-string "#<eof>" p))
        ((port? x) (write-string "#<port>" p))
        ((symbol? x) (write-string (symbol->string x) p))
        ((pair? x) (wrpair x d? p))
        ((number? x) (write-string (number->string x) p))
        ((null? x) (write-string "()" p))
        ((boolean? x) (write-string (if x "#t" "#f") p))
        ((char? x) (if d? (write-char x p) (wrchar x p)))
        ((string? x) (if d? (write-string x p) (wrstring x p)))
        ((vector? x) (wrvector x d? p))
        ((procedure? x) (write-string "#<procedure>" p))
        (else (write-string "#<unknown>" p)))))

  ;; write-string writes each character of s to p
  (define write-string
    (lambda (s p)
      (let ((n (string-length s)))
        (do ((i 0 (+ i 1)))
            ((= i n))
          (write-char (string-ref s i) p)))))

  ;; wrpair handles pairs and nonempty lists
  (define wrpair
    (lambda (x d? p)
      (write-char #\( p)
      (let loop ((x x))
        (wr (car x) d? p)
        (cond
          ((pair? (cdr x))
           (write-char #\space p)
           (loop (cdr x)))
          ((null? (cdr x)))
          (else
           (write-string " . " p)
           (wr (cdr x) d? p))))
      (write-char #\) p)))
```

```
;; wrchar handles characters, recognizing and printing the
;; special syntaxes for #\space and #\newline.  Used only when
;; d? is #f.
(define wrchar
  (lambda (x p)
    (case x
      ((#\newline) (write-string "#\\newline" p))
      ((#\space) (write-string "#\\space" p))
      (else (write-string "#\\" p)
            (write-char x p)))))

;; wrstring handles strings, inserting slashes where
;; necessary.  Used only when d? is #f.
(define wrstring
  (lambda (x p)
    (write-char #\" p)
    (let ((n (string-length x)))
      (do ((i 0 (+ i 1)))
          ((= i n))
          (let ((c (string-ref x i)))
            (if (or (char=? c #\") (char=? c #\\))
                (write-char #\\ p))
            (write-char c p))))
    (write-char #\" p)))

;; wrvector handles vectors
(define wrvector
  (lambda (x d? p)
    (write-string "#(" p)
    (let ((size (vector-length x)))
      (if (not (= size 0))
          (let ((last (- size 1)))
            (let loop ((i 0))
              (wr (vector-ref x i) d? p)
              (if (not (= i last))
                  (begin
                    (write-char #\space p)
                    (loop (+ i 1))))))))
    (write-char #\) p)))

;; write calls wr with d? set to #f
(set! write
  (lambda (x . rest)
    (if (null? rest)
        (wr x #f (current-output-port))
        (wr x #f (car rest)))))
```

```
;; display calls wr with d? set to #t
(set! display
  (lambda (x . rest)
    (if (null? rest)
        (wr x #t (current-output-port))
        (wr x #t (car rest)))))))
```

**Exercise 9.5.1.** Numbers are printed with the help of `number->string`. Correct printing of all Scheme numeric types, especially inexact numbers, is a complicated task. Handling exact integers and rational numbers is fairly straightforward, however. Modify the code to print exact integers and rational numbers directly (without `number->string`), but continue to use `number->string` for inexact and complex numbers.

**Exercise 9.5.2.** Modify `wr` and its helpers to direct their output to an internal buffer rather than to a port. Use the modified versions to implement a procedure `object->string` that, like `number->string`, returns a string containing a printed representation of its input. For example:

```
(object->string '(a b c))  ⇒  "(a b c)"
(object->string "hello")   ⇒  "\"hello\""
```

You may be surprised just how easy this change is to make.

## 9.6. Formatted Output

It is often necessary to print strings containing the printed representations of Scheme objects, especially numbers. Doing so with Scheme's standard output routines can be tedious. For example, the `tree-print` procedure of Section 9.4 requires a sequence of four calls to output routines to print a simple one-line message:

```
(write (tree-count node) p)
(write-char #\space p)
(display (tree-word node) p)
(newline p)
```

The formatted output facility defined in this section allows these four calls to be replaced by the single call to `fprintf` below.

```
(fprintf p "~s ~a~%" (tree-count node) (tree-word node))
```

`fprintf` expects a port argument, a *control string*, and an indefinite number of additional arguments that are inserted into the output as specified by the control string. In the example, the value of `(tree-count node)` is written first, in place of `~s`. This is followed by a space and the displayed value of `(tree-word node)`, in place of `~a`. The `~%` is replaced in the output with a newline.

.

The procedure `printf`, also defined in this section, is like `fprintf` except that no port argument is expected and output is sent to the current output port.

~s, ~a, and ~% are *format directives*; ~s causes the first unused argument after the control string to be printed to the output via `write`, ~a causes the first unused argument to be printed via `display`, and ~% simply causes a newline character to be printed. The simple implementation of `fprintf` below recognizes only one other format directive, ~~, which inserts a tilde into the output. For example,

```
(printf "The string ~s displays as ~~.~%" "~")
```

prints

```
The string "~" displays as ~.
```

---

```
(let ()
  ;; dofmt does all of the work.  It loops through the control string
  ;; recognizing format directives and printing all other characters
  ;; without interpretation.  A tilde at the end of a control string is
  ;; treated as an ordinary character.  No checks are made for proper
  ;; inputs.  Directives may be given in either lower or upper case.
  (define dofmt
    (lambda (p cntl args)
      (let ((nmax (- (string-length cntl) 1)))
        (let loop ((n 0) (a args))
          (if (<= n nmax)
              (let ((c (string-ref cntl n)))
                (if (and (char=? c #\~) (< n nmax))
                    (case (string-ref cntl (+ n 1))
                      ((#\a #\A)
                       (display (car a) p)
                       (loop (+ n 2) (cdr a)))
                      ((#\s #\S)
                       (write (car a) p)
                       (loop (+ n 2) (cdr a)))
                      ((#\%)
                       (newline p)
                       (loop (+ n 2) a))
                      ((#\~)
                       (write-char #\~ p)
                       (loop (+ n 2) a))
                      (else
                       (write-char c p)
                       (loop (+ n 1) a)))
                    (begin
                      (write-char c p)
                      (loop (+ n 1) a)))))))))
```

```
;; printf and fprintf differ only in that fprintf passes its
;; port argument to dofmt while printf passes the current output
;; port.
(set! printf
  (lambda (control . args)
    (dofmt (current-output-port) control args)))
(set! fprintf
  (lambda (p control . args)
    (dofmt p control args))))
```

**Exercise 9.6.1.** Using the optional radix argument to `number->string`, augment `printf` and `fprintf` with support for the following new format directives:

 a. ~b or ~B: print the next unused argument, which must be a number, in binary;

 b. ~o or ~O: print the next unused argument, which must be a number, in octal; and

 c. ~x or ~X: print the next unused argument, which must be a number, in hexadecimal.

For example:

```
(printf "#x~x #o~o #b~b~%" 16 8 2)
```

would print

```
#x10 #o10 #b10
```

**Exercise 9.6.2.** Add an "indirect" format directive, ~@, that treats the next unused argument, which must be a string, as if it were spliced into the current format string. For example:

```
(printf "--- ~@ ---" "> ~s <" '(a b c))
```

would print

```
---> (a b c) <---
```

**Exercise 9.6.3.** Implement `format`, a version of `fprintf` that places its output into a string instead of writing to a port. Make use of `object->string` from Exercise 9.5.2 to support the ~s and ~a directives.

```
(let ((x 3) (y 4))
  (format "~s + ~s = ~s" x y (+ x y)))  ⇒  "3 + 4 = 7"
```

**Exercise 9.6.4.** Modify `format`, `fprintf`, and `printf` to allow a field size to be specified after the tilde in the ~a and ~s format directives. For example, the directive

~10s would cause the next unused argument to be inserted into the output left-justified in a field of size 10. If the object requires more spaces than the amount specified, allow it to extend beyond the field.

```
(let ((x 'abc) (y '(def)))
  (format "(cons '~5s '~5s) = ~5s"
    x y (cons x y)))  ⇒  "(cons 'abc   '(def)) = (abc def)"
```

[*Hint*: Use format recursively.]

## 9.7. A Meta-Circular Interpreter for Scheme

The program described in this section is a *meta-circular* interpreter for Scheme, i.e., it is an interpreter *for* Scheme written *in* Scheme. The interpreter shows how small Scheme is when the core structure is considered independently from its syntactic extensions and primitives. It also illustrates interpretation techniques that can be applied equally well to languages other than Scheme.

The relative simplicity of the interpreter is somewhat misleading. An interpreter for Scheme written in Scheme can be quite a bit simpler than one written in most other languages. Here are a few reasons why this one is simpler.

- Tail calls are handled properly only because tail calls in the interpreter are handled properly by the host implementation. All that is required is that the interpreter itself be tail-recursive.

- First-class procedures in interpreted code are implemented by first-class procedures in the interpreter, which in turn are supported by the host implementation.

- First-class continuations created with call/cc are provided by the host implementation's call/cc.

- Primitive procedures such as cons and assq and services such as storage management are provided by the host implementation.

Converting the interpreter to run in a language other than Scheme may require explicit support for some or all of these items.

The interpreter stores lexical bindings in an *environment*, which is simply an *association list* (see page 6.3). Evaluation of a lambda expression results in the creation of a procedure within the scope of variables holding the environment and the lambda body. Subsequent application of the procedure combines the new bindings (the actual parameters) with the saved environment.

The interpreter handles only the core syntactic forms described in Section 3.1, and it recognizes bindings for only a handful of primitive procedures. It performs no error checking.

```
(interpret 3)  ⇒  3
```

```
(interpret '(cons 3 4))  ⇒  (3 . 4)
(interpret
  '((lambda (x . y)
      (list x y))
    'a 'b 'c 'd))  ⇒  (a (b c d))
(interpret
  '(((call/cc (lambda (k) k))
     (lambda (x) x))
    "HEY!"))  ⇒  "HEY!"
(interpret
  '((lambda (memq)
      (memq memq 'a '(b c a d e)))
    (lambda (memq x ls)
      (if (null? ls) #f
          (if (eq? (car ls) x)
              ls
              (memq memq x (cdr ls)))))))  ⇒  (a d e)
(interpret
  '((lambda (reverse)
      (set! reverse
        (lambda (ls new)
          (if (null? ls)
              new
              (reverse (cdr ls) (cons (car ls) new)))))
      (reverse '(a b c d e) '()))
   #f))  ⇒  (e d c b a)
```

---

```
(define interpret #f)
(let ()
  ;; primitive-environment contains a small number of primitive
  ;; procedures; it can be extended easily with additional primitives.
  (define primitive-environment
    `((apply . ,apply) (assq . ,assq) (call/cc . ,call/cc)
         (car . ,car) (cadr . ,cadr) (caddr . ,caddr)
         (cadddr . ,cadddr) (cddr . ,cddr) (cdr . ,cdr)
         (cons . ,cons) (eq? . ,eq?) (list . ,list)
         (map . ,map) (memv . ,memv) (null? . ,null?)
         (pair? . ,pair?) (read . ,read) (set-car! . ,set-car!)
         (set-cdr! . ,set-cdr!) (symbol? . ,symbol?)))
```

```scheme
;; new-env returns a new environment from a formal parameter
;; specification, a list of actual parameters, and an outer
;; environment.  The symbol? test identifies "improper"
;; argument lists.  Environments are association lists,
;; associating variables with values.
(define new-env
  (lambda (formals actuals env)
    (cond
      ((null? formals) env)
      ((symbol? formals) (cons (cons formals actuals) env))
      (else
       (cons (cons (car formals) (car actuals))
             (new-env (cdr formals) (cdr actuals) env))))))

;; lookup finds the value of the variable var in the environment
;; env, using assq.  Assumes var is bound in env.
(define lookup
  (lambda (var env)
    (cdr (assq var env))))

;; assign is similar to lookup but alters the binding of the
;; variable var by changing the cdr of the association pair
(define assign
  (lambda (var val env)
    (set-cdr! (assq var env) val)))

;; exec evaluates the expression, recognizing all core forms.
(define exec
  (lambda (exp env)
    (cond
      ((symbol? exp) (lookup exp env))
      ((pair? exp)
       (case (car exp)
         ((quote) (cadr exp))
         ((lambda)
          (lambda vals
            (let ((env (new-env (cadr exp) vals env)))
              (let loop ((exps (cddr exp)))
                (if (null? (cdr exps))
                    (exec (car exps) env)
                    (begin
                      (exec (car exps) env)
                      (loop (cdr exps))))))))
         ((if)
          (if (exec (cadr exp) env)
              (exec (caddr exp) env)
              (exec (cadddr exp) env)))
```

```
        ((set!)
         (assign (cadr exp)
                 (exec (caddr exp) env)
                 env))
        (else
         (apply (exec (car exp) env)
                (map (lambda (x) (exec x env))
                     (cdr exp))))))
      (else exp))))
;; interpret starts execution with the primitive environment.
(set! interpret
  (lambda (exp)
    (exec exp  primitive-environment)))))
```

**Exercise 9.7.1.** As written, the interpreter cannot interpret itself because it does not support several of the syntactic forms used in its implementation: `let` (named and unnamed), internal `define`, `case`, `cond`, and `begin`. Rewrite the code for the interpreter, using only core syntactic forms.

**Exercise 9.7.2.** After completing the preceding exercise, use the interpreter to run a copy of the interpreter, and use the copy to run another copy of the interpreter. Repeat this process to see how many levels deep it will go before the system grinds to a halt.

**Exercise 9.7.3.** At first glance, it might seem that the `lambda` case could be written more simply as follows.

```
((lambda)
 (lambda vals
   (let ((env (new-env (cadr exp) vals env)))
     (let loop ((exps (cddr exp)))
       (let ((val (exec (car exps) env)))
         (if (null? (cdr exps))
             val
             (loop (cdr exps))))))))
```

Why would this be incorrect? [*Hint*: What property of Scheme would be violated?]

**Exercise 9.7.4.** Try to make the interpreter more efficient by looking for ways to ask fewer questions or to allocate less storage space. [*Hint*: Before evaluation, convert lexical variable references into (`access` $n$), where $n$ represents the number of values in the environment association list in front of the value in question.]

**Exercise 9.7.5.** Scheme evaluates arguments to a procedure before applying the procedure and applies the procedure to the values of these arguments (*call-by-*

*value*). Modify the interpreter to pass arguments unevaluated and arrange to evaluate them upon reference (*call-by-name*). [*Hint*: Use `lambda` to delay evaluation.] You will need to create versions of the primitive procedures (`car`, `null?`, etc.) that take their arguments unevaluated.

## 9.8. Defining Abstract Objects

This example demonstrates a syntactic extension that facilitates the definition of simple abstract objects (see Section 2.9). This facility has unlimited potential as the basis for a complete object-oriented subsystem in Scheme.

Abstract objects are similar to basic data structures such as pairs and vectors. Rather than being manipulated via access and assignment operators, however, abstract objects respond to *messages*. The valid messages and the actions to be taken for each message are defined by code within the object itself rather than by code outside the object, resulting in more modular and potentially more secure programming systems. The data local to an abstract object is accessible only through the actions performed by the object in response to the messages.

A particular type of abstract object is defined with `define-object`, which has the general form

```
(define-object (name var₁ ...)
  ((var₂ val) ...)
  ((msg action) ...))
```

The first set of bindings ((*var₂ val*) ...) may be omitted. `define-object` defines a procedure that is called to create new abstract objects of the given type. This procedure is called *name*, and the arguments to this procedure become the values of the local variables *var₁* .... After the procedure is invoked, the variables *var₂* ... are bound to the values *val* ... in sequence (as with `let*`) and the messages *msg* ... are bound to the procedure values *action* ... in a mutually recursive fashion (as with `letrec`). Within these bindings, the new abstract object is created; this object is the value of the creation procedure.

The syntactic form `send-message` is used to send messages to abstract objects. (`send-message` *object msg arg* ...) sends *object* the message *msg* with arguments *arg* .... When an object receives a message, the *arg* ... become the parameters to the action procedure associated with the message, and the value returned by this procedure is returned by `send-message`.

The following examples should help to clarify how abstract objects are defined and used. The first example is a simple `kons` object that is similar to Scheme's built-in pair object type, except that to access or assign its fields requires sending it messages.

```
(define-object (kons kar kdr)
  ((get-car (lambda () kar))
   (get-cdr (lambda () kdr))
   (set-car! (lambda (x) (set! kar x)))
   (set-cdr! (lambda (x) (set! kdr x)))))
(define p (kons 'a 'b))
(send-message p get-car)  ⇒  a
(send-message p get-cdr)  ⇒  b
(send-message p set-cdr! 'c)
(send-message p get-cdr)  ⇒  c
```

The simple kons object does nothing but return or assign one of the fields
as requested. What makes abstract objects interesting is that they can be used to
restrict access or perform additional services. The following version of **kons** requires
that a password be given with any request to assign one of the fields. This password
is a parameter to the **kons** procedure.

```
(define-object (kons kar kdr pwd)
  ((get-car (lambda () kar))
   (get-cdr (lambda () kar))
   (set-car!
     (lambda (x p)
       (if (string=? p pwd)
           (set! kar x))))
   (set-cdr!
     (lambda (x p)
       (if (string=? p pwd)
           (set! kar x))))))
(define p1 (kons 'a 'b "magnificent"))
(send-message p1 set-car! 'c "magnificent")
(send-message p1 get-car)  ⇒  c
(send-message p1 set-car! 'd "please")
(send-message p1 get-car)  ⇒  c

(define p2 (kons 'x 'y "please"))
(send-message p2 set-car! 'z "please")
(send-message p2 get-car)  ⇒  z
```

One important ability of an abstract object is that it can keep statistics on
messages sent to it. The following version of **kons** counts accesses to the two fields.
This version also demonstrates the use of explicitly initialized local bindings.

```
(define-object (kons kar kdr)
  ((count 0))
  ((get-car
    (lambda ()
      (set! count (+ count 1))
      kar))
   (get-cdr
    (lambda ()
      (set! count (+ count 1))
      kdr))
   (accesses
    (lambda () count)))))
(define p (kons 'a 'b))
(send-message p get-car)   ⇒   a
(send-message p get-cdr)   ⇒   b
(send-message p accesses)  ⇒   2
(send-message p get-cdr)   ⇒   b
(send-message p accesses)  ⇒   3
```

The implementation of `define-object` is straightforward. The object definition is transformed into a definition of the object creation procedure. This procedure is the value of a `lambda` expression whose arguments are those specified in the definition. The body of the `lambda` consists of a `let*` expression to bind the local variables and a `letrec` expression to bind the message names to the action procedures. The body of the `letrec` is another `lambda` expression whose value represents the new object. The body of this `lambda` expression compares the messages passed in with the expected messages using a `case` expression and applies the corresponding action procedure to the remaining arguments.

For example, the definition

```
(define-object (kons kar kdr)
  ((count 0))
  ((get-car
    (lambda ()
      (set! count (+ count 1))
      kar))
   (get-cdr
    (lambda ()
      (set! count (+ count 1))
      kdr))
   (accesses
    (lambda () count)))))
```

is transformed into

```
(define kons
  (lambda (kar kdr)
    (let* ((count 0))
      (letrec ((get-car
                 (lambda ()
                   (set! count (+ count 1)) kar))
               (get-cdr
                 (lambda ()
                   (set! count (+ count 1)) kdr))
               (accesses (lambda () count)))
        (lambda (msg . args)
          (case msg
            ((get-car) (apply get-car args))
            ((get-cdr) (apply get-cdr args))
            ((accesses) (apply accesses args))
            (else
             (error 'kons "invalid message ~s"
               (cons msg args)))))))))
```

---

```
;;; define-object creates an object constructor that uses let* to bind
;;; local fields and letrec to define the exported procedures.  An
;;; object is itself a procedure that accepts messages corresponding
;;; to the names of the exported procedures.  The second pattern is
;;; used to allow the set of local fields to be omitted.
(define-syntax define-object
  (syntax-rules ()
    ((  (name . varlist)
        ((var1 val1) ...)
        ((var2 val2) ...))
     (define name
       (lambda varlist
         (let* ((var1 val1) ...)
           (letrec ((var2 val2) ...)
             (lambda (msg . args)
               (case msg
                 ((var2) (apply var2 args)) ...
                 (else
                  (error 'name "invalid message ~s"
                    (cons msg args)))))))))))
    ((_ (name . varlist)
        ((var2 val2) ...))
     (define-object (name . varlist)
       ()
       ((var2 val2) ...)))))
```

```
;;; send-message abstracts the act of sending a message from the act
;;; of applying a procedure and allows the message to be unquoted.
(define-syntax send-message
  (syntax-rules ()
    ((_ obj msg arg ...)
     (obj 'msg arg ...))))
```

**Exercise 9.8.1.** Use `define-object` to define the `stack` object type from Section 2.9.

**Exercise 9.8.2.** Use `define-object` to define a `queue` object type with operations similar to those described in Section 2.9.

**Exercise 9.8.3.** It is often useful to describe one object in terms of another. For example, the second `kons` object type could be described as the same as the first but with a password argument and different actions associated with the `set-car!` and `set-cdr!` messages. This is called *inheritance*; the new type of object is said to *inherit* attributes from the first. Modify `define-object` to support inheritance by allowing the optional declaration `(inherit object-name)` to appear after the message/action pairs. This will require saving some information about each object definition for possible use in subsequent object definitions. Conflicting argument names should be disallowed, but other conflicts should be resolved by using the initialization or action specified in the new object definition.

**Exercise 9.8.4.** Using the definition of `method` on page 205, define a complete vector-based object system. If your implementation of Scheme supports the definition of opaque records, use records instead of vectors to represent instances for greater security and efficiency. If done well, the resulting object system should be more efficient and easier to use than the system given above.

## 9.9. Fast Fourier Transform

The program described in this section uses Scheme's complex arithmetic to compute the discrete *Fourier transform* (DFT) of a sequence of values [2]. Discrete Fourier transforms are used to analyze and process sampled signal sequences in a wide variety of digital electronics applications such as pattern recognition, bandwidth compression, radar target detection, and weather surveillance.

The DFT of a sequence of $N$ input values,

$$\{x(n)\}_{n=0}^{N-1},$$

is the sequence of $N$ output values,

$$\{X(m)\}_{m=0}^{N-1},$$

each defined by the equation

$$X(m) = \sum_{n=0}^{N-1} x(n) e^{-i\frac{2\pi mn}{N}}.$$

It is convenient to abstract away the constant amount (for given $N$)

$$W_N = e^{-i\frac{2\pi}{N}},$$

in order to obtain the more concise but equivalent equation

$$X(m) = \sum_{n=0}^{N-1} x(n) W_N^{mn}.$$

A straightforward computation of the $N$ output values, each as a sum of $N$ intermediate values, requires on the order of $N^2$ operations. A *fast* Fourier transform (FFT), applicable when $N$ is a power of 2, requires only on the order of $N \log_2 N$ operations. Although usually presented as a rather complicated iterative algorithm, the fast Fourier transform is most concisely and elegantly expressed as a recursive algorithm.

The recursive algorithm, which is due to Sam Daniel [4], can be derived by manipulating the preceding summation as follows. We first split the summation into two summations and recombine them into one summation from 0 to $N/2 - 1$.

$$
\begin{aligned}
X(m) &= \sum_{n=0}^{N/2-1} x(n) W_N^{mn} + \sum_{n=N/2}^{N-1} x(n) W_N^{mn} \\
&= \sum_{n=0}^{N/2-1} [x(n) W_N^{mn} + x(n+N/2) W_N^{m(n+N/2)}]
\end{aligned}
$$

We then pull out the common factor $W_N^{mn}$.

$$X(m) = \sum_{n=0}^{N/2-1} [x(n) + x(n+N/2) W_N^{m(N/2)}] W_N^{mn}$$

We can reduce $W_N^{m(N/2)}$ to 1 when $m$ is even and $-1$ when $m$ is odd, since

$$W_N^{m(N/2)} = W_2^m = e^{-i\pi m} = \begin{cases} 1, & m \text{ even} \\ -1, & m \text{ odd}. \end{cases}$$

This allows us to specialize the summation for the even and odd cases of $m = 2k$

and $m = 2k + 1$, $0 \le k \le N/2 - 1$.

$$
\begin{aligned}
X(2k) &= \sum_{n=0}^{N/2-1} [x(n) + x(n + N/2)]W_N^{2kn} \\
&= \sum_{n=0}^{N/2-1} [x(n) + x(n + N/2)]W_{N/2}^{kn} \\
X(2k+1) &= \sum_{n=0}^{N/2-1} [x(n) - x(n + N/2)]W_N^{(2k+1)n} \\
&= \sum_{n=0}^{N/2-1} [x(n) - x(n + N/2)]W_N^{n}W_{N/2}^{kn}
\end{aligned}
$$

The resulting summations are DFTs of the $N/2$-element sequences

$$
\{x(n) + x(n + N/2)\}_{n=0}^{N/2-1}
$$

and

$$
\{[x(n) - x(n + N/2)]W_N^{n}\}_{n=0}^{N/2-1}.
$$

Thus, the DFT of an N-element sequence can be computed recursively by interlacing the DFTs of two $N/2$-element sequences. If we select a base case of two elements, we can describe a recursive fast Fourier transformation (RFFT) algorithm as follows. For $N = 2$,

$$
\begin{aligned}
RFFT\{x(n)\}_{n=0}^{1} &= \{X(m)\}_{m=0}^{1} \\
&= \{x(0) + x(1), [x(0) - x(1)]W_2^{0}\} \\
&= \{x(0) + x(1), x(0) - x(1)\},
\end{aligned}
$$

since $W_2^{0} = e^0 = 1$. For $N > 2$,

$$
\begin{aligned}
RFFT\{x(n)\}_{n=0}^{N-1} &= \{X(m)\}_{n=0}^{N-1} \\
&= \begin{cases} RFFT\{x(n) + x(n + N/2)\}_{n=0}^{N/2-1}, & m \text{ even} \\ RFFT\{(x(n) - x(n + N/2))W_N^{n}\}_{n=0}^{N/2-1}, & m \text{ odd} \end{cases}
\end{aligned}
$$

with the attendant interlacing of even and odd components.

The diagram which follows is adapted from one by Sam Daniel [4] and shows the computational structure of the RFFT algorithm. The first stage computes pairwise sums and differences of the first and second halves of the input; this stage is labeled the *butterfly* stage. The second stage recurs on the resulting subsequences. The third stage interlaces the output of the two recursive calls to RFFT, thus yielding the properly ordered sequence $\{X(m)\}_{m=0}^{N-1}$.

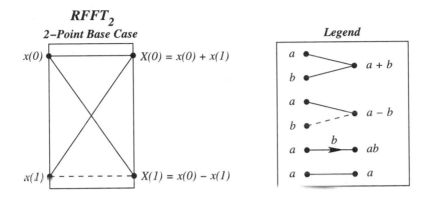

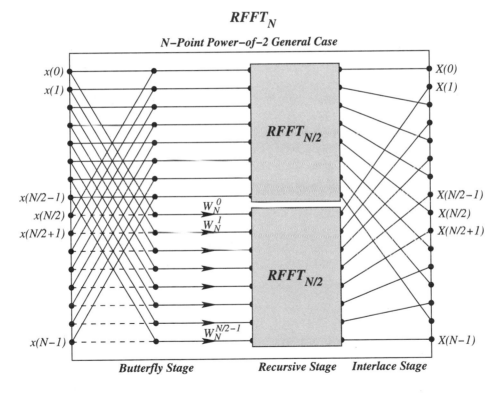

The procedure dft accepts a sequence (list) of values, x, the length of which is assumed to be a power of 2. dft precomputes a sequence of powers of $W_N$, $\{W_N^n\}_{n=0}^{N/2-1}$, and calls rfft to initiate the recursion. rfft follows the algorithm outlined above.

```
(define (dft x)
  (define (w-powers n)
    (let ((pi (* (acos 0.0) 2)))
      (let ((delta (/ (* -2.0i pi) n)))
        (let f ((n n) (x 0.0))
          (if (= n 0)
              '()
              (cons (exp x) (f (- n 2) (+ x delta))))))))))
  (define (evens w)
    (if (null? w)
        '()
        (cons (car w) (evens (cddr w)))))
  (define (interlace x y)
    (if (null? x)
        '()
        (cons (car x) (cons (car y) (interlace (cdr x) (cdr y))))))
  (define (split ls)
    (let split ((fast ls) (slow ls))
      (if (null? fast)
          (values '() slow)
          (call-with-values
            (lambda () (split (cddr fast) (cdr slow)))
            (lambda (front back)
              (values (cons (car slow) front) back))))))
  (define (butterfly x w)
    (call-with-values
      (lambda () (split x))
      (lambda (front back)
        (values
          (map + front back)
          (map * (map - front back) w)))))
  (define (rfft x w)
    (if (null? (cddr x))
        (let ((x0 (car x)) (x1 (cadr x)))
          (list (+ x0 x1) (- x0 x1)))
        (call-with-values
          (lambda () (butterfly x w))
          (lambda (front back)
            (let ((w (evens w)))
              (interlace (rfft front w) (rfft back w)))))))
  (rfft x (w-powers (length x))))
```

**Exercise 9.9.1.** Alter the algorithm to employ a base case of four points. What simplifications can be made to avoid multiplying any of the base case outputs by elements of w?

**Exercise 9.9.2.** Recode `dft` to accept a vector rather than a list as input, and have it produce a vector as output. Use lists internally if necessary, but do not simply convert the input to a list on entry and the output to a vector on exit.

**Exercise 9.9.3.** Rather than recomputing the powers of w on each step for a new number of points, the code simply uses the even numbered elements of the preceding list of powers. Show that doing so yields the proper list of powers. That is, show that (`evens (w-powers n)`) is equal to (`w-powers (/ n 2)`).

**Exercise 9.9.4.** The recursion step creates several intermediate lists that are immediately discarded. Recode the recursion step to avoid any unnecessary allocation.

**Exercise 9.9.5.** Each element of a sequence of input values may be regenerated from the discrete Fourier transform of the sequence via the equation

$$x(n) = \frac{1}{N} \sum_{m=0}^{N-1} X(m) e^{i \frac{2\pi mn}{N}}.$$

Noting the similarity between this equation and the original equation defining $X(m)$, create a modified version of `dft`, `inverse-dft`, that performs the inverse transformation. Verify that (`inverse-dft (dft` *seq*`)`) returns *seq* for several input sequences *seq*.

## 9.10. A Unification Algorithm

*Unification* [18] is a pattern-matching technique used in automated theorem proving, type-inference systems, computer algebra, and logic programming, e.g., Prolog [3].

A unification algorithm attempts to make two symbolic expressions equal by computing a unifying substitution for the expressions. A *substitution* is a function that replaces variables with other expressions. A substitution must treat all occurrences of a variable the same way, e.g., if it replaces one occurrence of the variable $x$ by $a$, it must replace all occurrences of $x$ by $a$. A unifying substitution, or *unifier*, for two expressions $e_1$ and $e_2$ is a substitution, $\sigma$, such that $\sigma(e_1) = \sigma(e_2)$.

For example, the two expressions $f(x)$ and $f(y)$ can be unified by substituting $x$ for $y$ (or $y$ for $x$). In this case, the unifier $\sigma$ could be described as the function that replaces $y$ with $x$ and leaves other variables unchanged. On the other hand, the two expressions $x + 1$ and $y + 2$ cannot be unified. It might appear that substituting 3 for $x$ and 2 for $y$ would make both expressions equal to 4 and hence equal to each other. The symbolic expressions, $3 + 1$ and $2 + 2$, however, still differ.

Two expressions may have more than one unifier. For example, the expressions $f(x, y)$ and $f(1, y)$ can be unified to $f(1, y)$ with the substitution of 1 for $x$. They may also be unified to $f(1, 5)$ with the substitution of 1 for $x$ and 5 for $y$. The first substitution is preferable, since it does not commit to the unnecessary replacement of $y$. Unification algorithms typically produce the *most general unifier*, or *mgu*, for two expressions. The mgu for two expressions makes no unnecessary substitutions; all other unifiers for the expressions are special cases of the mgu. In the example above, the first substitution is the mgu and the second is a special case.

For the purposes of this program, a symbolic expression can be a variable, a constant, or a function application. Variables are represented by Scheme symbols, e.g., x; a function application is represented by a list with the function name in the first position and its arguments in the remaining positions, e.g., (f x); and constants are represented by zero-argument functions, e.g., (a).

The algorithm presented here finds the mgu for two terms, if it exists, using a continuation passing style, or CPS (see Section 3.4), approach to recursion on subterms. The procedure unify takes two terms and passes them to a help procedure, uni, along with an initial (identity) substitution, a success continuation, and a failure continuation. The success continuation returns the result of applying its argument, a substitution, to one of the terms, i.e., the unified result. The failure continuation simply returns its argument, a message. Because control passes by explicit continuation within unify (always with tail calls), a return from the success or failure continuation is a return from unify itself.

Substitutions are procedures. Whenever a variable is to be replaced by another term, a new substitution is formed from the variable, the term, and the existing substitution. Given a term as an argument, the new substitution replaces occurrences of its saved variable with its saved term in the result of invoking the saved substitution on the argument expression. Intuitively, a substitution is a chain of procedures, one for each variable in the substitution. The chain is terminated by the initial, identity substitution.

```
(unify 'x 'y)  ⇒  y
(unify '(f x y) '(g x y))  ⇒  "clash"
(unify '(f x (h)) '(f (h) y))  ⇒  (f (h) (h))
(unify '(f (g x) y) '(f y x))  ⇒  "cycle"
(unify '(f (g x) y) '(f y (g x)))  ⇒  (f (g x) (g x))
(unify '(f (g x) y) '(f y z))  ⇒  (f (g x) (g x))
```

```scheme
(define unify #f)
(let ()
  ;; occurs? returns true if and only if u occurs in v
  (define occurs?
    (lambda (u v)
      (and (pair? v)
           (let f ((l (cdr v)))
             (and (pair? l)
                  (or (eq? u (car l))
                      (occurs? u (car l))
                      (f (cdr l))))))))
  ;; sigma returns a new substitution procedure extending s by
  ;; the substitution of u with v
  (define sigma
    (lambda (u v s)
      (lambda (x)
        (let f ((x (s x)))
          (if (symbol? x)
              (if (eq? x u) v x)
              (cons (car x) (map f (cdr x))))))))
  ;; try-subst tries to substitute u for v but may require a
  ;; full unification if (s u) is not a variable, and it may
  ;; fail if it sees that u occurs in v.
  (define try-subst
    (lambda (u v s ks kf)
      (let ((u (s u)))
        (if (not (symbol? u))
            (uni u v s ks kf)
            (let ((v (s v)))
              (cond
                ((eq? u v) (ks s))
                ((occurs? u v) (kf "cycle"))
                (else (ks (sigma u v s)))))))))
  ;; uni attempts to unify u and v with a continuation-passing
  ;; style that returns a substitution to the success argument
  ;; ks or an error message to the failure argument kf.  The
  ;; substitution itself is represented by a procedure from
  ;; variables to terms.
  (define uni
    (lambda (u v s ks kf)
      (cond
        ((symbol? u) (try-subst u v s ks kf))
        ((symbol? v) (try-subst v u s ks kf))
```

```
    ((and (eq? (car u) (car v))
          (= (length u) (length v)))
     (let f ((u (cdr u)) (v (cdr v)) (s s))
       (if (null? u)
           (ks s)
           (uni (car u)
                (car v)
                s
                (lambda (s) (f (cdr u) (cdr v) s))
                kf))))
    (else (kf "clash")))))
;; unify shows one possible interface to uni, where the initial
;; substitution is the identity procedure, the initial success
;; continuation returns the unified term, and the initial failure
;; continuation returns the error message.
(set! unify
  (lambda (u v)
    (uni u
         v
         (lambda (x) x)
         (lambda (s) (s u))
         (lambda (msg) msg)))))
```

**Exercise 9.10.1.** Modify unify so that it returns its substitution rather than the unified term. Apply this substitution to both input terms to verify that it returns the same result for each.

**Exercise 9.10.2.** As mentioned above, substitutions on a term are performed sequentially, requiring one entire pass through the input expression for each substituted variable. Represent the substitution differently so that only one pass through the expression need be made. Make sure that substitutions are performed not only on the input expression but also on any expressions you insert during substitution.

**Exercise 9.10.3.** Extend the continuation-passing style unification algorithm into an entire continuation-passing style logic programming system.

## 9.11. Multitasking with Engines

Engines are a high-level process abstraction supporting *timed preemption* [6, 10]. Engines may be used to simulate multiprocessing, implement light-weight threads, implement operating system kernels, and perform nondeterministic computations. The engine implementation is one of the more interesting applications of continuations in Scheme.

An engine is created by passing a thunk (procedure of no arguments) to `make-engine`. The body of the thunk is the computation to be performed by the engine. An engine itself is a procedure of three arguments:

1. *ticks*, a positive integer that specifies the amount of *fuel* to be given to the engine. An engine executes until this fuel runs out or until its computation finishes.

2. *complete*, a procedure of two arguments that specifies what to do if the computation finishes. Its arguments will be the amount of fuel left over and the result of the computation.

3. *expire*, a procedure of one argument that specifies what to do if the fuel runs out before the computation finishes. Its argument will be a new engine capable of continuing the computation from the point of interruption.

When an engine is applied to its arguments, it sets up a timer to fire in *ticks* time units. If the engine computation completes before the timer goes off, the system invokes *complete*, passing it the number of *ticks* left over and the value of the computation. If, on the other hand, the timer goes off before the engine computation completes, the system creates a new engine from the continuation of the interrupted computation and passes this engine to *expire*. *complete* and *expire* are invoked in the continuation of the engine invocation.

The following example creates an engine from a trivial computation, 3, and gives the engine 10 ticks.

```
(define eng
  (make-engine
    (lambda () 3)))
(eng 10
  (lambda (ticks value) value)
  (lambda (x) x))   ⇒   3
```

It is often useful to pass `list` as the *complete* procedure to an engine, causing the engine to return a list of the ticks remaining and the value if the computation completes.

```
(eng 10
  list
  (lambda (x) x))   ⇒   (9 3)
```

In the example above, the value was 3 and there were 9 ticks left over, i.e., it took only one unit of fuel to evaluate 3. (The fuel amounts given here are for illustration only. The actual amount may differ.)

Typically, the engine computation does not finish in one try. The following example displays the use of an engine to compute the 10th Fibonacci number (see Section 3.2) in steps.

```
(define fibonacci
  (lambda (n)
    (if (< n 2)
        n
        (+ (fibonacci (- n 1))
           (fibonacci (- n 2))))))
(define eng
  (make-engine
    (lambda ()
      (fibonacci 10))))
(eng 50
  list
  (lambda (new-eng)
    (set! eng new-eng)
    "expired"))  ⇒  "expired"
(eng 50
  list
  (lambda (new-eng)
    (set! eng new-eng)
    "expired"))  ⇒  "expired"
(eng 50
  list
  (lambda (new-eng)
    (set! eng new-eng)
    "expired"))  ⇒  "expired"
(eng 50
  list
  (lambda (new-eng)
    (set! eng new-eng)
    "expired"))  ⇒  (23 55)
```

Each time the engine's fuel ran out, the *expire* procedure assigned `eng` to the new engine. The entire computation required four allotments of 50 ticks to complete; of the last 50 it used all but 23. Thus, the total amount of fuel used was 177 ticks. This leads us to the following procedure, `mileage`, which uses engines to "time" a computation.

```
(define mileage
  (lambda (thunk)
    (let loop ((eng (make-engine thunk)) (total-ticks 0))
      (eng 50
        (lambda (ticks value)
          (+ total-ticks (- 50 ticks)))
        (lambda (new-eng)
          (loop new-eng (+ total-ticks 50)))))))

(mileage (lambda () (fibonacci 10)))   ⇒   177
```

The choice of 50 for the number of ticks to use each time is arbitrary, of course. It might make more sense to pass a much larger number, say 10000, in order to reduce the number of times the computation is interrupted.

The next procedure, round-robin, could be the basis for a simple time-sharing operating system. round-robin maintains a queue of processes (a list of engines) and cycles through the queue in a *round-robin* fashion, allowing each process to run for a set amount of time. round-robin returns a list of the values returned by the engine computations in the order that the computations complete.

```
(define round-robin
  (lambda (engs)
    (if (null? engs)
        '()
        ((car engs) 1
          (lambda (ticks value)
            (cons value (round-robin (cdr engs))))
          (lambda (eng)
            (round-robin
              (append (cdr engs) (list eng))))))))
```

Assuming the amount of computation corresponding to one tick is constant, the effect of round-robin is to return a list of the values sorted from the quickest to complete to the slowest to complete. Thus, when we call round-robin on a list of engines, each computing one of the Fibonacci numbers, the output list is sorted with the earlier Fibonacci numbers first, regardless of the order of the input list.

```
(round-robin
  (map (lambda (x)
         (make-engine
           (lambda ()
             (fibonacci x))))
       '(4 5 2 8 3 7 6 2)))   ⇒   (1 1 2 3 5 8 13 21)
```

More interesting things could happen if the amount of fuel varied each time through the loop. In this case, the computation would be nondeterministic, i.e., the results would vary from call to call.

The following syntactic form, `por` (parallel-or), returns the first of its expressions to complete with a true value. `por` is implemented with the procedure `first-true`, which is similar to `round-robin` but quits when any of the engines completes with a true value. If all of the engines complete, but none with a true value, `first-true` (and hence `por`) returns `#f`.

```
(define-syntax por
  (syntax-rules ()
    ((_ x ...)
     (first-true
       (list (make-engine (lambda () x)) ...)))))
(define first-true
  (lambda (engs)
    (if (null? engs)
        #f
        ((car engs) 1
          (lambda (ticks value)
            (or value (first-true (cdr engs))))
          (lambda (eng)
            (first-true
              (append (cdr engs) (list eng)))))))))
```

Even if one of the expressions is an infinite loop, `por` can still finish (as long as one of the other expressions completes and returns a true value).

```
(por 1 2)  ⇒  1
(por ((lambda (x) (x x)) (lambda (x) (x x)))
     (fibonacci 10))  ⇒  55
```

The first subexpression of the second `por` expression is nonterminating, so the answer is the value of the second subexpression.

Let's turn to the implementation of engines. Any preemptive multitasking primitive must have the ability to interrupt a running process after a given amount of computation. This ability is provided by a primitive timer interrupt mechanism in some Scheme implementations. We will construct a suitable one here.

Our timer system defines three procedures: `start-timer`, `stop-timer`, and `decrement-timer`, which can be described operationally as follows.

- (`start-timer` *ticks handler*) sets the timer to *ticks* and installs *handler* as the procedure to be invoked (without arguments) when the timer expires, i.e., reaches zero.

- (`stop-timer`) resets the timer and returns the number of ticks remaining.

- (`decrement-timer`) decrements the timer by one tick if the timer is on, i.e., if it is not zero. When the timer reaches zero, `decrement-timer` invokes the saved handler. If the timer has already reached zero, `decrement-timer` returns without changing the timer.

Code to implement these procedures is given along with the engine implementation below.

Using the timer system requires inserting calls to `decrement-timer` in appropriate places. Consuming a timer tick on entry to a procedure usually provides a sufficient level of granularity. This can be accomplished by using `timed-lambda` as defined below in place of `lambda`. `timed-lambda` simply invokes `decrement-timer` before executing the expressions in its body.

```
(define-syntax timed-lambda
  (syntax-rules ()
    ((_ formals exp1 exp2 ...)
     (lambda formals (decrement-timer) exp1 exp2 ...))))
```

It may be useful to redefine named `let` and `do` to use `timed-lambda` as well, so that recursions expressed with these constructs are timed. If you use this mechanism, do not forget to use the timed versions of `lambda` and other forms in code run within an engine, or no ticks will be consumed.

Now that we have a suitable timer, we can implement engines in terms of the timer and continuations. We use `call/cc` in two places in the engine implementation: (1) to obtain the continuation of the computation that invokes the engine so that we can return to that continuation when the engine computation completes or the timer expires, and (2) to obtain the continuation of the engine computation when the timer expires so that we can return to this computation if the newly created engine is subsequently run.

The state of the engine system is contained in two variables local to the engine system: `do-complete` and `do-expire`. When an engine is started, the engine assigns to `do-complete` and `do-expire` procedures that, when invoked, return to the continuation of the engine's caller to invoke *complete* or *expire*. The engine starts (or restarts) the computation by invoking the procedure passed as an argument to `make-engine` with the specified number of ticks. The ticks and the local procedure `timer-handler` are then used to start the timer.

Suppose that the timer expires before the engine computation completes. The procedure `timer-handler` is then invoked. It initiates a call to `start-timer` but obtains the ticks by calling `call/cc` with `do-expire`. Consequently, `do-expire` is called with a continuation that, if invoked, will restart the timer and continue the interrupted computation. `do-expire` creates a new engine from this continuation and arranges for the engine's *expire* procedure to be invoked with the new engine in the correct continuation.

If, on the other hand, the engine computation completes before the timer expires, the timer is stopped and the number of ticks remaining is passed along with the value to `do-complete`; `do-complete` arranges for the engine's *complete* procedure to be invoked with the ticks and value in the correct continuation.

Let's discuss a couple of subtle aspects to this code. The first concerns the method used to start the timer when an engine is invoked. The code would apparently be simplified by letting `new-engine` start the timer before it initiates or resumes the engine computation, instead of passing the ticks to the computation and letting it start the timer. Starting the timer within the computation, however, prevents ticks from being consumed prematurely. If the engine system itself consumes fuel, then an engine provided with a small amount of fuel may not progress toward completion. (It may, in fact, make negative progress.) If the software timer described above is used, this problem is actually avoided by compiling the engine-making code with the untimed version of `lambda`.

The second subtlety concerns the procedures created by `do-complete` and `do-expire` and subsequently applied by the continuation of the `call/cc` application. It may appear that `do-complete` could first invoke the engine's *complete* procedure, then pass the result to the continuation (and similarly for `do-expire`) as follows.

```
(escape (complete value ticks))
```

This would result in improper treatment of tail recursion, however. The problem is that the current continuation would not be replaced with the continuation stored in `escape` until the call to the `complete` procedure returns. Consequently, both the continuation of the running engine and the continuation of the engine invocation could be retained for an indefinite period of time, when in fact the actual engine invocation may appear to be tail-recursive. This is especially inappropriate because the engine interface encourages use of continuation-passing style and hence tail recursion. The round-robin scheduler and `first-true` provide good examples of this, since the *expire* procedure in each invokes engines tail-recursively.

We maintain proper treatment of tail recursion by arranging for `do-complete` and `do-expire` to escape from the continuation of the running engine before invoking the `complete` or `expire` procedures. Since the continuation of the engine invocation is a procedure application, passing it a procedure of no arguments results in application of the procedure in the continuation of the engine invocation.

```
(define start-timer #f)
(define stop-timer #f)
(define decrement-timer #f)
(let ((clock 0) (handler #f))
  (set! start-timer
    (lambda (ticks new-handler)
      (set! handler new-handler)
      (set! clock ticks)))
```

```
  (set! stop-timer
    (lambda ()
      (let ((time-left clock))
        (set! clock 0)
        time-left)))
  (set! decrement-timer
    (lambda ()
      (if (> clock 0)
          (begin
            (set! clock (- clock 1))
            (if (= clock 0) (handler)))))))
(define make-engine
  (let ((do-complete #f) (do-expire #f))
    (define timer-handler
      (lambda ()
        (start-timer (call/cc do-expire) timer-handler)))
    (define new-engine
      (lambda (resume)
        (lambda (ticks complete expire)
          ((call/cc
             (lambda (escape)
               (set! do-complete
                 (lambda (ticks value)
                   (escape (lambda () (complete ticks value)))))
               (set! do-expire
                 (lambda (resume)
                   (escape (lambda ()
                             (expire (new-engine resume))))))
               (resume ticks)))))))
    (lambda (proc)
      (new-engine
        (lambda (ticks)
          (start-timer ticks timer-handler)
          (let ((value (proc)))
            (let ((ticks (stop-timer)))
              (do-complete ticks value))))))))
```

**Exercise 9.11.1.** It may appear that the nested let expressions in the body of make-engine:

```
(let ((value (proc)))
  (let ((ticks (stop-timer)))
    (do-complete ticks value)))
```

could be replaced with:

```
(let ((value (proc)) (ticks (stop-timer)))
  (do-complete value ticks))
```

Why is this not correct?

**Exercise 9.11.2.** It would also be incorrect to replace the nested `let` expressions discussed in the preceding exercise with:

```
(let ((value (proc)))
  (do-complete value (stop-timer)))
```

Why?

**Exercise 9.11.3.** Modify the engine implementation to provide a procedure, `engine-return`, that returns immediately from an engine.

**Exercise 9.11.4.** Implement the kernel of a small operating system using engines for processes. Processes should request services (such as reading input from the user) by evaluating an expression of the form `(trap 'request)`. Use `call/cc` and `engine-return` from the preceding exercise to implement `trap`.

**Exercise 9.11.5.** Write the same operating-system kernel without using engines, building instead from continuations and timer interrupts.

**Exercise 9.11.6.** This implementation of engines does not allow one engine to call another, i.e., nested engines [6]. Modify the implementation to allow nested engines.

# Bibliography

[1] J. Michael Ashley and R. Kent Dybvig. An efficient implementation of multiple return values in Scheme. In *Proceedings of the 1994 ACM Conference on Lisp and Functional Programming*, 140 140, June 1994

[2] William Briggs and Van Emden Henson. *The DFT: An Owner's Manual for the Discrete Fourier Transform*. Society for Industrial and Applied Mathematics, Philadelphia, 1995.

[3] William F. Clocksin and Christopher S. Mellish. *Programming in Prolog*, second edition. Springer-Verlag, 1984.

[4] Sam M. Daniel. Efficient recursive FFT implementation in Prolog. In *Proceedings of the Second International Conference on the Practical Application of Prolog*, 175–185, 1994.

[5] R. Kent Dybvig. *Chez Scheme User's Guide: Version 7*. Cadence Research Systems, 2003. *http://www.scheme.com/csug7/*.

[6] R. Kent Dybvig and Robert Hieb. Engines from continuations. *Computer Languages*, 14(2):109–123, 1989.

[7] R. Kent Dybvig, Robert Hieb, and Carl Bruggeman. Syntactic abstraction in Scheme. *Lisp and Symbolic Computation*, 5(4):295–326, 1993.

[8] Daniel P. Friedman and Matthias Felleisen. *The Little Schemer*, fourth edition. MIT Press, 1996.

[9] Daniel P. Friedman, Christopher T. Haynes, and Eugene E. Kohlbecker. Programming with continuations. In P. Pepper, editor, *Program Transformation and Programming Environments*, 263–274. Springer-Verlag, 1984.

[10] Christopher T. Haynes and Daniel P. Friedman. Abstracting timed preemption with engines. *Computer Languages*, 12(2):109–121, 1987.

[11] Christopher T. Haynes, Daniel P. Friedman, and Mitchell Wand. Obtaining coroutines with continuations. *Computer Languages*, 11(3/4):143–153, 1986.

[12] Robert Hieb, R. Kent Dybvig, and Carl Bruggeman. Representing control in the presence of first-class continuations. In *Proceedings of the SIGPLAN*

*'90 Conference on Programming Language Design and Implementation*, 66–77, June 1990.

[13] IEEE Computer Society. *IEEE Standard for the Scheme Programming Language*, May 1991. IEEE Std 1178-1990.

[14] Richard Kelsey, William Clinger, Jonathan Rees, et al. The revised[5] report on the algorithmic language Scheme. *Higher Order and Symbolic Computation*, 11(1), 1999.

[15] Brian W. Kernighan and Dennis M. Ritchie. *The C Programming Language*, second edition. Prentice Hall, 1988.

[16] Peter Naur et al. Revised report on the algorithmic language ALGOL 60. *Communications of the ACM*, 6(1):1–17, January 1963.

[17] David A. Plaisted. Constructs for sets, quantifiers, and rewrite rules in Lisp. Technical Report UIUCDCS-R-84-1176, University of Illinois at Urbana-Champaign Department of Computer Science, June 1984.

[18] J. A. Robinson. A machine-oriented logic based on the resolution principle. *Journal of the ACM*, 12(1):23–41, 1965.

[19] Guy L. Steele Jr. *Common Lisp, the Language*, second edition. Digital Press, 1990.

[20] Guy L. Steele Jr. and Gerald J. Sussman. The revised report on Scheme, a dialect of Lisp. MIT AI Memo 452, Massachusetts Institute of Technology, January 1978.

[21] Gerald J. Sussman and Guy L. Steele Jr. Scheme: An interpreter for extended lambda calculus. *Higher-Order and Symbolic Computation*, 11(4):405–439, 1998. Reprinted from the AI Memo 349, MIT (1975), with a foreword.

[22] Oscar Waddell and R. Kent Dybvig. Extending the scope of syntactic abstraction. In *Conference Record of the Twenty Sixth Annual ACM Symposium on Principles of Programming Languages*, 203–213, January 1999.

[23] Oscar Waddell, R. Kent Dybvig, and Dipanwita Sarkar. Robust and effective transformation of letrec. In *Proceedings of the Third Workshop on Scheme and Functional Programming*, October 2002. Georgia Tech College of Computing Technical Report GIT-CC-02-48.

[24] Mitchell Wand. Continuation-based multiprocessing. *Higher-Order and Symbolic Computation*, 12(3):285–299, 1999. Reprinted from the proceedings of the 1980 Lisp Conference, with a foreword.

# Answers to Selected Exercises

**Exercise 2.2.1.** (Page 20)

   *a.* (+ (* 1.2 (- 2 1/3)) -8.7)

   *b.* (/ (+ 2/3 4/9) (- 5/11 4/3))

   *c.* (+ 1 (/ 1 (+ 2 (/ 1 (+ 1 1/2)))))

   *d.* (* (* (* (* (* (* 1 -2) 3) -4) 5) -6) 7) or (* 1 -2 3 -4 5 -6 7)

**Exercise 2.2.2.** (Page 20)

See Section 6.4.

**Exercise 2.2.3.** (Page 20)

   *a.* (car . cdr)

   *b.* (this (is silly))

   *c.* (is this silly?)

   *d.* (+ 2 3)

   *e.* (+ 2 3)

   *f.* +

   *g.* (2 3)

   *h.* #<procedure>

   *i.* cons

   *j.* 'cons

   *k.* quote

   *l.* 5

  *m.* 5

   *n.* 5

   *o.* 5

**Exercise 2.2.4.** (Page 20)

(car (cdr (car '((a b) (c d)))))  ⇒  b

(car (car (cdr '((a b) (c d)))))  ⇒  c

(car (cdr (car (cdr '((a b) (c d))))))  ⇒  d

**Exercise 2.2.5.** (Page 20)

'((a . b) ((c) d) ())

**Exercise 2.2.6.** (Page 21)

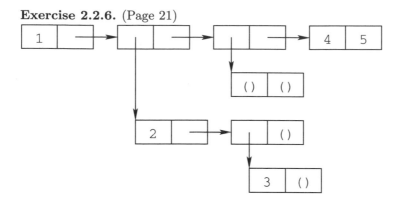

**Exercise 2.2.7.** (Page 21)
```
(car '((a b) (c d)))  ⇒  (a b)
(car (car '((a b) (c d))))  ⇒  a
(cdr (car '((a b) (c d))))  ⇒  (b)
(car (cdr (car '((a b) (c d)))))  ⇒  b
(cdr (cdr (car '((a b) (c d)))))  ⇒  ()
(cdr '((a b) (c d)))  ⇒  ((c d))
(car (cdr '((a b) (c d))))  ⇒  (c d)
(car (car (cdr '((a b) (c d)))))  ⇒  c
(cdr (car (cdr '((a b) (c d)))))  ⇒  (d)
(car (cdr (car (cdr '((a b) (c d))))))  ⇒  d
(cdr (cdr (car (cdr '((a b) (c d))))))  ⇒  ()
(cdr (cdr '((a b) (c d))))  ⇒  ()
```

**Exercise 2.2.8.** (Page 21)
See Section 2.3.

**Exercise 2.3.1.** (Page 22)

1. Evaluate the variables `list`, `+`, `-`, `*`, and `/`, yielding the list, addition, subtraction, multiplication, and division procedures.

2. Apply the list procedure to the addition, subtraction, multiplication, and division procedures, yielding a list containing these procedures in order.

3. Evaluate the variable `cdr`, yielding the cdr procedure.

4. Apply the cdr procedure to the list produced in step 2, yielding a list containing the subtraction, multiplication, and division procedures.

5. Evaluate the variable `car`, yielding the car procedure.

6. Apply the car procedure to the list produced in step 4, yielding the subtraction procedure.

7. Evaluate the constants 17 and 5, yielding 17 and 5.

8. Apply the subtraction procedure to 17 and 5, yielding 12.

Other orders are possible. For example, the variable `car` could have been evaluated before its argument.

**Exercise 2.4.1.** (Page 24)
  *a.* `(let ((x (* 3 a))) (+ (- x b) (+ x b)))`
  *b.* `(let ((x (list a b c))) (cons (car x) (cdr x)))`

**Exercise 2.4.2.** (Page 25)
The value is 54. The outer `let` binds x to 9, while the inner `let` binds x to 3 (9/3). The inner `let` evaluates to 6 $(3 + 3)$, and the outer `let` evaluates to 54 $(9 \times 6)$.

**Exercise 2.4.3.** (Page 25)
  *a.* `(let ((x0 'a) (y0 'b))`
  `   (list (let ((x1 'c)) (cons x1 y0))`
  `         (let ((y1 'd)) (cons x0 y1))))`
  *b.* `(let ((x0 '((a b) c)))`
  `   (cons (let ((x1 (cdr x0)))`
  `           (car x1))`
  `         (let ((x2 (car x0)))`
  `           (cons (let ((x3 (cdr x2)))`
  `                   (car x3))`
  `                 (cons (let ((x4 (car x2)))`
  `                         x4)`
  `                       (cdr x2))))))`

**Exercise 2.5.1.** (Page 29)
  *a.* `a`
  *b.* `(a)`
  *c.* `a`
  *d.* `()`

**Exercise 2.5.2.** (Page 29)
See page 30.

**Exercise 2.5.3.** (Page 29)
  *a.* no free variables
  *b.* `+`
  *c.* `f`
  *d.* `cons`, `f`, and `y`
  *e.* `cons` and `y`
  *f.* `cons`, `y`, and `z` (`y` also appears as a bound variable)

**Exercise 2.6.1.** (Page 32)
The program would loop indefinitely.

**Exercise 2.6.2.** (Page 33)
```
(define compose
  (lambda (p1 p2)
    (lambda (x)
      (p1 (p2 x)))))
```
```
(define cadr (compose car cdr))
(define cddr (compose cdr cdr))
```

**Exercise 2.6.3.** (Page 33)
```
(define caar (compose car car))
(define cadr (compose car cdr))
```
```
(define cdar (compose cdr car))
(define cddr (compose cdr cdr))
```
```
(define caaar (compose car caar))
(define caadr (compose car cadr))
(define cadar (compose car cdar))
(define caddr (compose car cddr))
```
```
(define cdaar (compose cdr caar))
(define cdadr (compose cdr cadr))
(define cddar (compose cdr cdar))
(define cdddr (compose cdr cddr))
```
```
(define caaaar (compose caar caar))
(define caaadr (compose caar cadr))
(define caadar (compose caar cdar))
(define caaddr (compose caar cddr))
(define cadaar (compose cadr caar))
(define cadadr (compose cadr cadr))
(define caddar (compose cadr cdar))
(define cadddr (compose cadr cddr))
```
```
(define cdaaar (compose cdar caar))
(define cdaadr (compose cdar cadr))
(define cdadar (compose cdar cdar))
(define cdaddr (compose cdar cddr))
(define cddaar (compose cddr caar))
(define cddadr (compose cddr cadr))
(define cdddar (compose cddr cdar))
(define cddddr (compose cddr cddr))
```

**Exercise 2.7.1.** (Page 39)
```
(define atom?
  (lambda (x)
    (not (pair? x)))))
```

**Exercise 2.7.2.** (Page 39)
```
(define shorter
  (lambda (ls1 ls2)
    (if (< (length ls2) (length ls1))
        ls2
        ls1)))
```

**Exercise 2.8.1.** (Page 44)
The structure of the output would be the mirror image of the structure of the input. For example, (a . b) would become (b . a) and ((a . b) . (c . d)) would become ((d . c) . (b . a)).

**Exercise 2.8.2.** (Page 44)
```
(define append
  (lambda (ls1 ls2)
    (if (null? ls1)
        ls2
        (cons (car ls1) (append (cdr ls1) ls2)))))
```

**Exercise 2.8.3.** (Page 44)
```
(define make-list
  (lambda (n x)
    (if (= n 0)
        '()
        (cons x (make-list (- n 1) x)))))
```

**Exercise 2.8.4.** (Page 45)
See pages 135 and 136.

**Exercise 2.8.5.** (Page 45)
```
(define shorter?
  (lambda (ls1 ls2)
    (and (not (null? ls2))
         (or (null? ls1)
             (shorter? (cdr ls1) (cdr ls2))))))
```

```
(define shorter
  (lambda (ls1 ls2)
    (if (shorter? ls2 ls1)
        ls2
        ls1)))
```

**Exercise 2.8.6.** (Page 45)
```
(define even?
  (lambda (x)
    (or (= x 0)
        (odd? (- x 1)))))
(define odd?
  (lambda (x)
    (and (not (= x 0))
         (even? (- x 1)))))
```

**Exercise 2.8.7.** (Page 45)
```
(define transpose
  (lambda (ls)
    (cons (map car ls) (map cdr ls))))
```

**Exercise 2.9.1.** (Page 52)
```
(define make-counter
  (lambda (init incr)
    (let ((next init))
      (lambda ()
        (let ((v next))
          (set! next (+ next incr))
          v)))))
```

**Exercise 2.9.2.** (Page 52)
```
(define make-stack
  (lambda ()
    (let ((ls '()))
      (lambda (msg . args)
        (case msg
          ((empty? mt?) (null? ls))
          ((push!) (set! ls (cons (car args) ls)))
          ((top) (car ls))
          ((pop!) (set! ls (cdr ls)))
          (else "oops"))))))
```

**Exercise 2.9.3.** (Page 53)
```
(define make-stack
  (lambda ()
    (let ((ls '()))
      (lambda (msg . args)
        (case msg
          ((empty? mt?) (null? ls))
          ((push!) (set! ls (cons (car args) ls)))
          ((top) (car ls))
          ((pop!) (set! ls (cdr ls)))
          ((ref) (list-ref ls (car args)))
          ((set!) (set-car! (list-tail ls (car args)) (cadr args)))
          (else "oops"))))))
```

**Exercise 2.9.4.** (Page 53)
```
(define make-stack
  (lambda (n)
    (let ((v (make-vector n)) (i -1))
      (lambda (msg . args)
        (case msg
          ((empty? mt?) (= i -1))
          ((push!)
           (set! i (+ i 1))
           (vector-set! v i (car args)))
          ((top) (vector-ref v i))
          ((pop!) (set! i (- i 1)))
          ((ref) (vector-ref v (- i (car args))))
          ((set!) (vector-set! v (- i (car args)) (cadr args)))
          (else "oops"))))))
```

**Exercise 2.9.5.** (Page 53)
Using *Chez Scheme*'s error:

```
(define emptyq?
  (lambda (q)
    (eq? (car q) (cdr q))))

(define getq
  (lambda (q)
    (if (emptyq? q)
        (error 'getq "the queue is empty")
        (car (car q)))))
```

```
(define delq!
  (lambda (q)
    (if (emptyq? q)
        (error 'delq! "the queue is empty")
        (set-car! q (cdr (car q)))))))
```

**Exercise 2.9.6.** (Page 53)

```
(define make-queue
  (lambda ()
    (cons '() '())))

(define putq!
  (lambda (q v)
    (let ((p (cons v '())))
      (if (null? (car q))
          (begin
            (set-car! q p)
            (set-cdr! q p))
          (begin
            (set-cdr! (cdr q) p)
            (set-cdr! q p))))))

(define getq
  (lambda (q)
    (car (car q))))

(define delq!
  (lambda (q)
    (if (eq? (car q) (cdr q))
        (begin
          (set-car! q '())
          (set-cdr! q '()))
        (set-car! q (cdr (car q))))))
```

**Exercise 2.9.7.** (Page 54)

The behavior depends upon the Scheme implementation. When asked to print
a cyclic structure, Chez Scheme prints a warning that the output is cyclic, then
proceeds to print a representation of the output that reflects its cyclic structure.
Similarly, when the built-in `length` is passed a cyclic list, Chez Scheme signals an
error to that effect. The definition of `length` on page 40 will simply loop indefinitely.

**Exercise 2.9.8.** (Page 54)
```
(define race
  (lambda (hare tortoise)
    (if (pair? hare)
        (let ((hare (cdr hare)))
          (if (pair? hare)
              (and (not (eq? hare tortoise))
                   (race (cdr hare) (cdr tortoise)))
              (null? hare)))
        (null? hare)))))

(define list?
  (lambda (x)
    (race x x)))
```

**Exercise 3.1.1.** (Page 61)
```
(let ((x (memv 'a ls))) (and x (memv 'b x)))   →
  ((lambda (x) (and x (memv 'b x))) (memv 'a ls))   →
  ((lambda (x) (if x (and (memv 'b x)) #f)) (memv 'a ls))   →
  ((lambda (x) (if x (memv 'b x) #f)) (memv 'a ls))
```

**Exercise 3.1.2.** (Page 61)
```
(or (memv x '(a b c)) (list x))   →
  (let ((t (memv x '(a b c)))) (if t t (or (list x))))   →
  ((lambda (t) (if t t (list x))) (or (memv x '(a b c))))   →
  ((lambda (t) (if t t (list x))) (memv x '(a b c)))
```

**Exercise 3.1.3.** (Page 61)
See page 88.

**Exercise 3.1.4.** (Page 62)
```
(define-syntax when
  (syntax-rules ()
    ((_ e0 e1 e2 ...)
     (if e0 (begin e1 e2 ...)))))

(define-syntax unless
  (syntax-rules ()
    ((_ e0 e1 e2 ...)
     (when (not e0) e1 e2 ...))))
```

**Exercise 3.2.1.** (Page 69)
Tail-recursive: `even?` and `odd?`, `race`, `fact` in second definition of `factorial`, `fib` in second version of `fibonacci`. Nontail-recursive: `sum`, `factorial`, `fib` in first version of `fibonacci`. Both: `factor`.

**Exercise 3.2.2.** (Page 69)
```
(define factor
  (lambda (n)
    (letrec ((f (lambda (n i)
                  (cond
                    ((>= i n) (list n))
                    ((integer? (/ n i))
                     (cons i (f (/ n i) i)))
                    (else (f n (+ i 1)))))))
      (f n 2))))
```

**Exercise 3.2.3.** (Page 69)
Yes, but we need two named **let** expressions, one for **even?** and one for **odd?**.

```
(let even? ((x 20))
  (or (= x 0)
      (let odd? ((x (- x 1)))
        (and (not (= x 0))
             (even? (- x 1))))))
```

**Exercise 3.2.4.** (Page 70)
```
(define fibcount1 0)
(define fibonacci1
  (lambda (n)
    (let fib ((i n))
      (set! fibcount1 (+ fibcount1 1))
      (cond
        ((= i 0) 0)
        ((= i 1) 1)
        (else (+ (fib (- i 1)) (fib (- i 2))))))))
(define fibcount2 0)
(define fibonacci2
  (lambda (n)
    (if (= n 0)
        0
        (let fib ((i n) (a1 1) (a2 0))
          (set! fibcount2 (+ fibcount2 1))
          (if (= i 1)
              a1
              (fib (- i 1) (+ a1 a2) a1))))))
```

The counts for (fibonacci 10) are 177 and 10, for (fibonacci 20) are 21891 and 20, and for (fibonacci 30) are 2692537 and 30. While the number of calls made by the second is directly proportional to the input, the number of calls made by the second grows rapidly (exponentially, in fact) as the input value increases.

**Exercise 3.2.5.** (Page 70)
See page 201.

**Exercise 3.2.6.** (Page 70)
A call in the last subexpression of an **or** expression in tail position would not be a tail call with the modified definition of **or**. For the **even?/odd?** example, the resulting definition of **even?** would no longer be tail recursive and for very large inputs might exhaust available space.

**Exercise 3.2.7.** (Page 70)
The first of the three versions of **factor** below directly addresses the identified problems by stopping at $\sqrt{n}$, avoiding the redundant division, and skipping the even factors after 2. Stopping at $\sqrt{n}$ probably yields the biggest savings, followed by skipping even factors greater than 2. Avoiding the redundant division is less important, since it occurs only when a factor is found.

```
(define factor
  (lambda (n)
    (let f ((n n) (i 2) (step 1))
      (if (> i (sqrt n))
          (list n)
          (let ((n/i (/ n i)))
            (if (integer? n/i)
                (cons i (f n/i i step))
                (f n (+ i step) 2)))))))
```

The second version replaces (> i (sqrt n)) with (> (* i i) n), since * is typically much faster than **sqrt**.

```
(define factor
  (lambda (n)
    (let f ((n n) (i 2) (step 1))
      (if (> (* i i) n)
          (list n)
          (let ((n/i (/ n i)))
            (if (integer? n/i)
                (cons i (f n/i i step))
                (f n (+ i step) 2)))))))
```

The third version uses **gcd** (see page 147) to avoid most of the divisions, since **gcd** should be faster than /.

```
(define factor
  (lambda (n)
    (let f ((n n) (i 2) (step 1))
      (if (> (* i i) n)
          (list n)
          (if (= (gcd n i) 1)
              (f n (+ i step) 2)
              (cons i (f (/ n i) i step)))))))
```

To see the difference these changes make, time each version of **factor**, including the original, in your Scheme system to see which performs better. Try a variety of inputs, including larger ones like (+ (expt 2 100) 1).

**Exercise 3.3.1.** (Page 74)
```
(let ((k.n (call/cc (lambda (k) (cons k 0)))))
  (let ((k (car k.n)) (n (cdr k.n)))
    (write n)
    (newline)
    (k (cons k (+ n 1)))))
```

Or with multiple values (see Section 5.7):

```
(call-with-values
  (lambda () (call/cc (lambda (k) (values k 0))))
  (lambda (k n)
    (write n)
    (newline)
    (k k (+ n 1))))
```

**Exercise 3.3.2.** (Page 74)
```
(define product
  (lambda (ls)
    (if (null? ls)
        1
        (if (= (car ls) 0)
            0
            (let ((n (product (cdr ls))))
              (if (= n 0) 0 (* n (car ls))))))))
```

**Exercise 3.3.3.** (Page 74)
If one of the processes returns without calling **pause**, it returns to the call to **pause** that first caused it to run, or to the original call to **start** if it was the first process in the list. Here is a reimplementation of the system that allows a process to **quit** explicitly. If other processes are active, the **lwp** system continues to run. Otherwise, control returns to the continuation of the original call to **start**.

```
(define lwp-list '())
(define lwp
  (lambda (thunk)
    (set! lwp-list (append lwp-list (list thunk)))))
(define start
  (lambda ()
    (call/cc
      (lambda (k)
        (set! quit-k k)
        (next)))))
(define next
  (lambda ()
    (let ((p (car lwp-list)))
      (set! lwp-list (cdr lwp-list))
      (p))))
(define pause
  (lambda ()
    (call/cc
      (lambda (k)
        (lwp (lambda () (k #f)))
        (next)))))
(define quit
  (lambda (v)
    (if (null? lwp-list)
        (quit-k v)
        (next))))
```

**Exercise 3.3.4.** (Page 74)
```
(define lwp-queue (make-queue))
(define lwp
  (lambda (thunk)
    (putq! lwp-queue thunk)))
(define start
  (lambda ()
    (let ((p (getq lwp-queue)))
      (delq! lwp-queue)
      (p))))
(define pause
  (lambda ()
    (call/cc
      (lambda (k)
        (lwp (lambda () (k #f)))
        (start)))))
```

**Exercise 3.4.1.** (Page 77)
```
(define reciprocal
  (lambda (n success failure)
    (if (= n 0)
        (failure)
        (success (/ 1 n)))))
```

**Exercise 3.4.2.** (Page 77)
```
(define retry #f)

(define factorial
  (lambda (x)
    (let f ((x x) (k (lambda (x) x)))
      (if (= x 0)
          (begin (set! retry k) (k 1))
          (f (- x 1) (lambda (y) (k (* x y)))))))))
```

**Exercise 3.4.3.** (Page 77)
```
(define map/k
  (lambda (p ls k)
    (if (null? ls)
        (k '())
        (p (car ls)
           (lambda (x)
             (map/k p (cdr ls)
               (lambda (ls)
                 (k (cons x ls)))))))))
(define reciprocals
  (lambda (ls)
    (map/k (lambda (x k) (if (= x 0) "zero found" (k (/ 1 x))))
           ls
           (lambda (x) x))))
```

**Exercise 3.5.1.** (Page 81)
```
(define-syntax complain
  (syntax-rules ()
    ((_ ek msg exp) (ek (list msg exp)))))
```

**Exercise 3.5.2.** (Page 81)
```
(define calc
  (lambda (exp)
    (call/cc
      (lambda (ek)
        (define do-calc
          (lambda (exp)
            (cond
              ((number? exp) exp)
              ((and (list? exp) (= (length exp) 3))
               (let ((op (car exp)) (args (cdr exp)))
                 (case op
                   ((add) (apply-op + args))
                   ((sub) (apply-op - args))
                   ((mul) (apply-op * args))
                   ((div) (apply-op / args))
                   (else (complain "invalid operator" op)))))
              (else (complain "invalid expression" exp)))))
        (define apply-op
          (lambda (op args)
            (op (do-calc (car args)) (do-calc (cadr args)))))
        (define complain
          (lambda (msg exp)
            (ek (list msg exp))))
        (do-calc exp)))))
```

**Exercise 3.5.3.** (Page 81)
Using *Chez Scheme*'s error:

```
(define calc #f)
(let ()
  (define do-calc
    (lambda (exp)
      (cond
        ((number? exp) exp)
        ((and (list? exp) (= (length exp) 3))
         (let ((op (car exp)) (args (cdr exp)))
           (case op
             ((add) (apply-op + args))
             ((sub) (apply-op - args))
             ((mul) (apply-op * args))
             ((div) (apply-op / args))
             (else (complain "invalid operator" op)))))
        (else (complain "invalid expression" exp)))))
  (define apply-op
    (lambda (op args)
```

```
      (op (do-calc (car args)) (do-calc (cadr args)))))
  (define complain
    (lambda (msg exp)
      (error 'calc "~a ~s" msg exp)))
  (set! calc
    (lambda (exp)
      (do-calc exp))))
```

**Exercise 3.5.4.** (Page 81)
This adds sqrt, times (an alias for mul), and expt along with minus.

```
(let ()
  (define do-calc
    (lambda (ek exp)
      (cond
        ((number? exp) exp)
        ((and (list? exp) (= (length exp) 2))
         (let ((op (car exp)) (args (cdr exp)))
           (case op
             ((minus) (apply-op1 ek - args))
             ((sqrt) (apply-op1 ek sqrt args))
             (else (complain ek "invalid unary operator" op)))))
        ((and (list? exp) (= (length exp) 3))
         (let ((op (car exp)) (args (cdr exp)))
           (case op
             ((add) (apply-op2 ek + args))
             ((sub) (apply-op2 ek - args))
             ((mul times) (apply-op2 ek * args))
             ((div) (apply-op2 ek / args))
             ((expt) (apply-op2 ek expt args))
             (else (complain ek "invalid binary operator" op)))))
        (else (complain ek "invalid expression" exp)))))
  (define apply-op1
    (lambda (ek op args)
      (op (do-calc ek (car args)))))
  (define apply-op2
    (lambda (ek op args)
      (op (do-calc ek (car args)) (do-calc ek (cadr args)))))
  (define complain
    (lambda (ek msg exp)
      (ek (list msg exp))))
  (set! calc
    (lambda (exp)
      (call/cc
        (lambda (ek)
          (do-calc ek exp))))))
```

# Formal Syntax of Scheme

The formal grammars and accompanying text appearing here describe the syntax of Scheme programs and data. Consult the Summary of Forms and Procedures and the individual descriptions given in Chapters 4 through 8 for additional details on specific syntactic forms.

Programs and data are formed from tokens, whitespace, and comments. Tokens include identifiers, booleans, numbers, characters, strings, open and close parentheses, the open vector parenthesis #(, the dotted pair marker . (dot), the quotation marks ' and ', and the unquotation marks , and ,@. Whitespace consists of spaces and newline characters and in some implementations also consists of other characters, such as tabs or form feeds. A comment consists of a semicolon ( ; ) followed by any number of characters up to the next line break. A token may be surrounded by any number of whitespace characters and comments. Identifiers, numbers, characters, and dot are delimited by whitespace, the start of a comment, an open or close parenthesis, or a string quote.

In the productions below, ⟨empty⟩ stands for the empty string. An item followed by an asterisk ( * ) represents zero or more occurrences of the item, and an item followed by a raised plus sign ( + ) represents one or more occurrences. Spacing between items within a production appears for readability only and should be treated as if it were not present.

**Programs.** A program consists of a sequence of definitions and expressions.

⟨program⟩ ⟶ ⟨form⟩*
⟨form⟩ ⟶ ⟨definition⟩ | ⟨expression⟩

**Definitions.** Definitions include variable and syntax definitions, **begin** forms containing zero or more definitions, **let-syntax** and **letrec-syntax** forms expanding into zero or more definitions, and derived definitions. Derived definitions are syntactic extensions that expand into some form of definition. A transformer expression is a **syntax-rules** form or some other expression that produces a transformer.

⟨definition⟩ ⟶ ⟨variable definition⟩
   | ⟨syntax definition⟩
   | (**begin** ⟨definition⟩*)
   | (**let-syntax** (⟨syntax binding⟩*) ⟨definition⟩*)
   | (**letrec-syntax** (⟨syntax binding⟩*) ⟨definition⟩*)
   | ⟨derived definition⟩
⟨variable definition⟩ ⟶ (**define** ⟨variable⟩ ⟨expression⟩)
   | (**define** (⟨variable⟩ ⟨variable⟩*) ⟨body⟩)
   | (**define** (⟨variable⟩ ⟨variable⟩* . ⟨variable⟩) ⟨body⟩)
⟨variable⟩ ⟶ ⟨identifier⟩
⟨body⟩ ⟶ ⟨definition⟩* ⟨expression⟩+
⟨syntax definition⟩ ⟶ (**define-syntax** ⟨keyword⟩ ⟨transformer expression⟩)
⟨keyword⟩ ⟶ ⟨identifier⟩
⟨syntax binding⟩ ⟶ (⟨keyword⟩ ⟨transformer expression⟩)

**Expressions.** Expressions include core expressions, `let-syntax` or `letrec-syntax` forms expanding into a sequence of one or more expressions, and derived expressions. The core expressions are self-evaluating constants, variable references, applications, and `quote`, `lambda`, `if`, and `set!` expressions. Derived expressions include `and`, `begin`, `case`, `cond`, `delay`, `do`, `let`, `let*`, `letrec`, `or`, and `quasiquote` expressions plus syntactic extensions that expand into some form of expression.

⟨expression⟩ ⟶ ⟨constant⟩
   | ⟨variable⟩
   | (**quote** ⟨datum⟩) | ' ⟨datum⟩
   | (**lambda** ⟨formals⟩ ⟨body⟩)
   | (**if** ⟨expression⟩ ⟨expression⟩ ⟨expression⟩) | (**if** ⟨expression⟩ ⟨expression⟩)
   | (**set!** ⟨variable⟩ ⟨expression⟩)
   | ⟨application⟩
   | (**let-syntax** (⟨syntax binding⟩*) ⟨expression⟩+)
   | (**letrec-syntax** (⟨syntax binding⟩*) ⟨expression⟩+)
   | ⟨derived expression⟩
⟨constant⟩ ⟶ ⟨boolean⟩ | ⟨number⟩ | ⟨character⟩ | ⟨string⟩
⟨formals⟩ ⟶ ⟨variable⟩ | (⟨variable⟩*) | (⟨variable⟩+ . ⟨variable⟩)
⟨application⟩ ⟶ (⟨expression⟩ ⟨expression⟩*)

**Identifiers.** Identifiers may denote variables, keywords, or symbols, depending upon context. They are formed from sequences of letters, digits, and special characters. With three exceptions, identifiers cannot begin with a character that can also begin a number, i.e., they cannot begin with ., +, -, or a digit. The three exceptions are the identifiers ..., +, and -. Case is insignificant in identifiers so that, for example, `newspaper`, `NewsPaper`, and `NEWSPAPER` all represent the same identifier.

⟨identifier⟩ ⟶ ⟨initial⟩ ⟨subsequent⟩* | + | - | ...
⟨initial⟩ ⟶ ⟨letter⟩ | ! | @ | $ | % | & | * | / | : | < | = | > | ? | ~ | _ | ^
⟨subsequent⟩ ⟶ ⟨initial⟩ | ⟨digit⟩ | . | + | -
⟨letter⟩ ⟶ a | b | ... | z
⟨digit⟩ ⟶ 0 | 1 | ... | 9

**Data.** Data include booleans, numbers, characters, strings, symbols, lists, and vectors. Case is insignificant in the syntax for booleans, numbers, and character names, but it is significant in other character constants and in strings. For example, `#T` is equivalent to `#t`, `#E1E3` is equivalent to `#e1e3`, `#X2aBc` is equivalent to `#x2abc`, and `#\NewLine` is equivalent to `#\newline`; but `#\A` is distinct from `#\a` and `"String"` is distinct from `"string"`.

⟨datum⟩ ⟶ ⟨boolean⟩ | ⟨number⟩ | ⟨character⟩ | ⟨string⟩ | ⟨symbol⟩ | ⟨list⟩ | ⟨vector⟩
⟨boolean⟩ ⟶ #t | #f
⟨number⟩ ⟶ ⟨num 2⟩ | ⟨num 8⟩ | ⟨num 10⟩ | ⟨num 16⟩
⟨character⟩ ⟶ #\ ⟨any character⟩ | #\newline | #\space
⟨string⟩ ⟶ " ⟨string character⟩* "
⟨string character⟩ ⟶ \" | \\ | ⟨any character other than " or \⟩
⟨symbol⟩ ⟶ ⟨identifier⟩
⟨list⟩ ⟶ (⟨datum⟩*) | (⟨datum⟩+ . ⟨datum⟩) | ⟨abbreviation⟩
⟨abbreviation⟩ ⟶ ' ⟨datum⟩ | ` ⟨datum⟩ | , ⟨datum⟩ | ,@ ⟨datum⟩
⟨vector⟩ ⟶ #(⟨datum⟩*)

**Numbers.** Numbers can appear in one of four radices: 2, 8, 10, and 16, with 10 the default. The first several productions below are parameterized by the radix, $r$, and each represents four productions, one for each of the four possible radices. Numbers that contain radix points or exponents are constrained to appear in radix 10, so ⟨decimal $r$⟩ is valid only when $r$ is 10.

⟨num $r$⟩ ⟶ ⟨prefix $r$⟩ ⟨complex $r$⟩
⟨complex $r$⟩ ⟶ ⟨real $r$⟩ | ⟨real $r$⟩ @ ⟨real $r$⟩
    | ⟨real $r$⟩ + ⟨imag $r$⟩ | ⟨real $r$⟩ - ⟨imag $r$⟩
    | + ⟨imag $r$⟩ | - ⟨imag $r$⟩
⟨imag $r$⟩ ⟶ i | ⟨ureal $r$⟩ i
⟨real $r$⟩ ⟶ ⟨sign⟩ ⟨ureal $r$⟩
⟨ureal $r$⟩ ⟶ ⟨uinteger $r$⟩ | ⟨uinteger $r$⟩ / ⟨uinteger $r$⟩ | ⟨decimal $r$⟩
⟨uinteger $r$⟩ ⟶ ⟨digit $r$⟩+ #*
⟨prefix $r$⟩ ⟶ ⟨radix $r$⟩ ⟨exactness⟩ | ⟨exactness⟩ ⟨radix $r$⟩
⟨decimal 10⟩ ⟶ ⟨uinteger 10⟩ ⟨exponent⟩
    | . ⟨digit 10⟩+ #* ⟨suffix⟩
    | ⟨digit 10⟩+ . ⟨digit 10⟩* #* ⟨suffix⟩
    | ⟨digit 10⟩+ #+ . #* ⟨suffix⟩

⟨suffix⟩ ⟶ ⟨empty⟩ | ⟨exponent⟩

⟨exponent⟩ ⟶ ⟨exponent marker⟩ ⟨sign⟩ ⟨digit 10⟩$^+$

⟨exponent marker⟩ ⟶ e | s | f | d | l

⟨sign⟩ ⟶ ⟨empty⟩ | + | -

⟨exactness⟩ ⟶ ⟨empty⟩ | #i | #e

⟨radix 2⟩ ⟶ #b

⟨radix 8⟩ ⟶ #o

⟨radix 10⟩ ⟶ ⟨empty⟩ | #d

⟨radix 16⟩ ⟶ #x

⟨digit 2⟩ ⟶ 0 | 1

⟨digit 8⟩ ⟶ 0 | 1 | ... | 7

⟨digit 10⟩ ⟶ ⟨digit⟩

⟨digit 16⟩ ⟶ ⟨digit⟩ | a | b | c | d | e | f

# Summary of Forms

The table that follows summarizes the Scheme syntactic forms and procedures described in Chapters 4 through 8. It shows the category of the form and the page number where it is defined. The category states whether the form describes a syntactic form or a procedure.

| Form | Category | Page |
|---|---|---|
| $'obj$ | syntax | 121 |
| $(*\ num\ \ldots)$ | procedure | 143 |
| $(+\ num\ \ldots)$ | procedure | 142 |
| $,obj$ | syntax | 122 |
| $,@obj$ | syntax | 122 |
| $(-\ num_1)$ | procedure | 143 |
| $(-\ num_1\ num_2\ num_3\ \ldots)$ | procedure | 143 |
| $(/\ num_1)$ | procedure | 143 |
| $(/\ num_1\ num_2\ num_3\ \ldots)$ | procedure | 143 |
| $(<\ real_1\ real_2\ real_3\ \ldots)$ | procedure | 141 |
| $(<=\ real_1\ real_2\ real_3\ \ldots)$ | procedure | 141 |
| $(=\ num_1\ num_2\ num_3\ \ldots)$ | procedure | 141 |
| $(>\ real_1\ real_2\ real_3\ \ldots)$ | procedure | 141 |
| $(>=\ real_1\ real_2\ real_3\ \ldots)$ | procedure | 141 |
| $`obj$ | syntax | 122 |
| $(\texttt{abs}\ real)$ | procedure | 146 |
| $(\texttt{acos}\ num)$ | procedure | 152 |
| $(\texttt{and}\ exp\ \ldots)$ | syntax | 97 |
| $(\texttt{angle}\ num)$ | procedure | 150 |
| $(\texttt{append}\ list\ \ldots)$ | procedure | 136 |
| $(\texttt{apply}\ procedure\ obj\ \ldots\ list)$ | procedure | 95 |
| $(\texttt{asin}\ num)$ | procedure | 152 |
| $(\texttt{assoc}\ obj\ alist)$ | procedure | 138 |
| $(\texttt{assq}\ obj\ alist)$ | procedure | 138 |
| $(\texttt{assv}\ obj\ alist)$ | procedure | 138 |
| $(\texttt{atan}\ num)$ | procedure | 152 |

| | | |
|---|---|---|
| (atan $real_1$ $real_2$) | procedure | 152 |
| (begin $exp_1$ $exp_2$ ...) | syntax | 96 |
| (boolean? $obj$) | procedure | 129 |
| (bound-identifier=? $identifier_1$ $identifier_2$) | procedure | 193 |
| (caaaar $pair$) | procedure | 134 |
| (caaadr $pair$) | procedure | 134 |
| (caaar $pair$) | procedure | 134 |
| (caadar $pair$) | procedure | 134 |
| (caaddr $pair$) | procedure | 134 |
| (caadr $pair$) | procedure | 134 |
| (caar $pair$) | procedure | 134 |
| (cadaar $pair$) | procedure | 134 |
| (cadadr $pair$) | procedure | 134 |
| (cadar $pair$) | procedure | 134 |
| (caddar $pair$) | procedure | 134 |
| (cadddr $pair$) | procedure | 134 |
| (caddr $pair$) | procedure | 134 |
| (cadr $pair$) | procedure | 134 |
| (call-with-current-continuation $procedure$) | procedure | 104 |
| (call-with-input-file $filename$ $proc$) | procedure | 172 |
| (call-with-output-file $filename$ $proc$) | procedure | 176 |
| (call-with-values $producer$ $consumer$) | procedure | 111 |
| (car $pair$) | procedure | 133 |
| (case $exp_0$ $clause_1$ $clause_2$ ...) | syntax | 99 |
| (cdaaar $pair$) | procedure | 134 |
| (cdaadr $pair$) | procedure | 134 |
| (cdaar $pair$) | procedure | 134 |
| (cdadar $pair$) | procedure | 134 |
| (cdaddr $pair$) | procedure | 134 |
| (cdadr $pair$) | procedure | 134 |
| (cdar $pair$) | procedure | 134 |
| (cddaar $pair$) | procedure | 134 |
| (cddadr $pair$) | procedure | 134 |
| (cddar $pair$) | procedure | 134 |
| (cdddar $pair$) | procedure | 134 |
| (cddddr $pair$) | procedure | 134 |
| (cdddr $pair$) | procedure | 134 |
| (cddr $pair$) | procedure | 134 |
| (cdr $pair$) | procedure | 133 |
| (ceiling $real$) | procedure | 146 |
| (char->integer $char$) | procedure | 156 |
| (char-alphabetic? $char$) | procedure | 155 |

| | | |
|---|---|---|
| (char-ci<=? $char_1$ $char_2$ $char_3$ ...) | procedure | 154 |
| (char-ci<? $char_1$ $char_2$ $char_3$ ...) | procedure | 154 |
| (char-ci=? $char_1$ $char_2$ $char_3$ ...) | procedure | 154 |
| (char-ci>=? $char_1$ $char_2$ $char_3$ ...) | procedure | 154 |
| (char-ci>? $char_1$ $char_2$ $char_3$ ...) | procedure | 154 |
| (char-downcase *char*) | procedure | 156 |
| (char-lower-case? *letter*) | procedure | 155 |
| (char-numeric? *char*) | procedure | 155 |
| (char-ready?) | procedure | 175 |
| (char-ready? *input-port*) | procedure | 175 |
| (char-upcase *char*) | procedure | 156 |
| (char-upper-case? *letter*) | procedure | 155 |
| (char-whitespace? *char*) | procedure | 156 |
| (char<=? $char_1$ $char_2$ $char_3$ ...) | procedure | 153 |
| (char<? $char_1$ $char_2$ $char_3$ ...) | procedure | 153 |
| (char=? $char_1$ $char_2$ $char_3$ ...) | procedure | 153 |
| (char>=? $char_1$ $char_2$ $char_3$ ...) | procedure | 153 |
| (char>? $char_1$ $char_2$ $char_3$ ...) | procedure | 153 |
| (char? *obj*) | procedure | 131 |
| (close-input-port *input-port*) | procedure | 172 |
| (close-output-port *output-port*) | procedure | 175 |
| (complex? *obj*) | procedure | 130 |
| (cond $clause_1$ $clause_2$ ...) | syntax | 98 |
| (cons $obj_1$ $obj_2$) | procedure | 133 |
| *constant* | syntax | 121 |
| (cos *num*) | procedure | 152 |
| (current-input-port) | procedure | 171 |
| (current-output-port) | procedure | 175 |
| (datum->syntax-object *template-identifier* *obj*) | procedure | 197 |
| (define *var* *exp*) | syntax | 89 |
| (define ($var_0$ $var_1$ ...) $exp_1$ $exp_2$ ...) | syntax | 89 |
| (define ($var_0$ . $var_r$) $exp_1$ $exp_2$ ...) | syntax | 89 |
| (define ($var_0$ $var_1$ $var_2$ ... . $var_r$) $exp_1$ $exp_2$ ...) | syntax | 89 |
| (define-syntax *keyword* *exp*) | syntax | 184 |
| (delay *exp*) | syntax | 108 |
| (denominator *rat*) | procedure | 149 |
| (display *obj*) | procedure | 178 |
| (display *obj* *output-port*) | procedure | 178 |
| (do (($var$ $val$ $update$) ...) ($test$ $res$ ...) $exp$ ...) | syntax | 101 |
| (dynamic-wind *in* *body* *out*) | procedure | 105 |
| (eof-object? *obj*) | procedure | 174 |
| (eq? $obj_1$ $obj_2$) | procedure | 123 |

| | | |
|---|---|---|
| (equal? $obj_1$ $obj_2$) | procedure | 127 |
| (eqv? $obj_1$ $obj_2$) | procedure | 125 |
| (eval *obj env-spec*) | procedure | 116 |
| (even? *int*) | procedure | 145 |
| (exact->inexact *num*) | procedure | 148 |
| (exact? *num*) | procedure | 141 |
| (exp *num*) | procedure | 151 |
| (expt $num_1$ $num_2$) | procedure | 148 |
| (floor *real*) | procedure | 146 |
| (fluid-let-syntax ((*keyword exp*) ...) $form_1$ $form_2$ ...) | syntax | 186 |
| (for-each *procedure* $list_1$ $list_2$ ...) | procedure | 103 |
| (force *promise*) | procedure | 109 |
| (free-identifier=? $identifier_1$ $identifier_2$) | procedure | 193 |
| (gcd *int* ...) | procedure | 147 |
| (generate-temporaries *list*) | procedure | 199 |
| (identifier? *obj*) | procedure | 193 |
| (if *test consequent alternative*) | syntax | 97 |
| (if *test consequent*) | syntax | 97 |
| (imag-part *num*) | procedure | 150 |
| (inexact->exact *num*) | procedure | 148 |
| (inexact? *num*) | procedure | 141 |
| (input-port? *obj*) | procedure | 171 |
| (integer->char *int*) | procedure | 158 |
| (integer? *obj*) | procedure | 130 |
| (interaction-environment) | procedure | 117 |
| (lambda *formals* $exp_1$ $exp_2$ ...) | syntax | 86 |
| (lcm *int* ...) | procedure | 147 |
| (length *list*) | procedure | 135 |
| (let ((*var val*) ...) $exp_1$ $exp_2$ ...) | syntax | 87 |
| (let *name* ((*var val*) ...) $exp_1$ $exp_2$ ...) | syntax | 100 |
| (let* ((*var val*) ...) $exp_1$ $exp_2$ ...) | syntax | 88 |
| (let-syntax ((*keyword exp*) ...) $form_1$ $form_2$ ...) | syntax | 185 |
| (letrec ((*var val*) ...) $exp_1$ $exp_2$ ...) | syntax | 88 |
| (letrec-syntax ((*keyword exp*) ...) $form_1$ $form_2$ ...) | syntax | 185 |
| (list *obj* ...) | procedure | 134 |
| (list->string *list*) | procedure | 163 |
| (list->vector *list*) | procedure | 166 |
| (list-ref *list* *n*) | procedure | 135 |
| (list-tail *list* *n*) | procedure | 135 |
| (list? *obj*) | procedure | 134 |
| (load *filename*) | procedure | 179 |
| (log *num*) | procedure | 151 |

| | | |
|---|---|---|
| (magnitude *num*) | procedure | 150 |
| (make-polar *real₁ real₂*) | procedure | 150 |
| (make-rectangular *real₁ real₂*) | procedure | 150 |
| (make-string *n*) | procedure | 160 |
| (make-string *n char*) | procedure | 160 |
| (make-vector *n*) | procedure | 164 |
| (make-vector *n obj*) | procedure | 164 |
| (map *procedure list₁ list₂ ...*) | procedure | 102 |
| (max *real₁ real₂ ...*) | procedure | 147 |
| (member *obj list*) | procedure | 137 |
| (memq *obj list*) | procedure | 137 |
| (memv *obj list*) | procedure | 137 |
| (min *real₁ real₂ ...*) | procedure | 147 |
| (modulo *int₁ int₂*) | procedure | 145 |
| (negative? *real*) | procedure | 144 |
| (newline) | procedure | 178 |
| (newline *output-port*) | procedure | 178 |
| (not *obj*) | procedure | 97 |
| (null-environment *version*) | procedure | 117 |
| (null? *obj*) | procedure | 129 |
| (number->string *num*) | procedure | 153 |
| (number->string *num radix*) | procedure | 153 |
| (number? *obj*) | procedure | 130 |
| (numerator *rat*) | procedure | 149 |
| (odd? *int*) | procedure | 145 |
| (open-input-file *filename*) | procedure | 171 |
| (open-output-file *filename*) | procedure | 175 |
| (or *exp ...*) | syntax | 98 |
| (output-port? *obj*) | procedure | 175 |
| (pair? *obj*) | procedure | 130 |
| (peek-char) | procedure | 174 |
| (peek-char *input-port*) | procedure | 174 |
| (positive? *real*) | procedure | 144 |
| (*procedure exp ...*) | syntax | 95 |
| (procedure? *obj*) | procedure | 132 |
| (quasiquote *obj*) | syntax | 122 |
| (quote *obj*) | syntax | 121 |
| (quotient *int₁ int₂*) | procedure | 145 |
| (rational? *obj*) | procedure | 130 |
| (rationalize *real₁ real₂*) | procedure | 149 |
| (read) | procedure | 173 |
| (read *input-port*) | procedure | 173 |

| | | |
|---|---|---|
| `(read-char)` | procedure | 174 |
| `(read-char` *input-port*`)` | procedure | 174 |
| `(real-part` *num*`)` | procedure | 149 |
| `(real?` *obj*`)` | procedure | 130 |
| `(remainder` *int₁ int₂*`)` | procedure | 145 |
| `(reverse` *list*`)` | procedure | 137 |
| `(round` *real*`)` | procedure | 146 |
| `(scheme-report-environment` *version*`)` | procedure | 117 |
| `(set!` *var exp*`)` | syntax | 91 |
| `(set-car!` *pair obj*`)` | procedure | 133 |
| `(set-cdr!` *pair obj*`)` | procedure | 134 |
| `(sin` *num*`)` | procedure | 152 |
| `(sqrt` *num*`)` | procedure | 151 |
| `(string` *char* `...)` | procedure | 160 |
| `(string->list` *string*`)` | procedure | 163 |
| `(string->number` *string*`)` | procedure | 152 |
| `(string->number` *string radix*`)` | procedure | 152 |
| `(string->symbol` *string*`)` | procedure | 167 |
| `(string-append` *string* `...)` | procedure | 161 |
| `(string-ci<=?` *string₁ string₂ string₃* `...)` | procedure | 160 |
| `(string-ci<?` *string₁ string₂ string₃* `...)` | procedure | 160 |
| `(string-ci=?` *string₁ string₂ string₃* `...)` | procedure | 160 |
| `(string-ci>=?` *string₁ string₂ string₃* `...)` | procedure | 160 |
| `(string-ci>?` *string₁ string₂ string₃* `...)` | procedure | 160 |
| `(string-copy` *string*`)` | procedure | 161 |
| `(string-fill!` *string char*`)` | procedure | 162 |
| `(string-length` *string*`)` | procedure | 160 |
| `(string-ref` *string n*`)` | procedure | 161 |
| `(string-set!` *string n char*`)` | procedure | 161 |
| `(string<=?` *string₁ string₂ string₃* `...)` | procedure | 158 |
| `(string<?` *string₁ string₂ string₃* `...)` | procedure | 158 |
| `(string=?` *string₁ string₂ string₃* `...)` | procedure | 158 |
| `(string>=?` *string₁ string₂ string₃* `...)` | procedure | 158 |
| `(string>?` *string₁ string₂ string₃* `...)` | procedure | 158 |
| `(string?` *obj*`)` | procedure | 131 |
| `(substring` *string start end*`)` | procedure | 162 |
| `(symbol->string` *symbol*`)` | procedure | 168 |
| `(symbol?` *obj*`)` | procedure | 132 |
| `(syntax` *template*`)` | syntax | 192 |
| `(syntax-case` *exp* (*literal* `...`) *clause* `...)` | syntax | 191 |
| `(syntax-object->datum` *obj*`)` | procedure | 197 |
| `(syntax-rules` (*literal* `...`) *clause* `...)` | syntax | 187 |

| | | |
|---|---|---|
| (tan *num*) | procedure | 152 |
| (transcript-off) | procedure | 179 |
| (transcript-on *filename*) | procedure | 179 |
| (truncate *real*) | procedure | 146 |
| (unquote *obj*) | syntax | 122 |
| (unquote-splicing *obj*) | syntax | 122 |
| (values *obj* ...) | procedure | 110 |
| *variable* | syntax | 85 |
| (vector *obj* ...) | procedure | 164 |
| (vector->list *vector*) | procedure | 166 |
| (vector-fill! *vector obj*) | procedure | 165 |
| (vector-length *vector*) | procedure | 164 |
| (vector-ref *vector n*) | procedure | 165 |
| (vector-set! *vector n obj*) | procedure | 165 |
| (vector? *obj*) | procedure | 132 |
| (with-input-from-file *filename thunk*) | procedure | 173 |
| (with-output-to-file *filename thunk*) | procedure | 177 |
| (with-syntax ((*pattern val*) ...) $exp_1$ $exp_2$ ...) | syntax | 196 |
| (write *obj*) | procedure | 177 |
| (write *obj output-port*) | procedure | 177 |
| (write-char *char*) | procedure | 178 |
| (write-char *char output-port*) | procedure | 178 |
| (zero? *num*) | procedure | 144 |

# Index

! (exclamation point), 8
" (double quote), 158
# (hash), 140
#\, 153
#b (binary), 140
#d (decimal), 140
#f, 7, 35, 122
#o (octal), 140
#t, 7, 35, 122
#x (hexadecimal), 140
' (quote), 17, 22, 57, *121*
(), 7, 18
*, 16, *143*
+, 16, *142*
, (unquote), *122*
,@ (unquote-splicing), *122*
-, 16, *143*
->, 8
. (dot), 19
... (ellipses), 59, 187
/, 16, *143*
; (comment), 7, 277
<, *141*
<=, *141*
=, *141*
=>, 98
>, *141*
>=, *141*
? (question mark), 8, 36
_ (underscore), 59, 189, 203
' (quasiquote), *122*

abs, 33, *146*, 150

abstract objects, 51, 238
acos, *152*
actual parameters, 26, 86
Algol 60, 5
and, 35, 86, *97*
angle, *150*
append, 44, *136*
apply, *95*
arbitrary precision, 139
asin, *152*
assignment, 91
assignments, 45, 91
assoc, *138*
association list, 138, 234
assq, *138*
assv, *138*
atan, *152*
atom?, 39
auxiliary keywords, 59, 187

base case, 40
be-like-begin, 202
begin, 49, 58, 90, *96*, 277
binary trees, 132
binding, 4
block structure, 4
boolean values, 7
boolean?, *129*
bound-identifier=?, *193*
brackets ( [ ] ), 7, 132
break, 198

C, 224
caaaar, *134*

caaadr, *134*

caaar, *134*

caadar, *134*

caaddr, *134*

caadr, *134*

caar, *134*

caar, cadr, ..., cddddr, 33

cadaar, *134*

cadadr, *134*

cadar, *134*

caddar, *134*

cadddr, *134*

caddr, *134*

cadr, 30, 31, 33, *134*

call-by-name, 238

call-by-value, 237

call-with-current-continuation, 71, *104*, 107, 113, 256

call-with-input-file, *172*

call-with-output-file, *176*

call-with-values, 110, *111*

call/cc, 71, 104, 107, 113, 255, 256

car, 18, 132, *133*

case, 52, *99*, 196

cdaaar, *134*

cdaadr, *134*

cdaar, *134*

cdadar, *134*

cdaddr, *134*

cdadr, *134*

cdar, *134*

cddaar, *134*

cddadr, *134*

cddar, *134*

cdddar, *134*

cddddr, *134*

cdddr, *134*

cddr, 30, 33, *134*

cdr, 18, 36, 132, *133*

ceiling, *146*

char->integer, *156*

char-alphabetic?, *155*

char-ci<=?, *154*

char-ci<?, *154*

char-ci=?, *154*

char-ci>=?, *154*

char-ci>?, *154*

char-downcase, *156*

char-lower-case?, *155*

char-numeric?, *155*

char-ready?, *175*

char-upcase, *156*

char-upper-case?, *155*

char-whitespace?, *156*

char<=?, *153*

char<?, *153*

char=?, *153*

char>=?, *153*

char>?, *153*

char?, *131*

characters, 153

*Chez Scheme*, ix, 37, 40, 114, 216

circular lists, 133

close-input-port, *172*

close-output-port, *175*

comments, 7, 277

Common Lisp, 6

compiler, 4

*complete*, *see* engines

complex numbers, 139, 242

complex?, *130*, 139

compose, 33

cond, 38, 42, *98*, 196

conditionals, 97

cons, 19, *133*

cons cell, 132

consing, 19

constant, *121*

constants, 21, 121

continuation passing style, 248

continuation-passing style, 75

continuations, 5, 70, 105, 250

control structures, 95

core syntactic forms, 4, 22, 57, 234

cos, *152*
CPS, 75
current-input-port, *171*
current-output-port, *175*
cyclic lists, 54

d (double), 140
data, 121
datum, 279
datum->syntax-object, *197*, 205, 209
define, 29, 77, *89*
define-integrable, 206
define-object, 238
define-structure, 207
define-syntax, 59, 183, *184*, 220
defining syntactic extensions, 58
definitions, 277
defun syntax, 31, 58
delay, *108*
delayed evaluation, 238
delq!, 52
denominator, *149*
derived expression, 278
describe-segment, 112
display, *178*, 228
divisors, 100, 102
do, *101*, 201
dot ( . ), 19
dotted pair, 19, 133
double, 26, 31
double quotes, 158
double-any, 29
double-cons, 26, 31
doubler, 31
doubly recursive, 67
dxdy, 111
dynamic allocation, 3
dynamic-wind, *105*

ellipses ( ... ), 59, 187
else, 98, 99
empty list, 7, 18

engines, 250
environment, 234
eof object, 171
eof-object?, 171, *174*
eq?, *123*
equal?, *127*
equivalence predicates, 123
eqv?, 36, *125*
error, 37, 216
errors, 8
eval, *116*
even?, 45, 63, 78, *145*
exact->inexact, *148*
exact?, 139, *141*
exactness, 139, 148
exactness preserving, 139
exclamation point ( ! ), 8
exp, *151*
expansion, 57
*expire*, *see* engines
expressions, 7
expt, *148*
extended examples, 213

f (single), 140
factor, 68–70
factorial, 66, 73, 101
false, 7, 35
fast Fourier transform (FFT), 242
fenders, 191, 193
fibonacci, 66, 92, 101, 252
Fibonacci numbers, 66, 92
file, 171
first-class data values, 3
first-class procedures, 5
flip-flop, 91
floating point, 139
floor, *146*
fluid binding, 106
fluid-let-syntax, *186*, 206
for-each, *103*
force, *109*

formal parameters, 26, 28, 86
formatted output, 231
fprintf, 231
free variable, 27
free-identifier=?, *193*
frequency, 224

garbage collector, 3
gcd, *147*
generate-temporaries, *199*
getq, 52
goodbye, 40

hare and tortoise, 54, 64
hash ( # ), 140

identifier-syntax, 204, 205
identifier?, *193*
identifiers, 6, 7, 278
if, 33, 34, 38, 49, 57, *97*
imag-part, *150*
implicit begin, 96
improper list, 19, 132
include, 198
inexact->exact, *148*
inexact?, 139, *141*
inheritance, 242
input-port?, *171*
integer->char, *158*
integer-divide, 76
integer?, *130*, 139
integers, 139
integrable procedures, 206
interaction-environment, *117*
internal define-syntax, 183
internal definitions, 77, 86, 90
internal state, 47
interpret, 234
interpreter, 4, 234
iteration, 5, 43, 65, 100–103

keywords, 4, 59, 184

l (long), 140
lambda, 25, 28, 57, *86*
lazy, 49
lazy evaluation, 49, 108
lcm, *147*
length, 40, *135*
let, 23, 27, 62, *87*, *100*
let*, 61, *88*
let-bound variables, 23
let-syntax, 183, *185*, 203, 277, 278
let-values, 115, 200
letrec, 63, 78, *88*, 90, 199
letrec-syntax, 183, *185*, 203, 277, 278
lexical scoping, 4, 5, 24, 61
light-weight threads, 250
Lisp, ix, 5
lisp-cdr, 36
list, 19, 30, 31, *134*
list constants, 7
list->string, *163*
list->vector, *166*
list-copy, 41
list-ref, *135*
list-tail, *135*
list?, 54, 64, 65, 78, *134*
lists, 17, 18, 132
literals, 187
load, 13, *179*
local variable bindings, 87
log, *151*
loop, 198
looping, 5

macros, 183
magnitude, 146, *150*
make-counter, 48, 52
make-list, 44
make-polar, *150*
make-promise, 109, 113
make-queue, 52
make-rectangular, *150*

make-stack, 50, 52
make-string, *160*
make-vector, *164*
map, 43, 45, *102*, 223
map1, 44
mapping, 43, 102, 103
matrix multiplication, 213
max, *147*
member, *137*
memq, *137*
memv, 41, *137*
merge, 219
messages, 50, 238
meta-circular interpreter, 234
method, 205
min, *147*
modulo, *145*
mul, 214
multiple values, 8
multiprocessing, 250
mutually recursive procedures, 63, 88

named let, 64, 68, 100
naming conventions, 7
negative?, *144*
nested engines, 258
nested let expressions, 88
newline, *178*
nondeterministic computations, 250, 253
nonlocal exits, 104, 105
not, 34, *97*
null-environment, *117*
null?, 36, *129*
number->string, *153*
number?, 37, *130*
numbers, 16, 139, 279
numerator, *149*

object identity, 123
object-oriented programming, 205, 238

objects, 3
occur free, 27, 29
odd?, 45, 63, 78, *145*
open-input-file, *171*
open-output-file, *175*
operating system, 253, 258
operations on objects, 121
operator precedence, 16
or, 34, 35, 61, *98*
order of evaluation, 22, 95
output-port?, *175*

pair?, 37, *130*
pairs, 19, 132
pattern variable, 187
pattern variables, 59, 191
patterns, 187
peek-char, *174*
*Petite Chez Scheme*, ix
pointers, 4
por (parallel-or), 254
ports, 171
positive?, *144*
predicates, 8, 36, 122
prefix notation, 15, 16
primitive procedures, 4
printf, 232
procedure application, 16, 17, 21, 26, 95
procedure definition, 5, 30, 89
procedure?, *132*
procedures, 25, 85, 86
product, 72, 76
program, 277
proper list, 19, 54, 132
putq!, 52

quadratic-formula, 46
quasiquote ( ` ), *122*
question mark ( ? ), 8, 36
queue, 51
quote ( ' ), 17, 22, 57, *121*

quotient, *145*

rational numbers, 139
rational?, *130*, 139
rationalize, *149*
read, *173*
read-char, *174*
real numbers, 139
real-part, *149*
real?, *130*, 139
rec, 200
reciprocal, 15, 35, 37, 77
recursion, 5, 39, 62, 100
recursion step, 40
recursive procedure, 40
remainder, *145*
remv, 42
retry, 73, 77
reverse, *137*
Revised Reports, ix, 3
round, *146*
round-robin, 253

s (short), 140
Scheme standard, ix, 3
scheme-report-environment, *117*
scope, 24
segment-length, 111
segment-slope, 111
semicolon ( ; ), 7, 277
sequence, 202
sequencing, 96
set!, 45, 57, *91*
set-car!, *133*
set-cdr!, 54, *134*
set-of, 220
sets, 220
shadowing, 4, 24, 30
shhh, 48
shorter, 39, 45
shorter?, 45
side effects, 8, 96

sin, *152*
sort, 218
split, 112
sqrt, *151*
square, 14
stack objects, 50
streams, 109
string, *160*
string->list, *163*
string->number, *152*
string->symbol, *167*
string-append, *161*
string-ci<=?, *160*
string-ci<?, *160*
string-ci=?, *160*
string-ci>=?, *160*
string-ci>?, *160*
string-copy, *161*
string-fill!, *162*
string-length, *160*
string-ref, *161*
string-set!, *161*
string<=?, *158*
string<?, *158*
string=?, *158*
string>=?, *158*
string>?, *158*
string?, 37, *131*
strings, 14, 158
structured forms, 6
structures, 207
substring, *162*
sum, 62
symbol table, 167
symbol->string, *168*
symbol?, 37, *132*
symbols, 18, 166
syntactic extensions, 5, 22, 57, 58,
          183, 277
syntactic forms, 17, 57, 183, 277
syntax, *192*
syntax-case, 183, *191*

syntax-object->datum, *197*
syntax-rules, 183, *187*, 192, 221

tail call, 5, 65
tail recursion, 5, 65
tan, *152*
tconc, 51
tell, 48
templates, 188
threads, 250
thunk, 49, 105
*ticks*, *see* engines
timed preemption, 250
timer interrupts, 254
tokens, 277
top-level definitions, 29, 89
trace, 40
tracing, 40
transcript, 13, 179
transcript-off, 13, *179*
transcript-on, 13, *179*
transformer, 59
tree-copy, 42
true, 7, 35
truncate, *146*
type predicates, 37

underscore ( _ ), 59, 189, 203
unification, 247
unify, 248
unless, 62
unquote ( , ), *122*
unquote-splicing ( ,@ ), *122*
unspecified, 8
unwind-protect (in Lisp), 105

values, 110, *110*
variable binding, 23, 85
variable reference, *85*
variables, 4, 18, 22, 29, 45
vector, *164*
vector->list, *166*

vector-fill!, *165*
vector-length, *164*
vector-ref, *165*
vector-set!, *165*
vector?, *132*
vectors, 53, 164, 215

when, 62
whitespace, 156, 277
whitespace characters, 7
winders, *see* dynamic-wind
with-input-from-file, *173*
with-output-to-file, *177*
with-syntax, *196*
write, *177*, *228*
write-char, *178*

x++, 204

zero?, *144*